Left-Handed Banjo G Tuning Photo Chord Book

MEL BAY

Visit us on the Web at www.melbay.com — E-mail us at email@melbay.com

TUNING THE BANJO

G - BLUEGRASS

The 5 strings are tuned to a piano as shown.

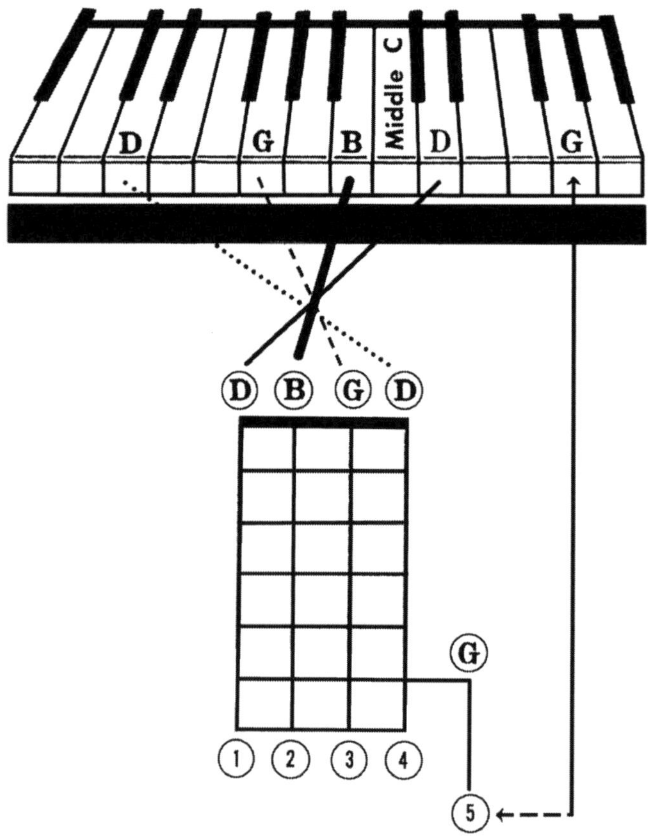

ACTUAL PITCH

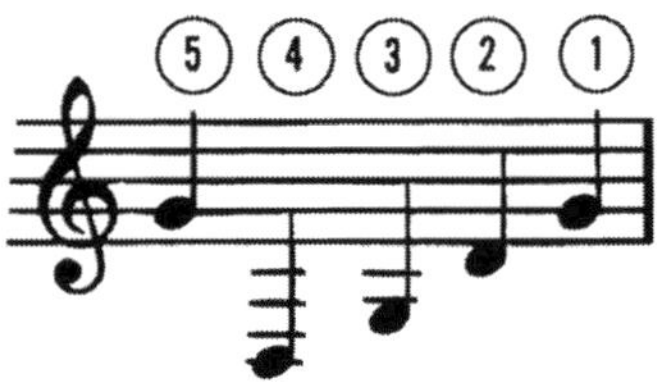

THIS IS BASIC 'G' TUNING

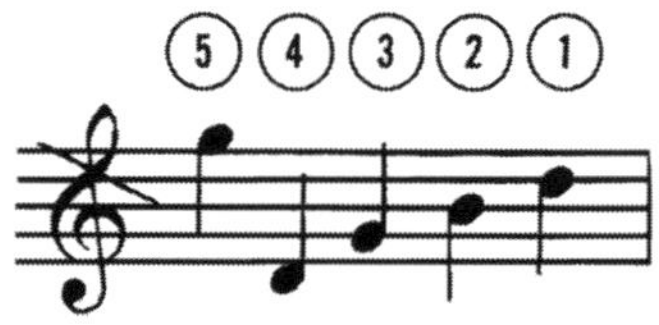

(BANJO NOTATION)

Banjo music written an octave higher than the actual sound, will be indicated by 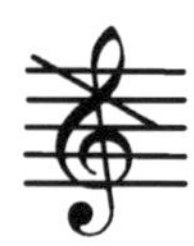

When the music is written exactly as heard, it will be indicated by 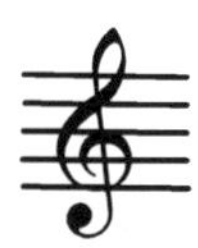

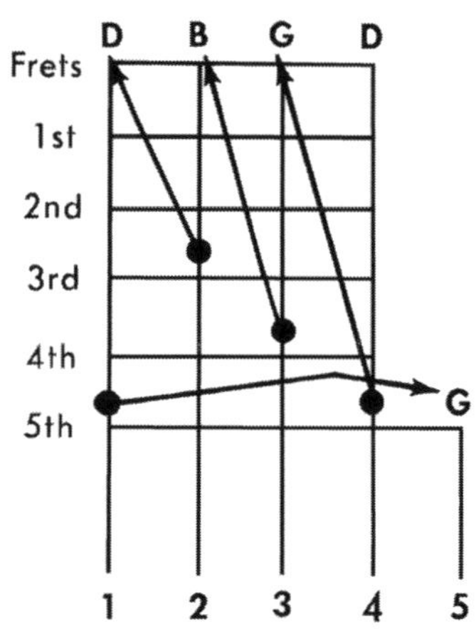

ANOTHER WAY TO TUNE

Tune the first string to 'D' (Next above middle C)

Tune 2nd string, noted at 3rd fret, to same pitch as open first string.

Tune 3rd string, noted at 4th fret, to same pitch as open second string.

Tune the 5th string, to sound the same as the 1st string noted at the 5th fret.

Table of Contents

C Chords 4

D♭/C♯ Chords 8

D Chords 12

E♭/D♯ Chords 16

E Chords...20

F Chords...24

G♭/F♯ Chords 28

G Chords 32

A♭/G♯ Chords 36

A Chords...40

B♭/A♯ Chords 44

B Chords 48

C Chords

C Major*

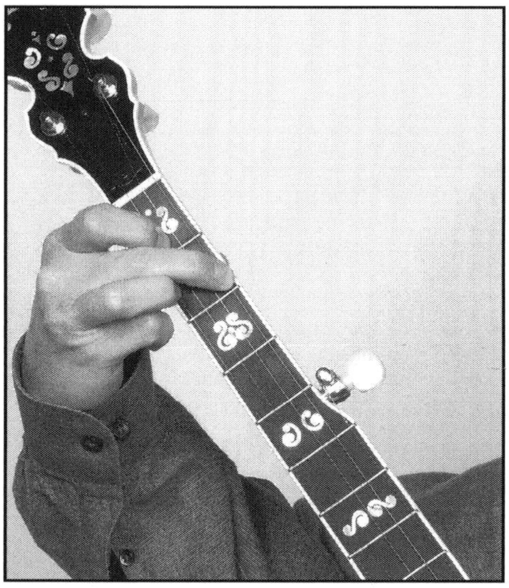

Root - 3rd - 5th
C - E - G

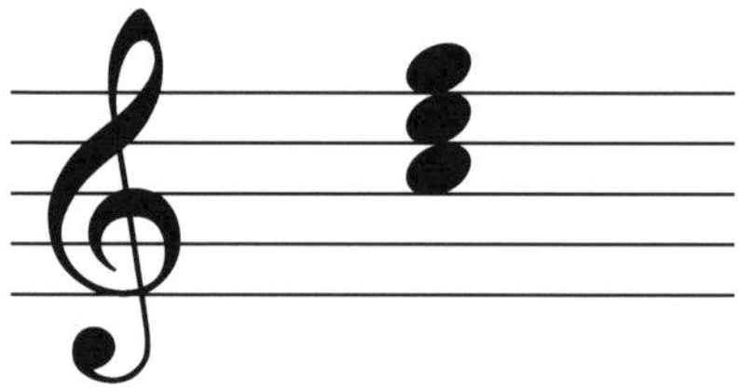

C

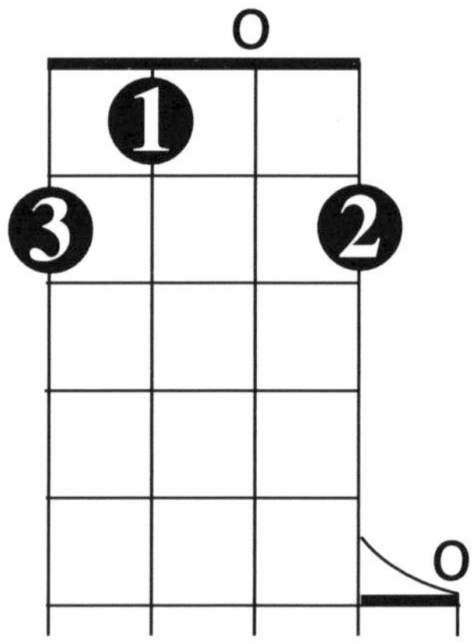

C Minor

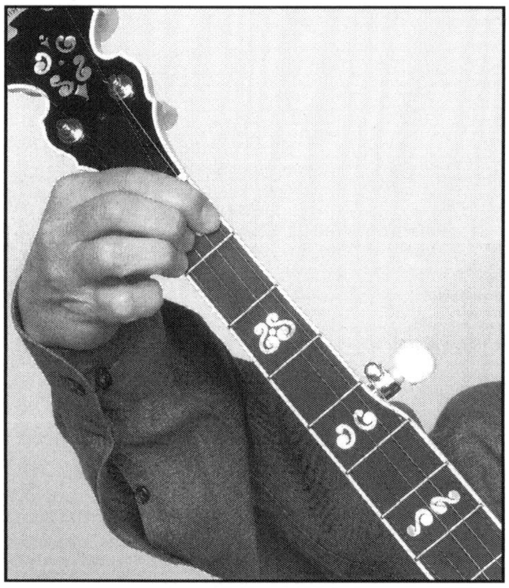

Root - ♭3rd - 5th
C - E♭ - G

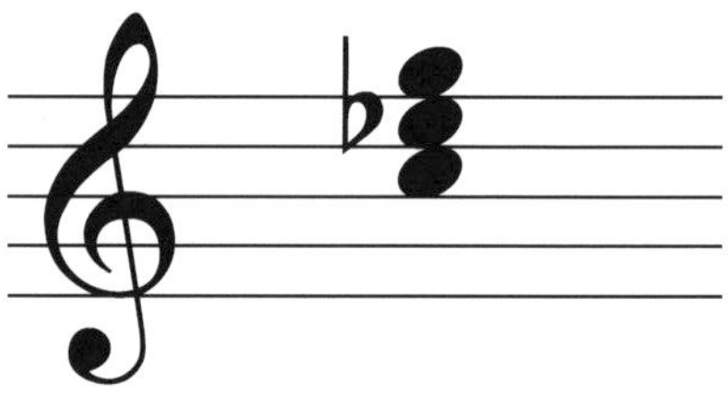

Cm

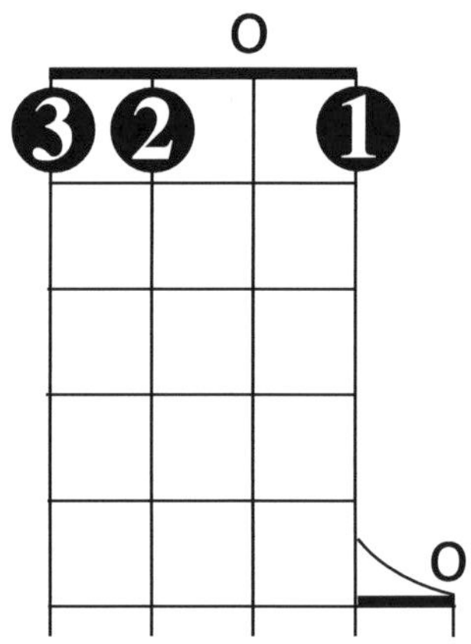

C Seventh

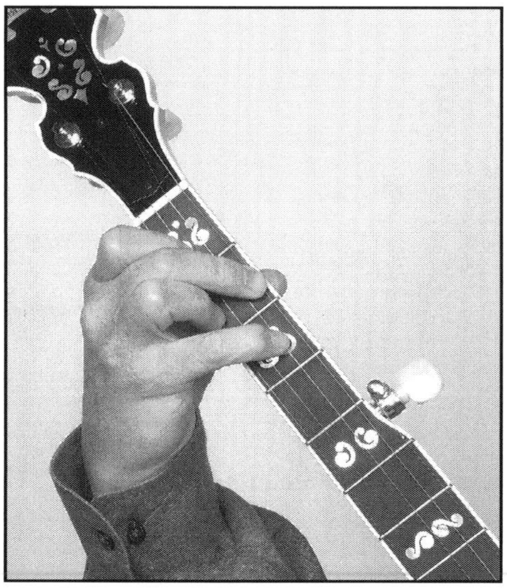

Root - 3rd - 5th - ♭7th
C - E - G - B♭

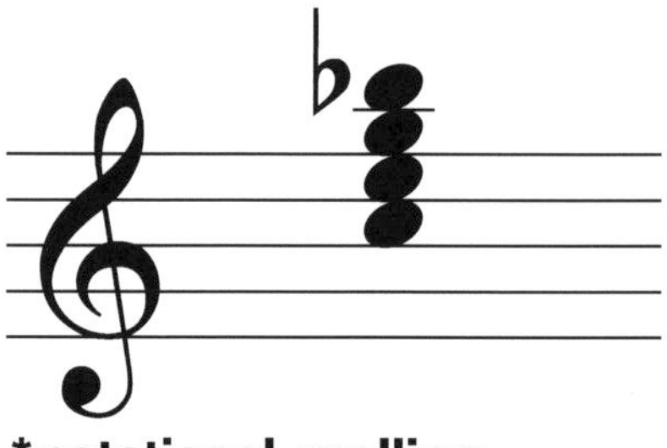

C7

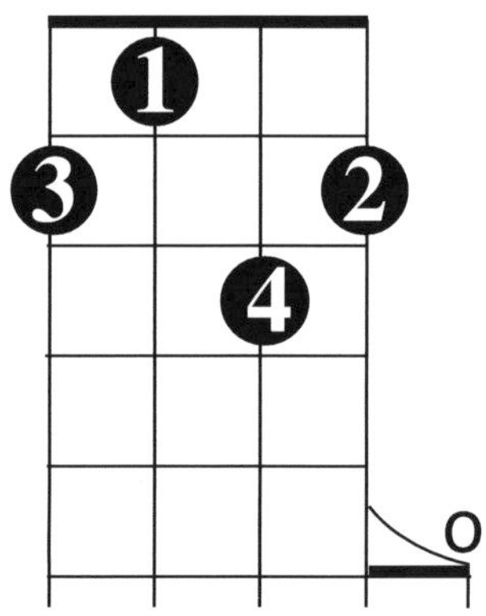

***notational spelling not necessarily the same as voicing of pictured chord inversion.**

C Chords

X = Do not play 5th string

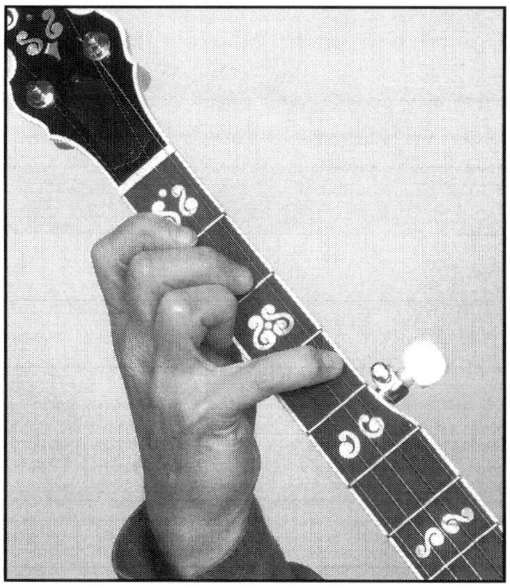

C Diminished

Root - ♭3rd - ♭5th - ♭♭7th
C - E♭ - G♭ - B♭♭

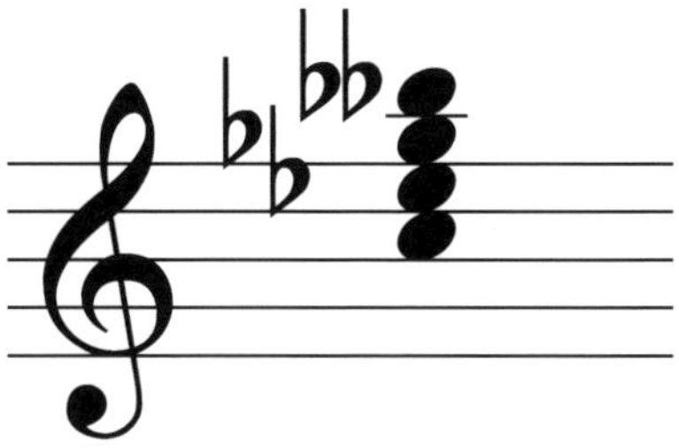

C° or Cdim

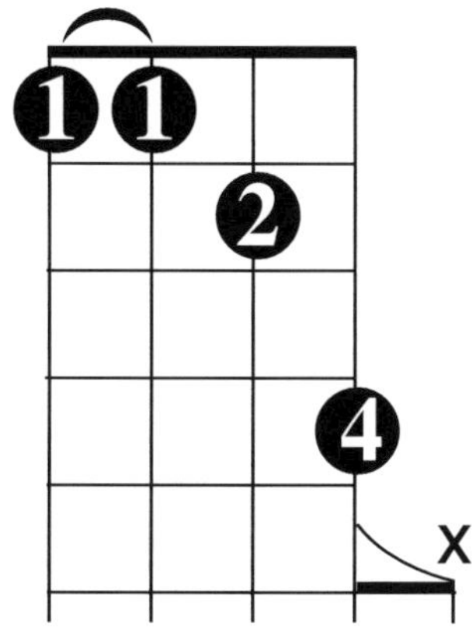

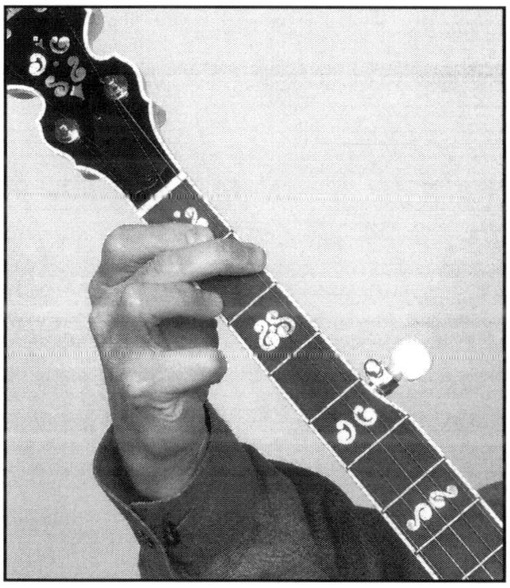

C Augmented

Root - 3rd - ♯5th
C - E - G♯

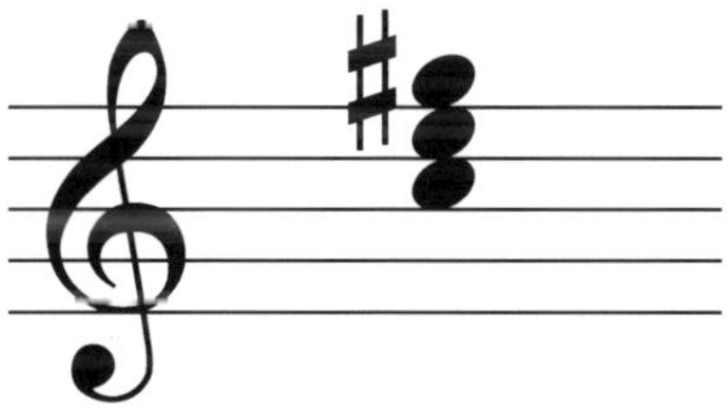

C+ or Caug

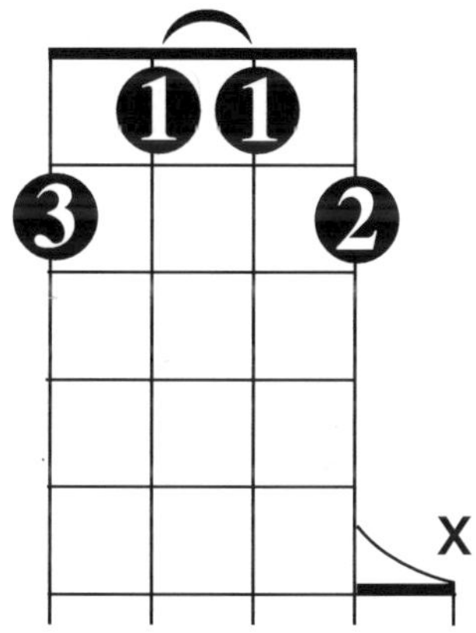

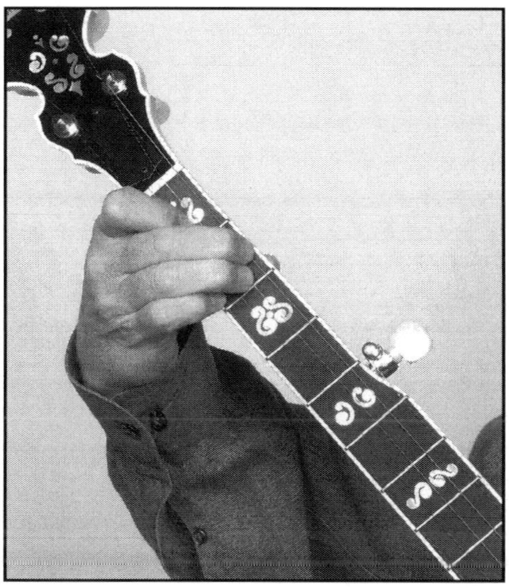

C Sixth

Root - 3rd - 5th - 6th
C - E - G - A

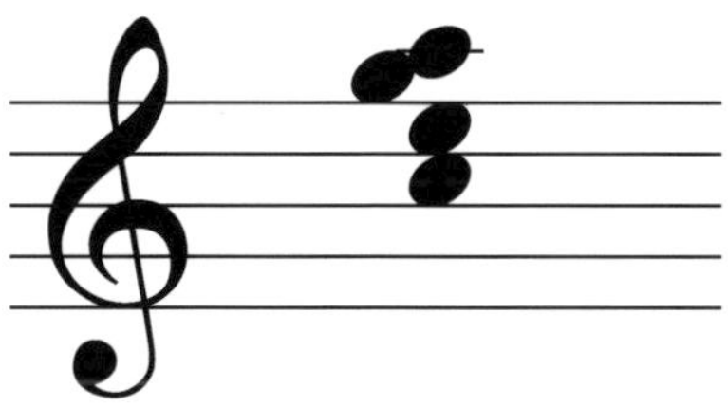

C6

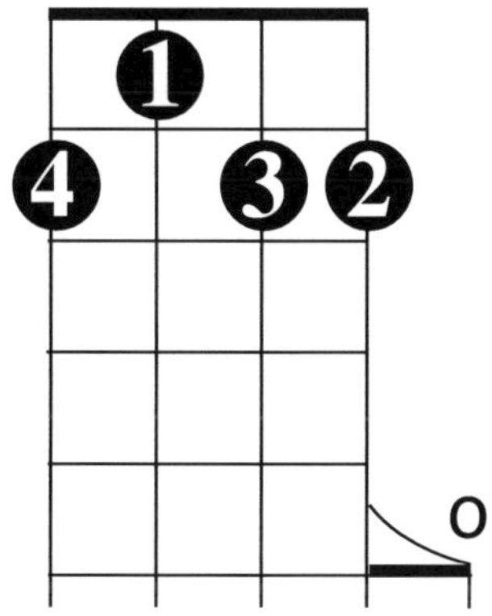

C Chords

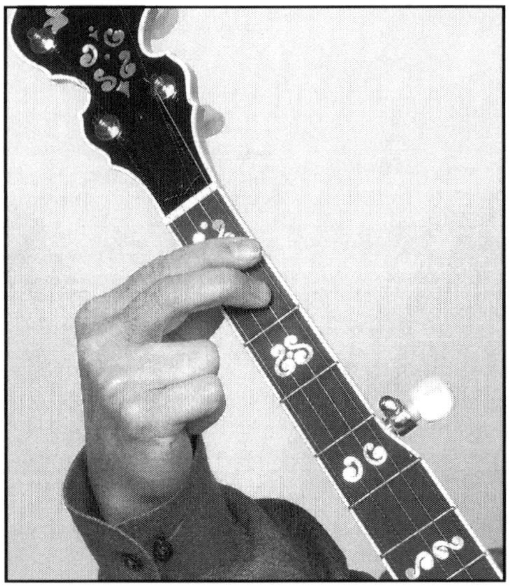

C Minor Sixth

Root - ♭3rd - 5th - 6th
C - E♭ - G - A

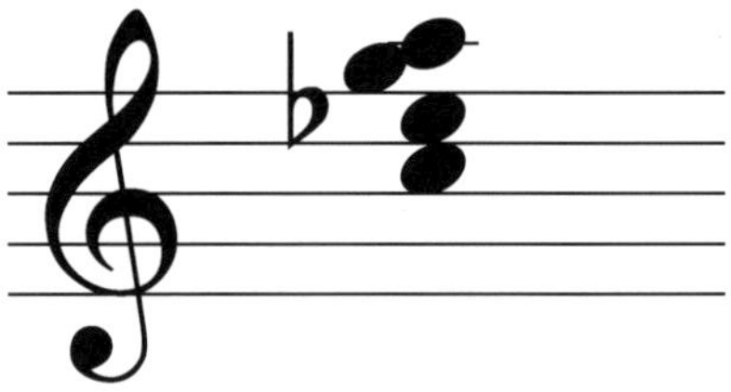

Cm6

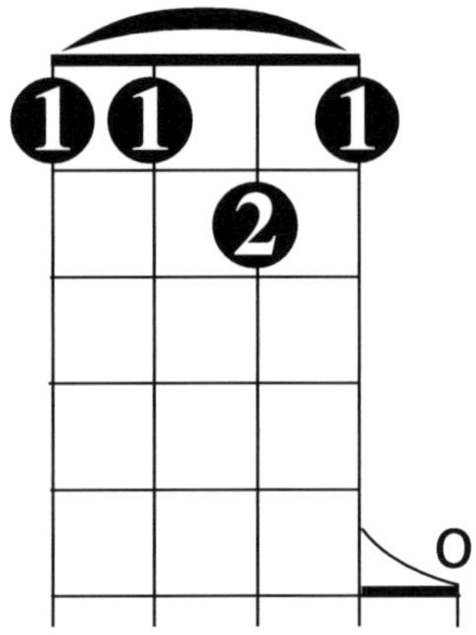

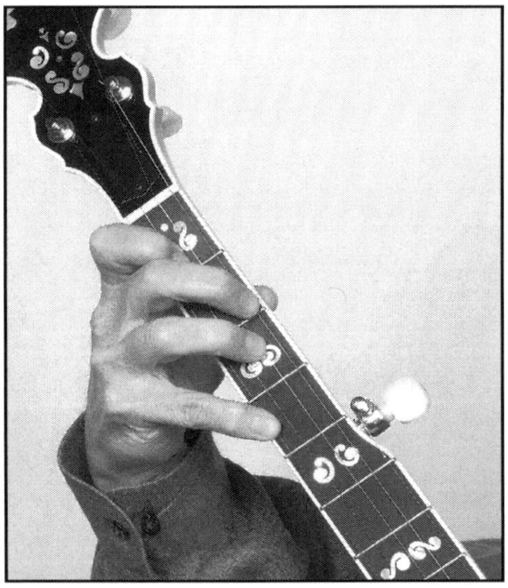

C Seven Flat Five

Root - 3rd - ♭5th - ♭7th
C - E - G♭ - B♭

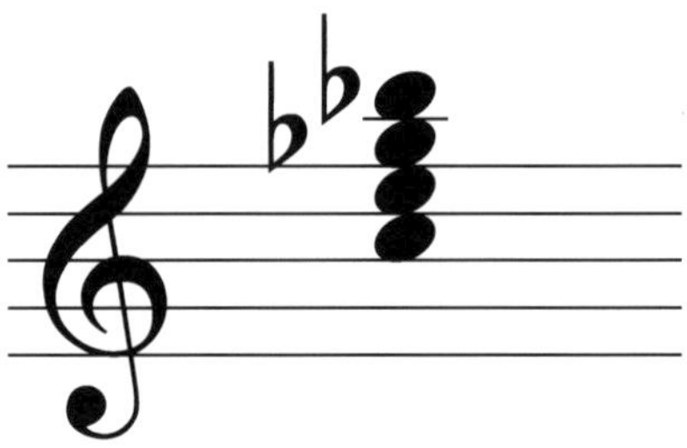

C7♭5

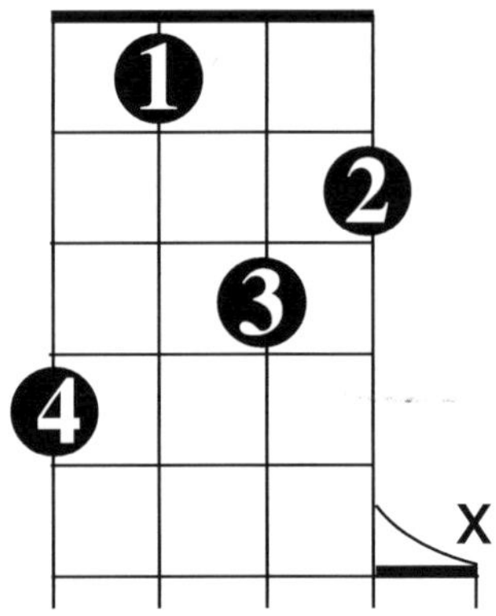

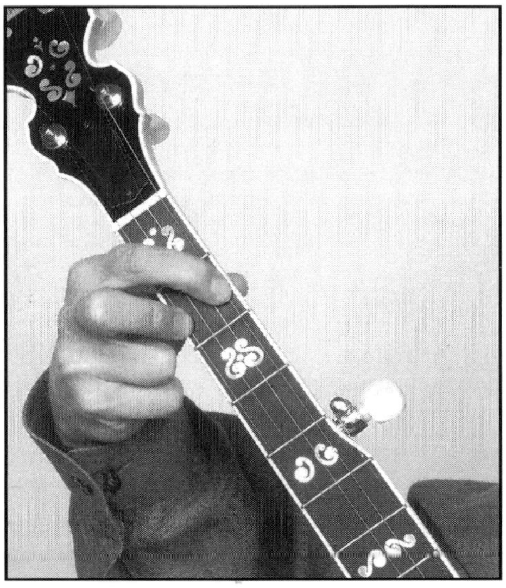

C Major Seventh

Root - 3rd - 5th - 7th
C - E - G - B

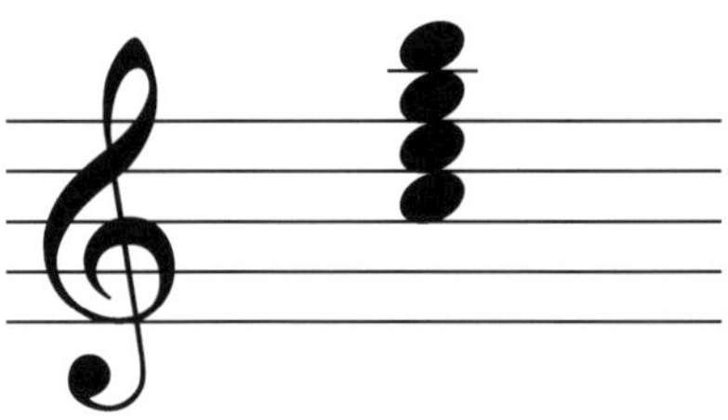

CMaj7

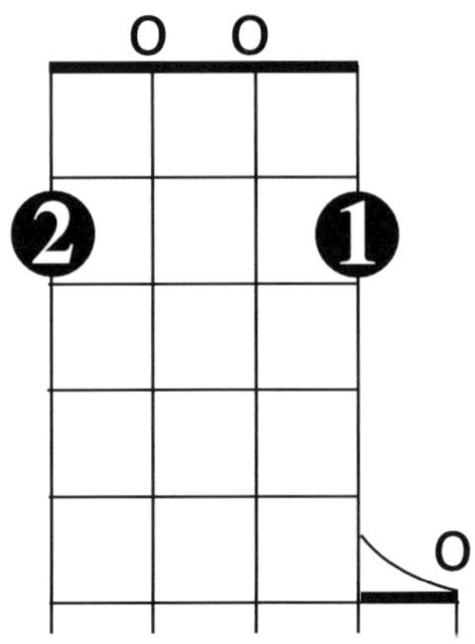

C Chords

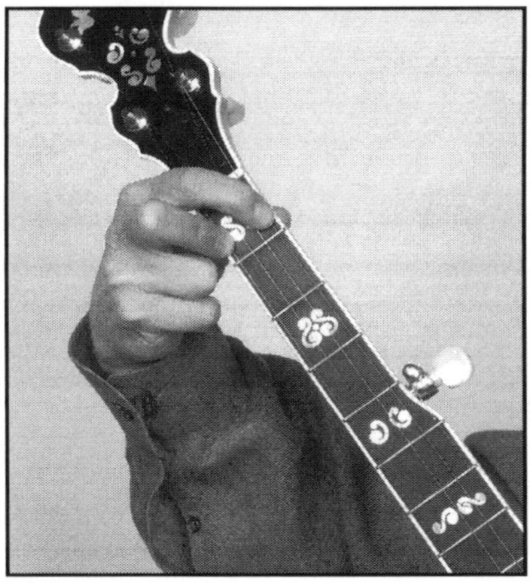

C Major Seventh Flat Third

Root - ♭3rd - 5th - 7th
C - E♭ - G - B

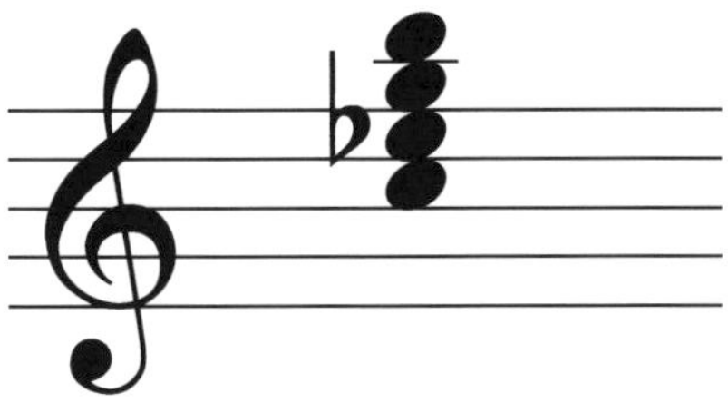

CMaj7♭3

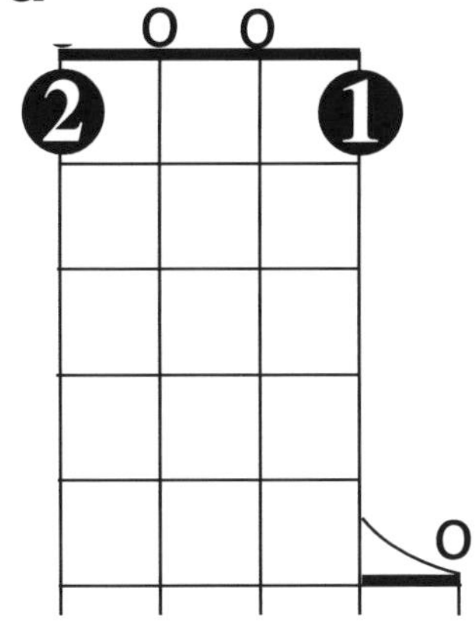

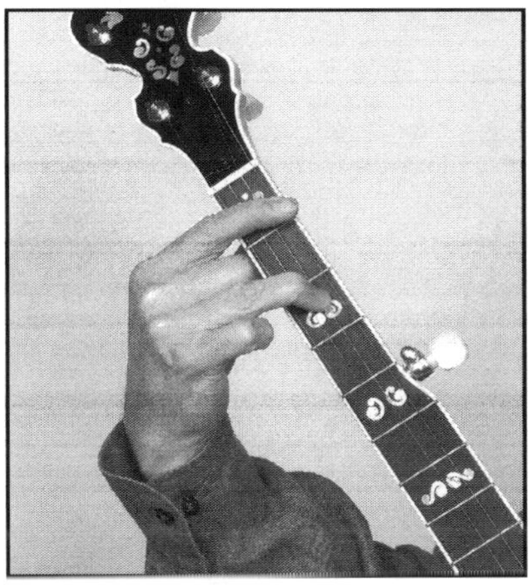

C Minor Seventh

Root - ♭3rd - 5th - ♭7th
C - E♭ - G - B♭

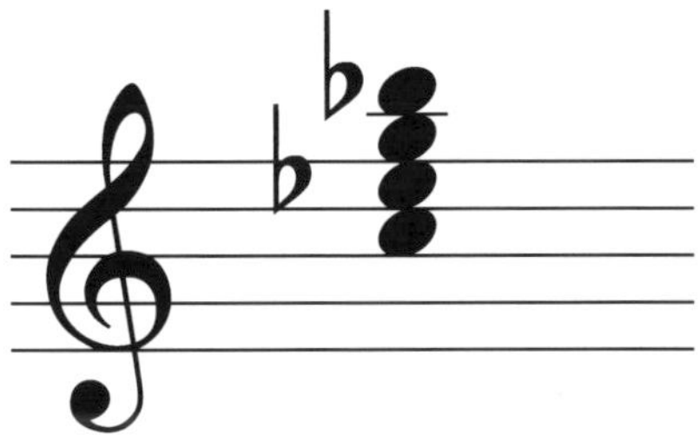

Cm7

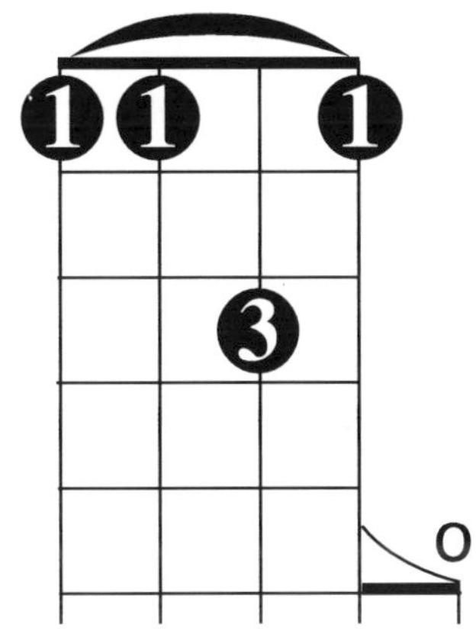

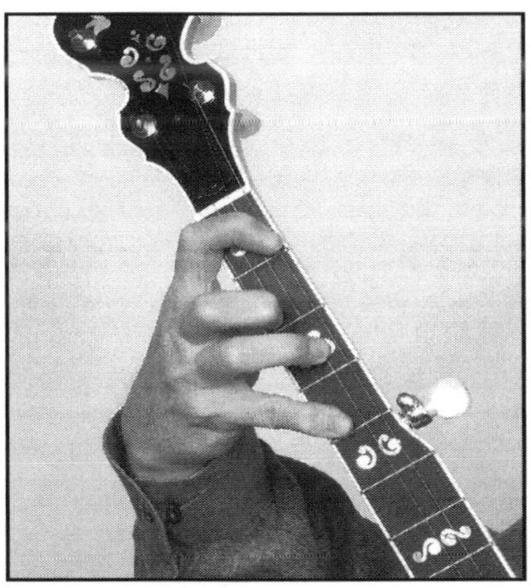

C Minor Seventh Flat Five*

Root - ♭3rd - ♭5th - ♭7th
C - E♭ - G♭ - B♭

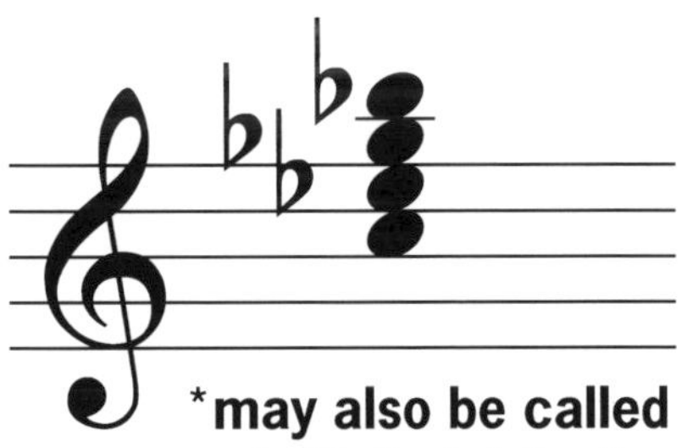

*may also be called half diminished

Cm7♭5

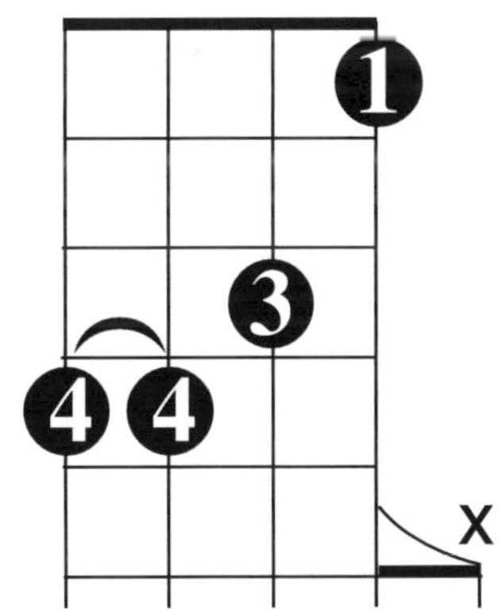

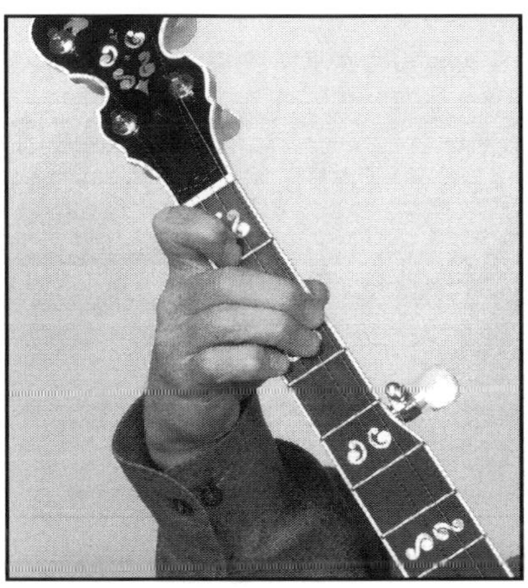

C Seventh Suspended Fourth

Root - 4th - 5th - ♭7th
C - F - G - B♭

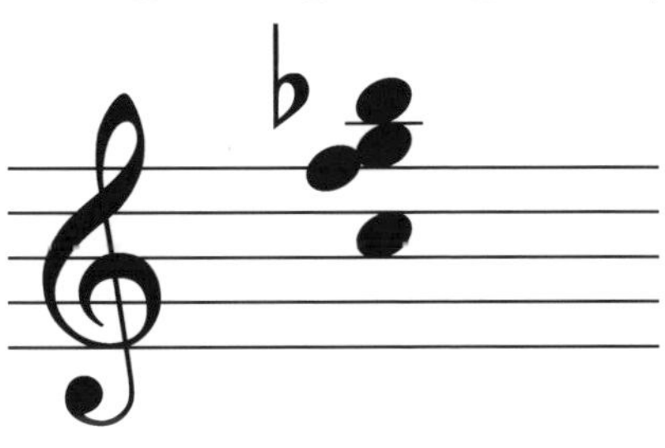

C7sus4

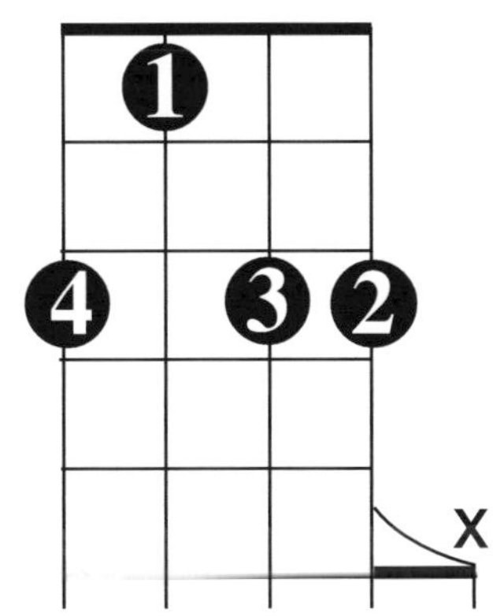

D♭/C♯ Chords

D♭ Major

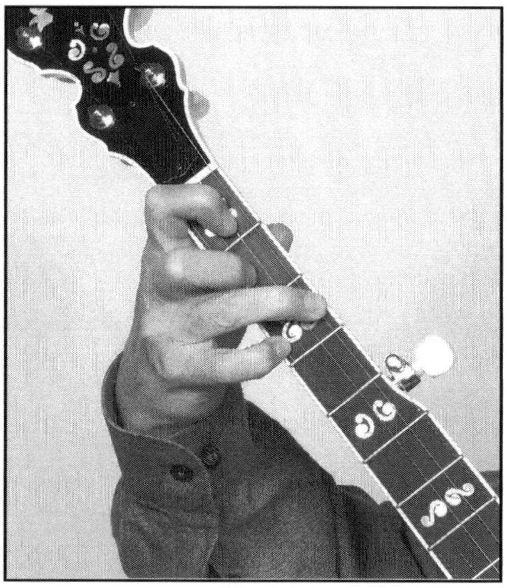

Root - 3rd - 5th
D♭ - F - A♭
C♯ - E♯ - G♯

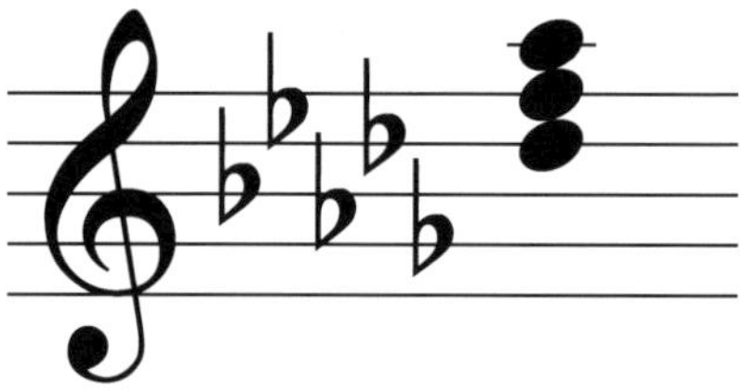

D♭

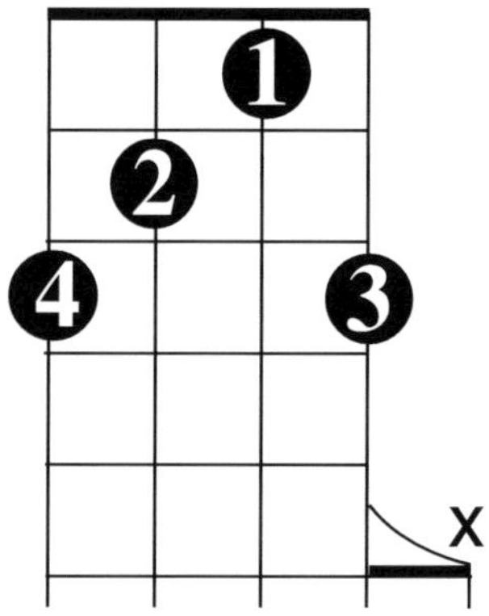

D♭ Minor

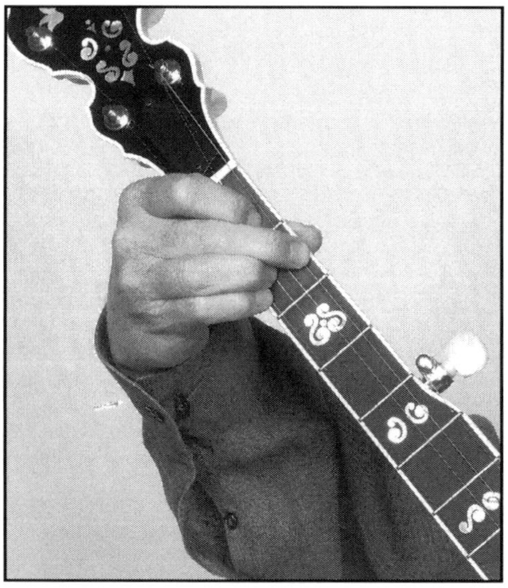

Root - ♭3rd - 5th
D♭ - F♭ - A♭
C♯ - E♮ - G♯

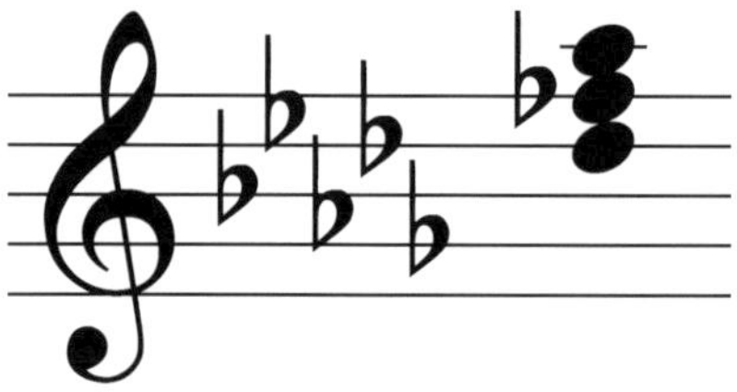

D♭m

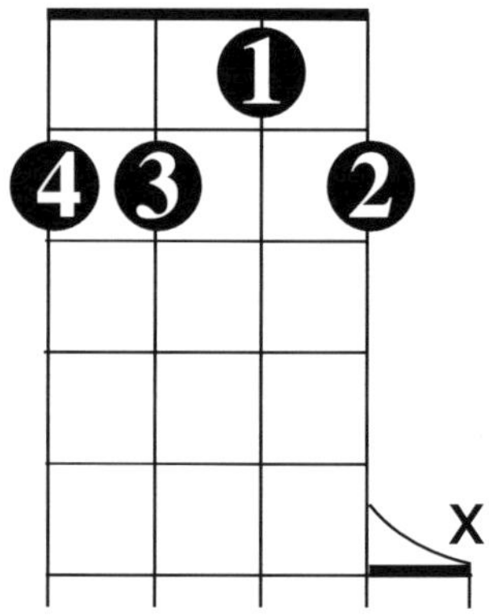

D♭ Seventh

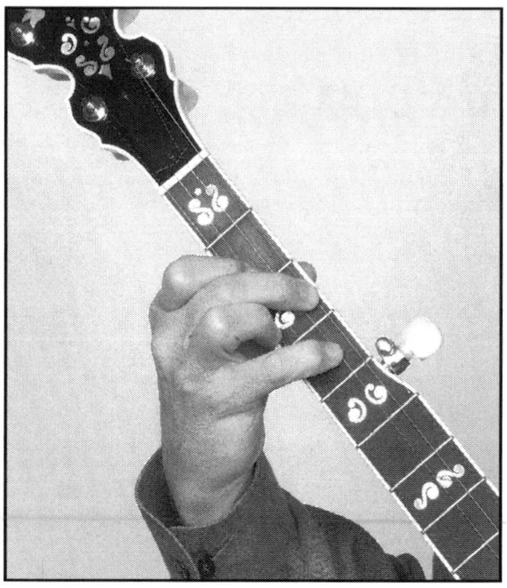

Root - 3rd - 5th - ♭7th
D♭ - F - A♭ - C♭
C♯ - E♯ - G♯ - B

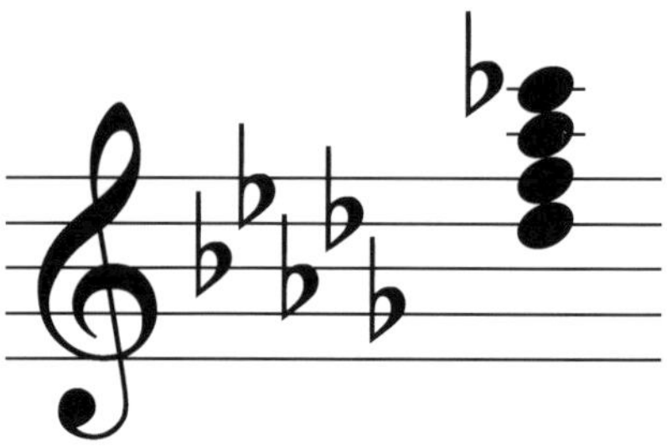

D♭7

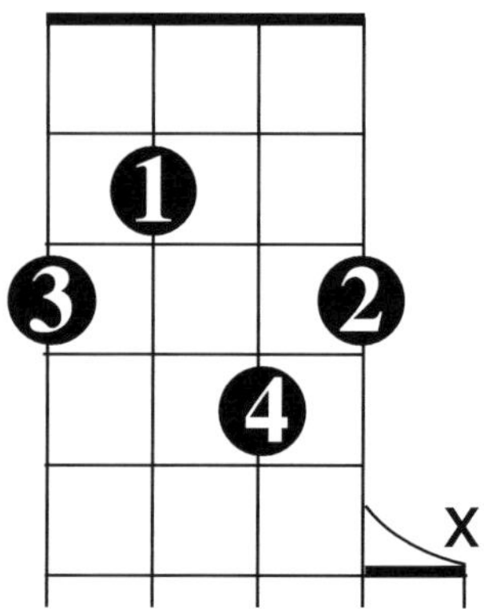

D♭/C♯ Chords

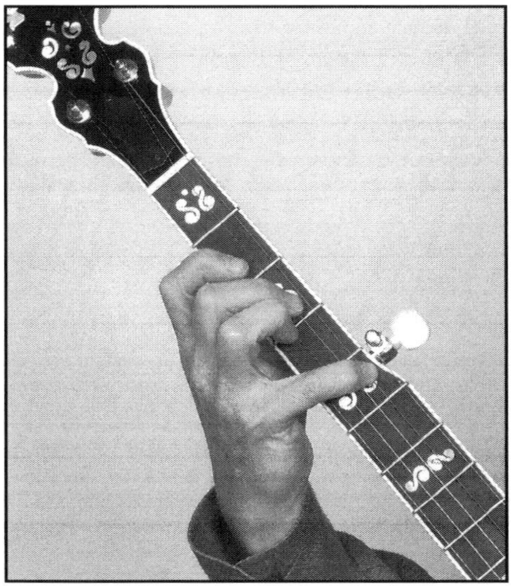

D♭ Diminished

Root - ♭3rd - ♭5th - 𝄫7th
D♭ - F♭ - A𝄫 - C𝄫
C♯ - E - G - B♭

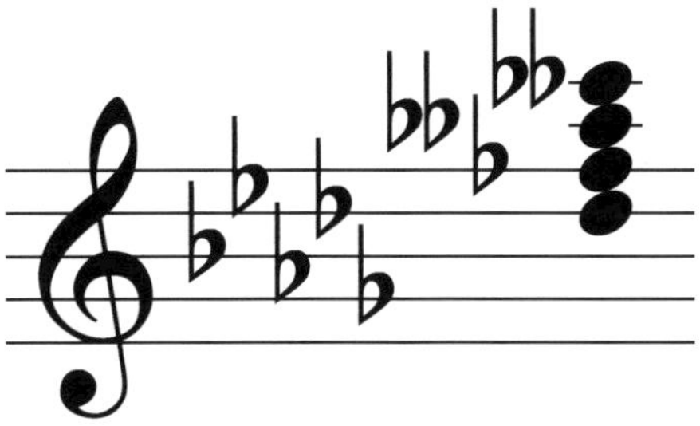

D♭°

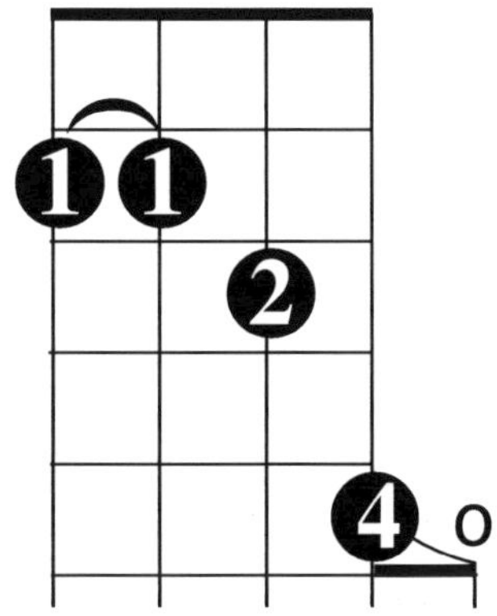

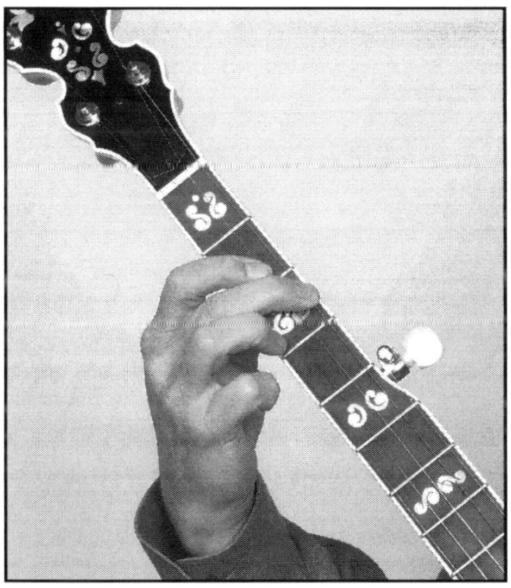

D♭ Augmented

Root - 3rd - ♯5th
D♭ - F - A♮
C♯ - E♯ - G𝄪

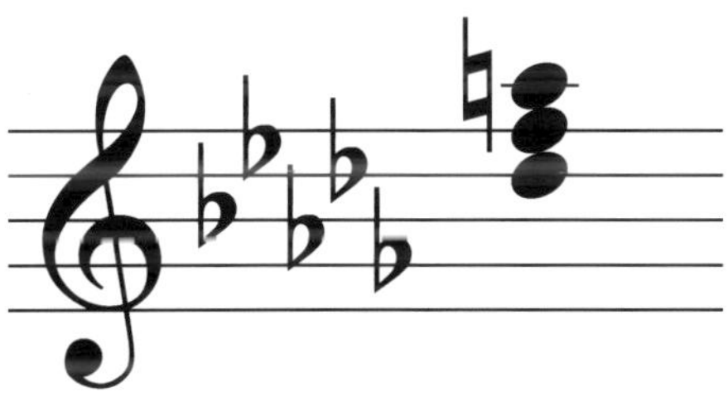

D♭+

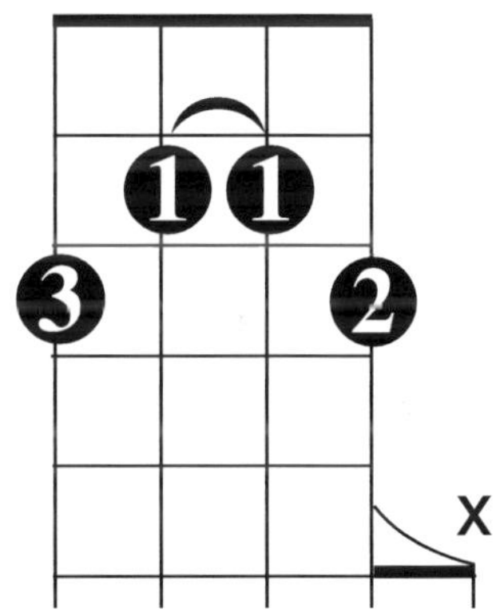

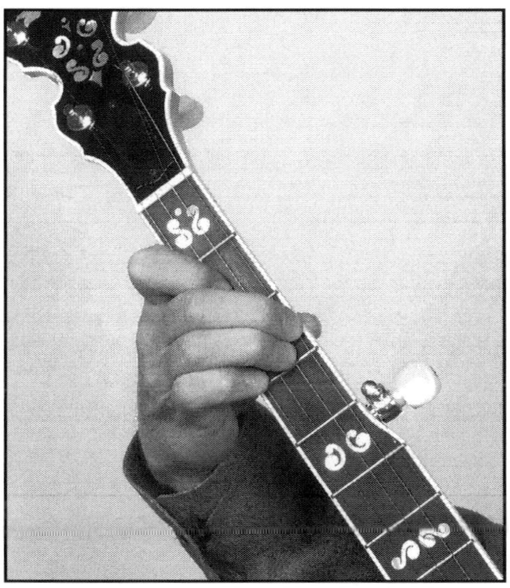

D♭ Sixth

Root - 3rd - 5th - 6th
D♭ - F - A♭ - B♭
C♯ - E♯ - G♯ - A♯

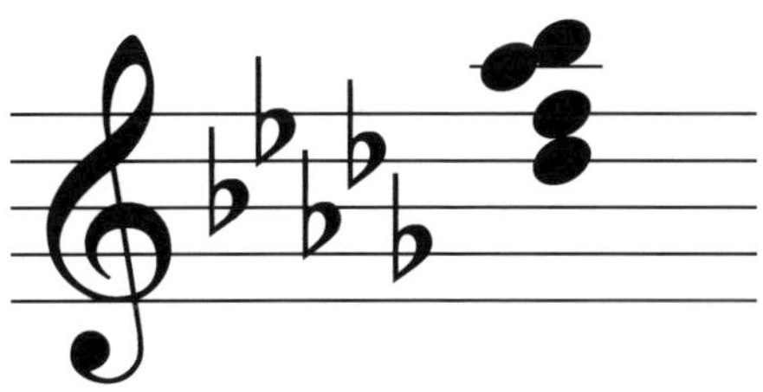

D♭6

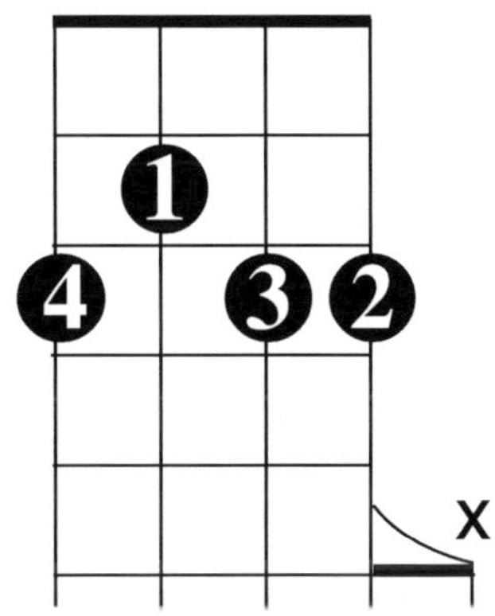

D♭/C♯ Chords

D♭ Minor Sixth

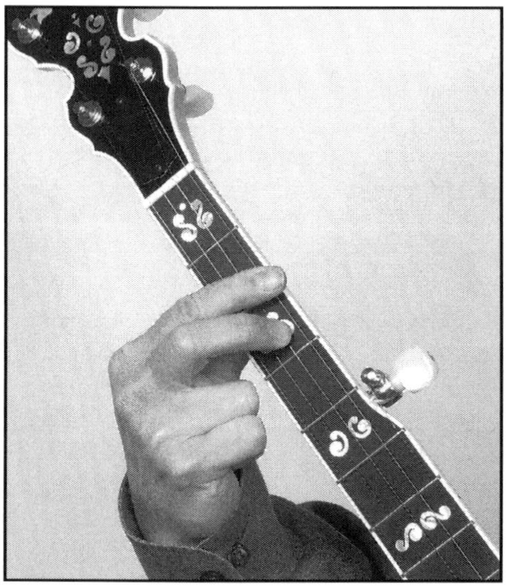

Root - ♭3rd - 5th - 6th
D♭ - F♭ - A♭ - B♭
C♯ - E - G♯ - A♯

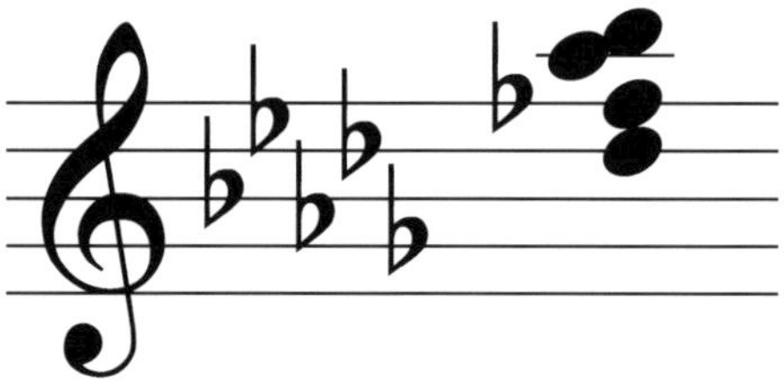

D♭m6

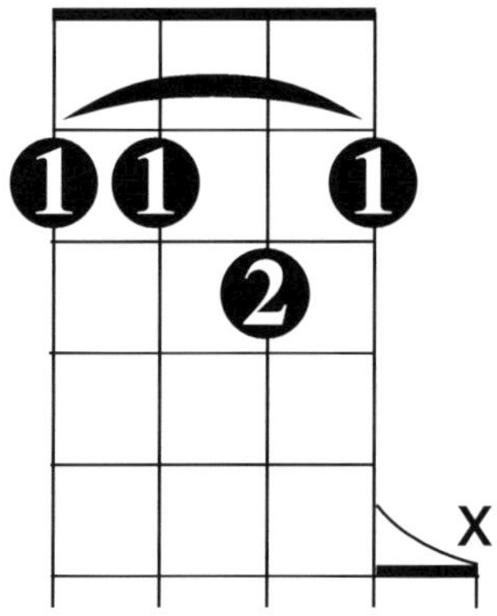

D♭ Seven Flat Five

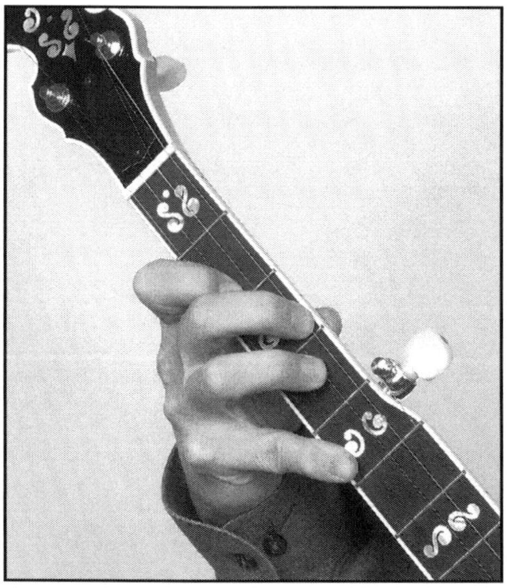

Root - 3rd - ♭5th - ♭7th
D♭ - F - A♭♭ - C♭
C♯ - E♯ - G♮ - B

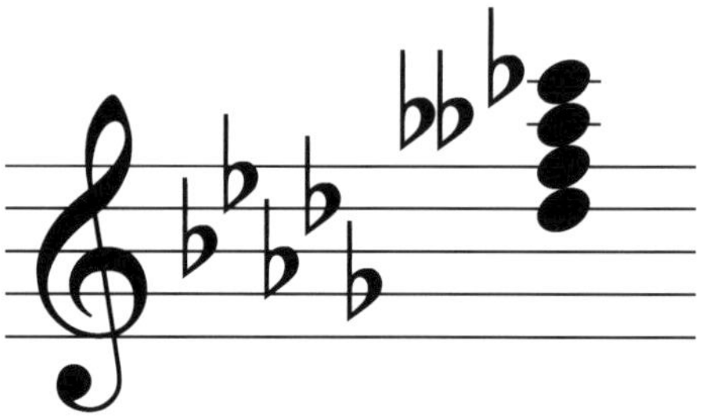

D♭7♭5

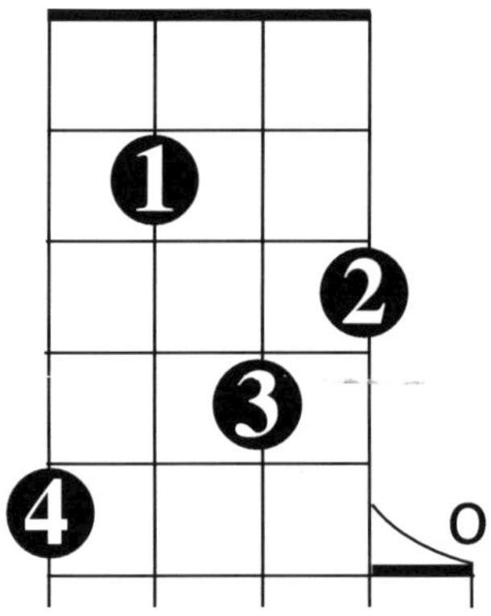

D♭ Major Seventh

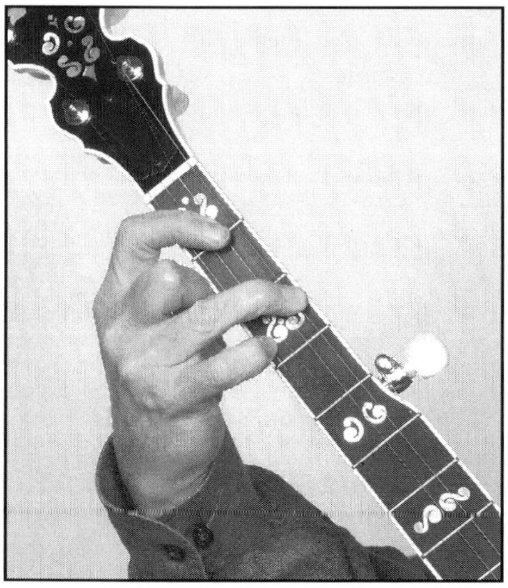

Root - 3rd - 5th - 7th
D♭ - F - A♭ - C
C♯ - E♯ - G♯ - B♯

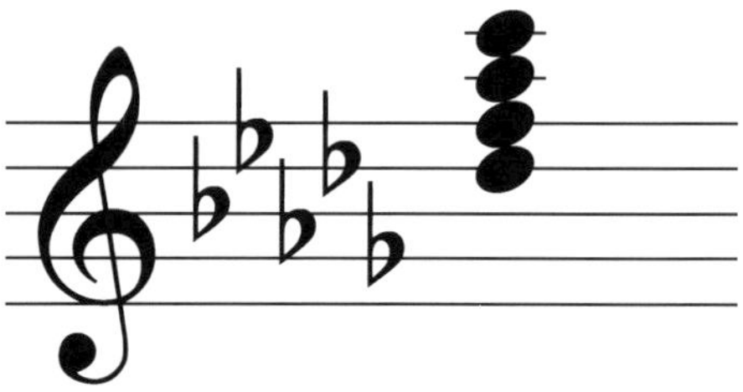

D♭Maj7

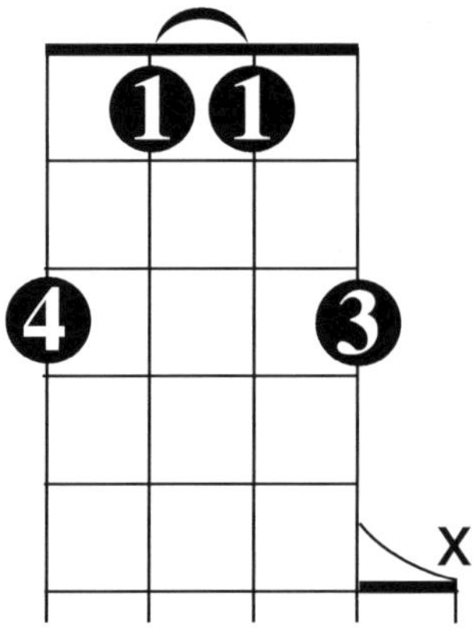

D♭/C♯ Chords

D♭ Major Seventh Flat Third

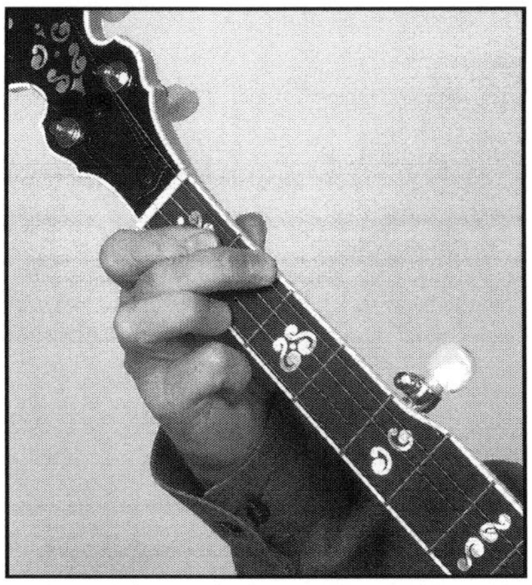

Root - ♭3rd - 5th - 7th
D♭ - F♭ - A♭ - C
C♯ - E - G♯ - B♯

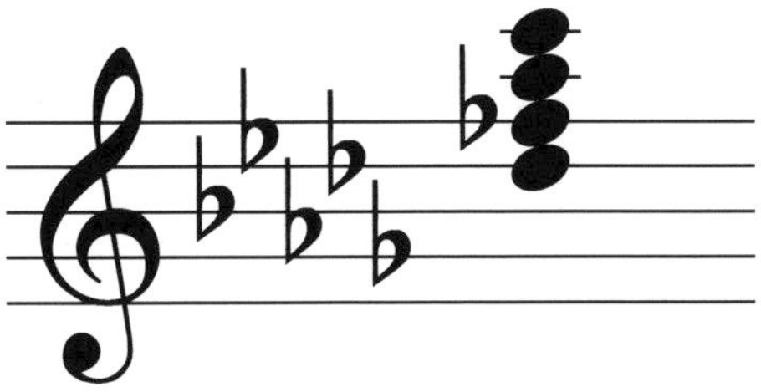

D♭Maj7♭3

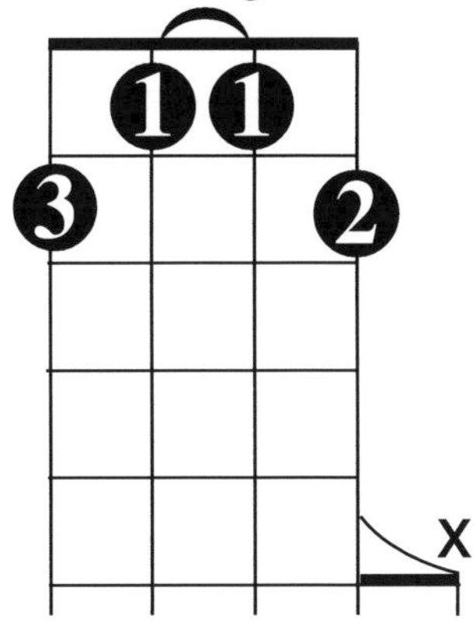

D♭ Minor Seventh

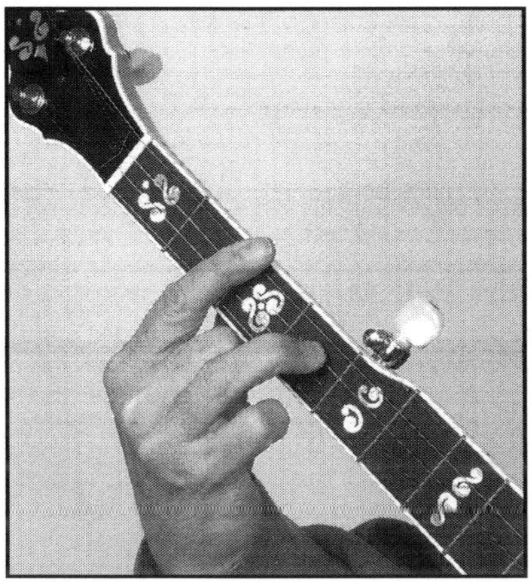

Root - ♭3rd - 5th - ♭7th
D♭ - F♭ - A♭ - C♭
C♯ - E - G♯ - B♮

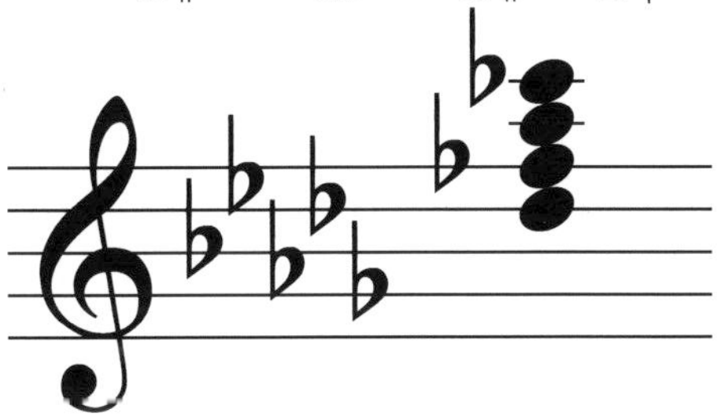

D♭m7

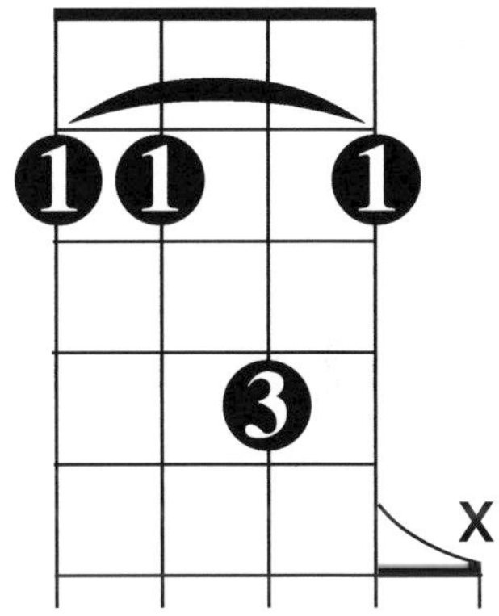

D♭ Minor Seventh Flat Five

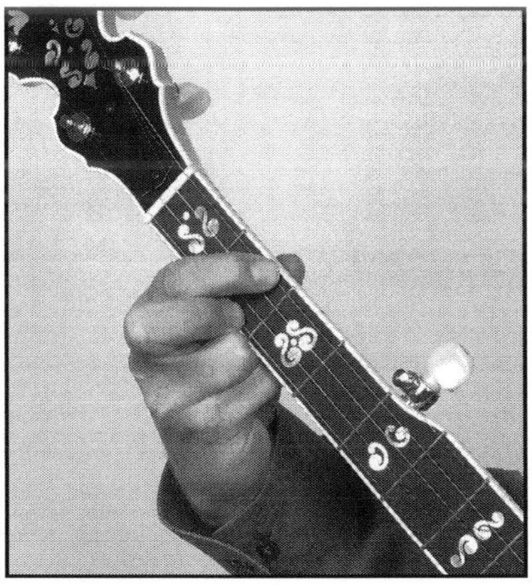

Root - ♭3rd - ♭5th - ♭7th
D♭ - F♭ - A𝄫 - C♭
C♯ - E - G - B

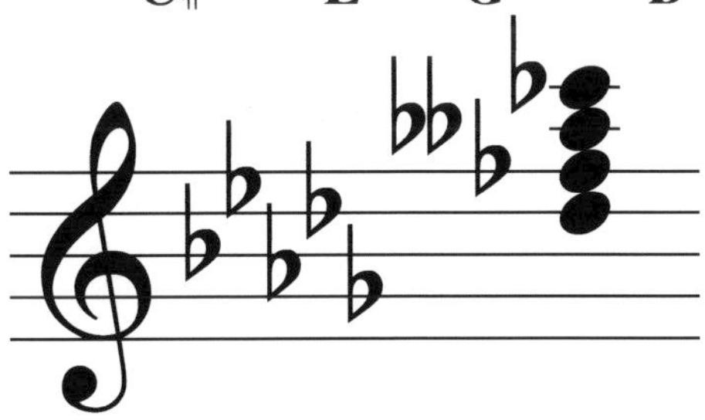

D♭m7♭5

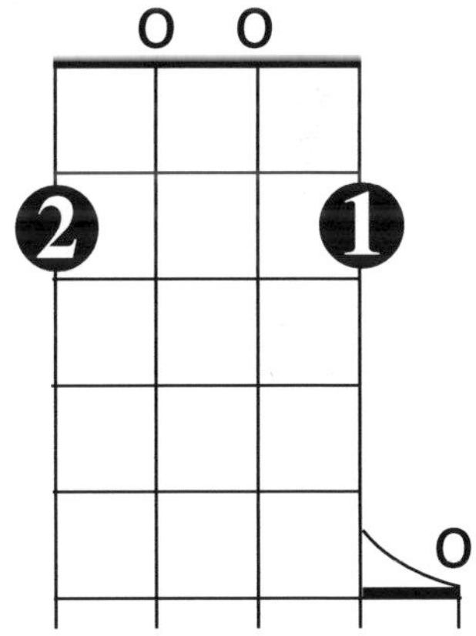

D♭ Seventh Suspended Fourth

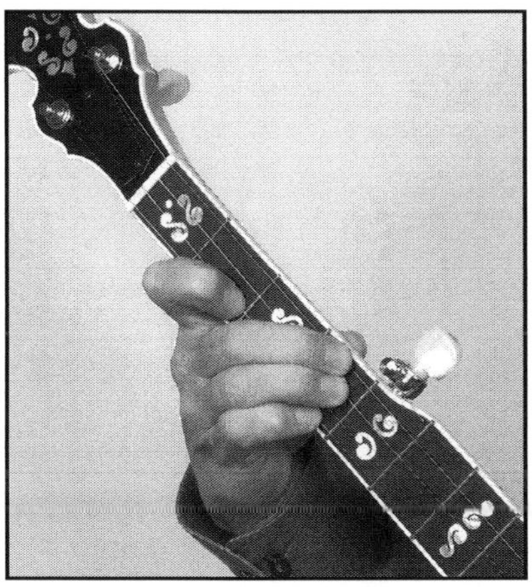

Root - 4th - 5th - ♭7th
D♭ - G♭ - A♭ - C♭
C♯ - F♯ - G♯ - B

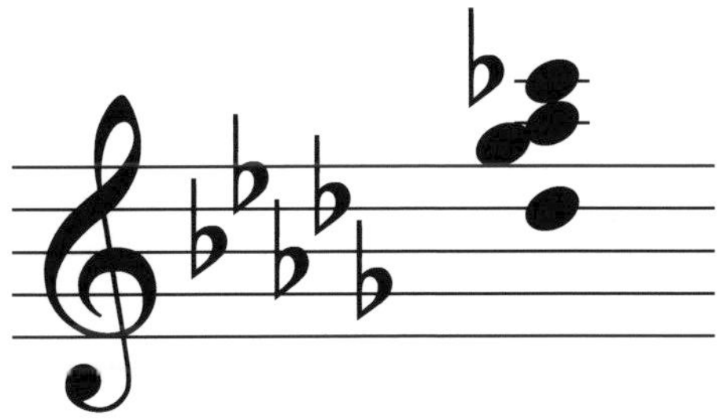

D♭7sus4

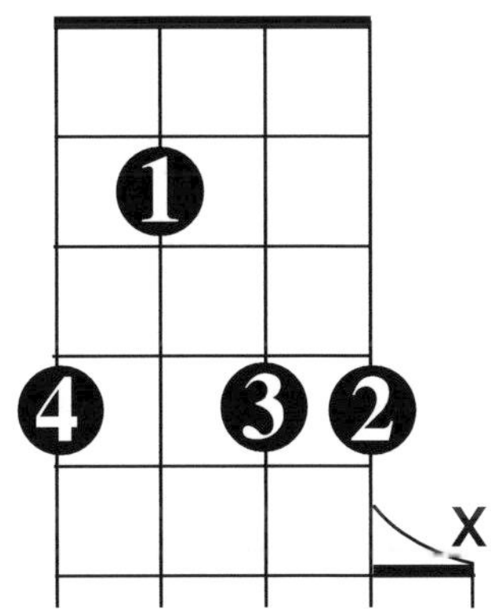

D Chords

D Major

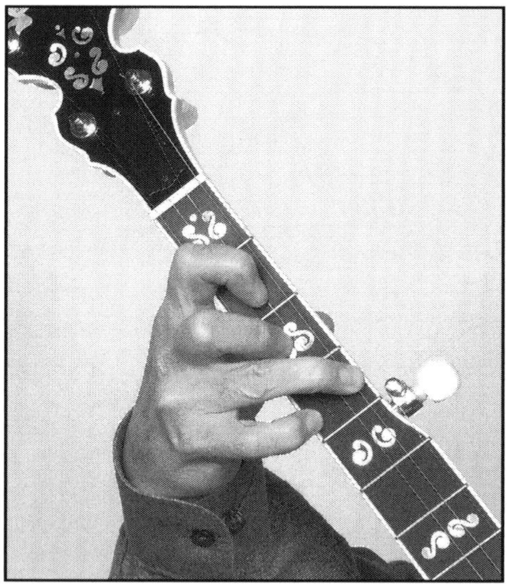

Root - 3rd - 5th
D - F♯ - A

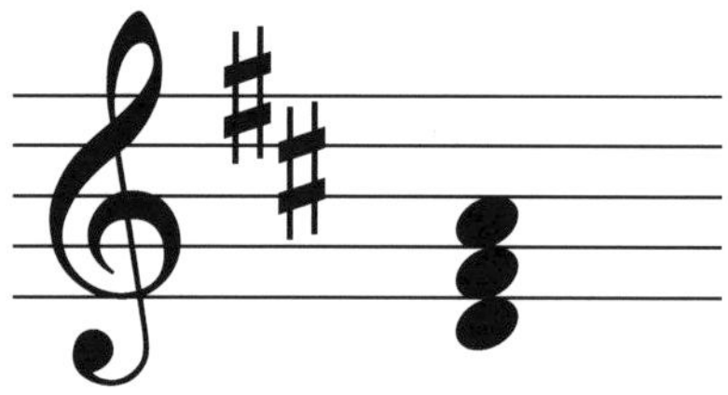

D

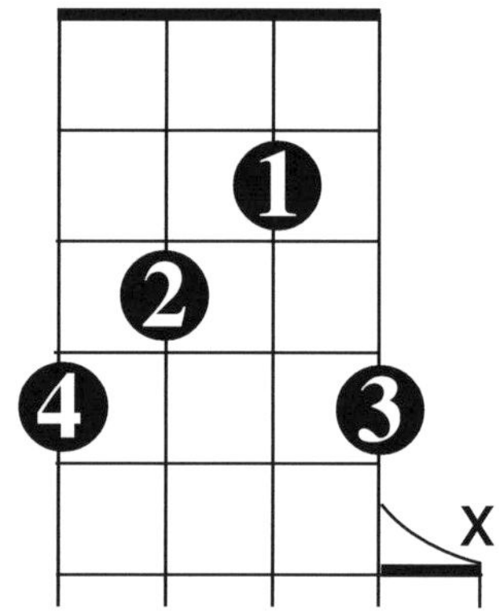

D Minor

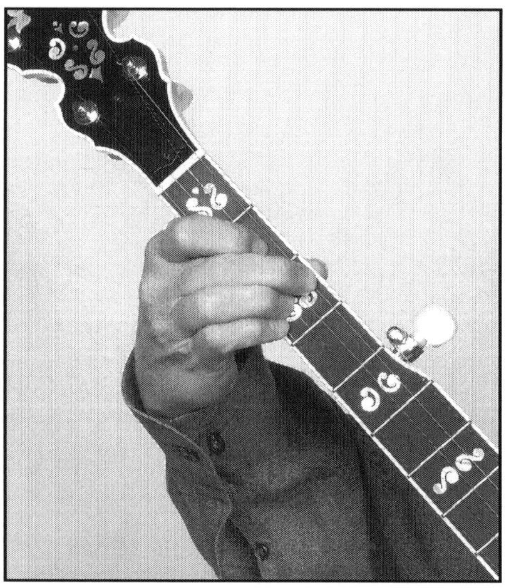

Root - ♭3rd - 5th
D - F♮ - A

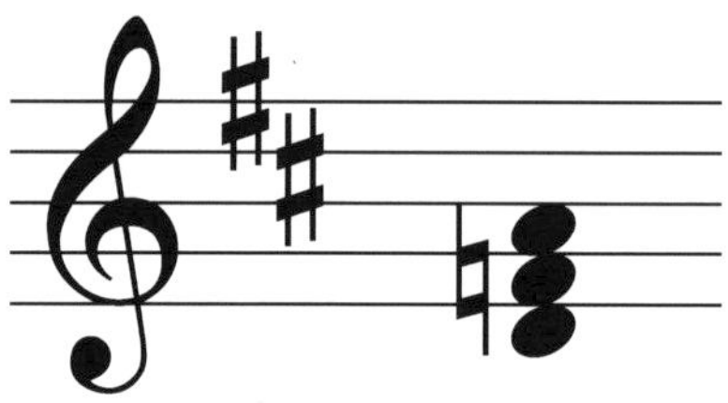

Dm

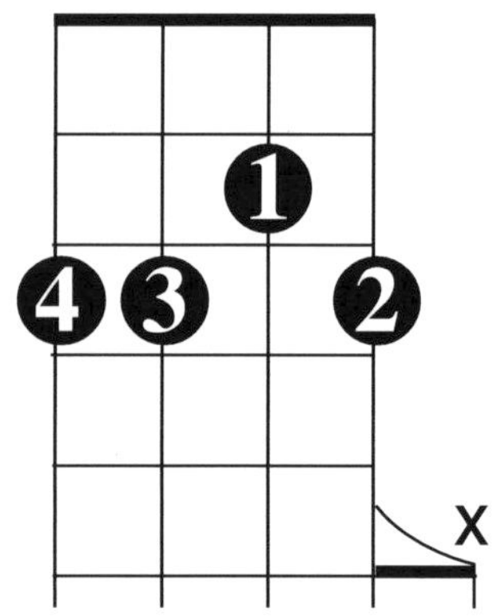

D Seventh

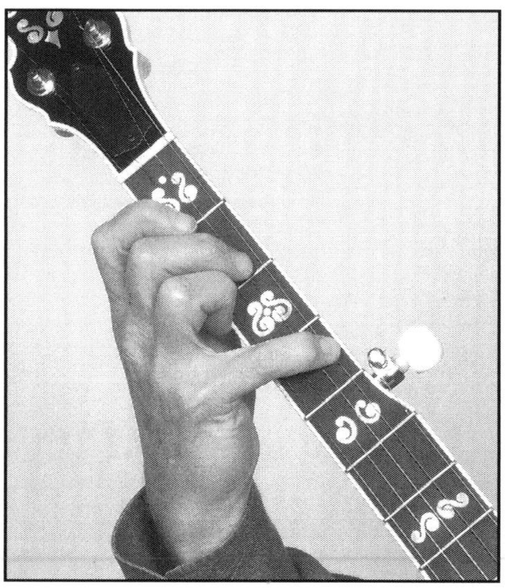

Root - 3rd - 5th - ♭7th
D - F♯ - A - C♮

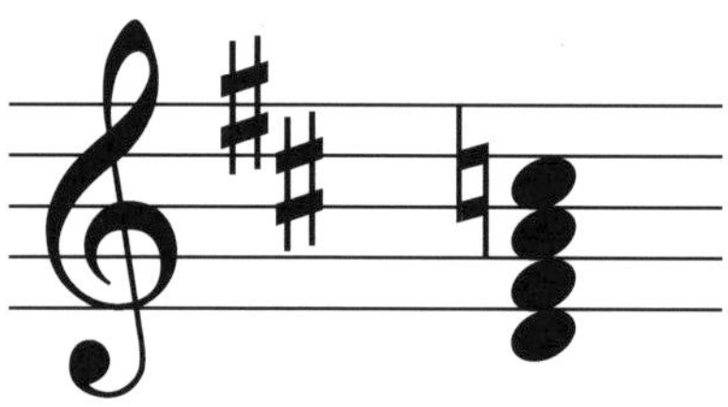

D7

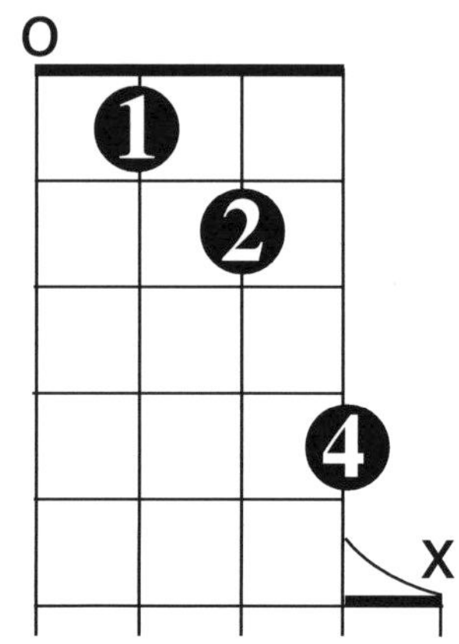

D Chords

D Diminished

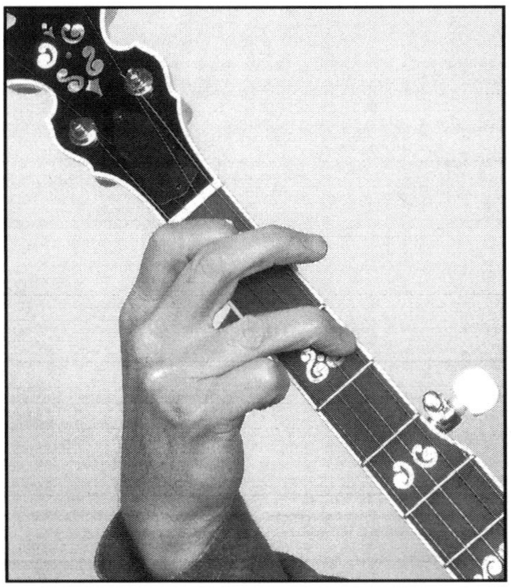

Root - ♭3rd - ♭5th - ♭♭7th
D - F♮ - A♭ - C♭

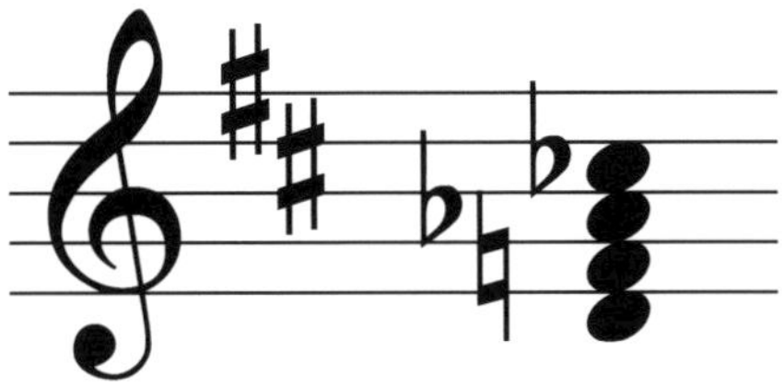

D°

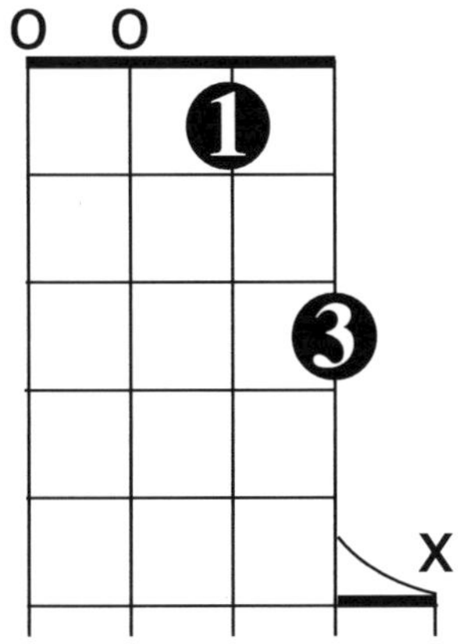

D Augmented

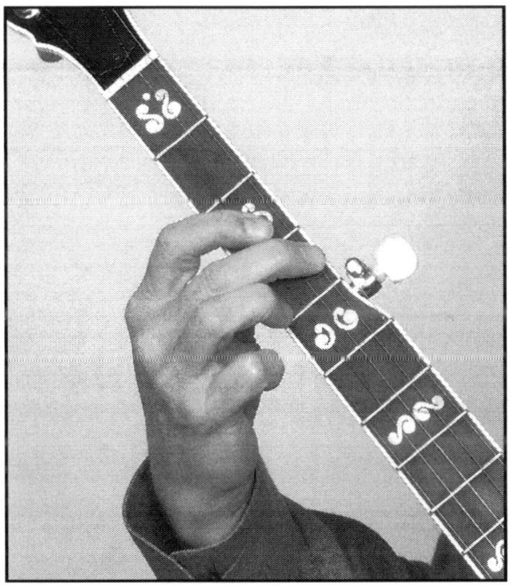

Root - 3rd - ♯5th
D - F♯ - A♯

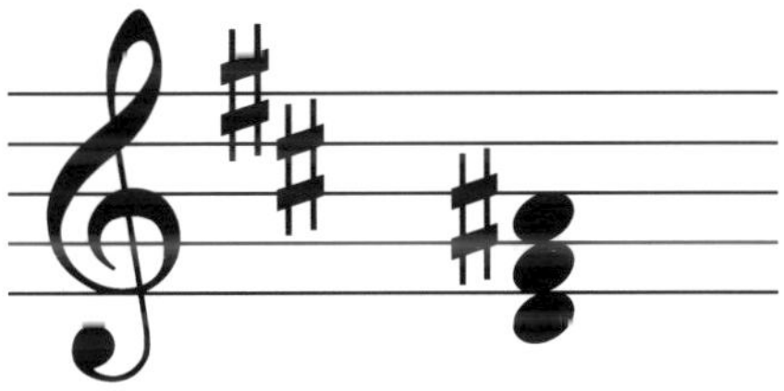

D+

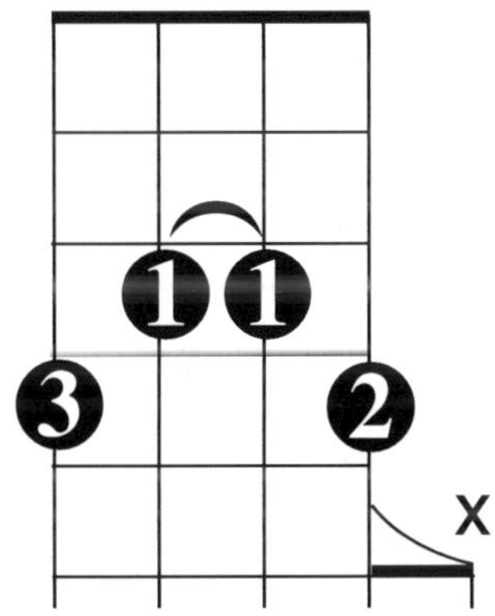

D Sixth

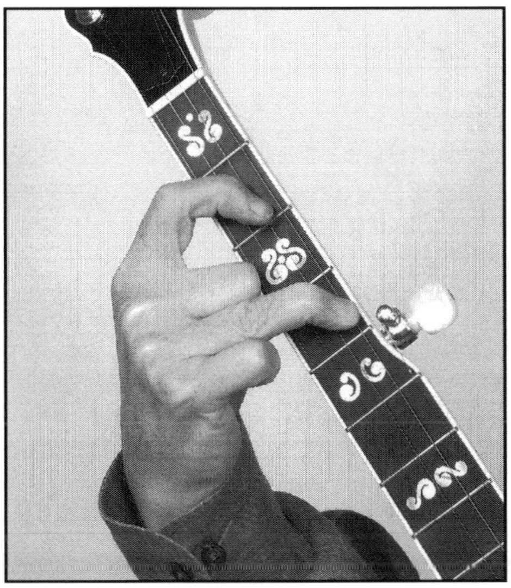

Root - 3rd - 5th - 6th
D - F♯ - A - B

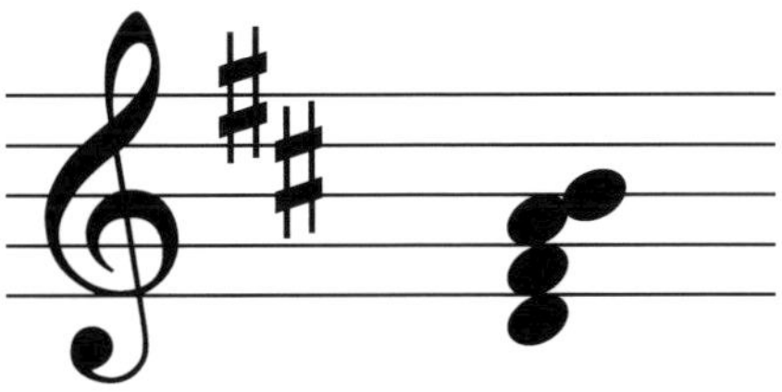

D6

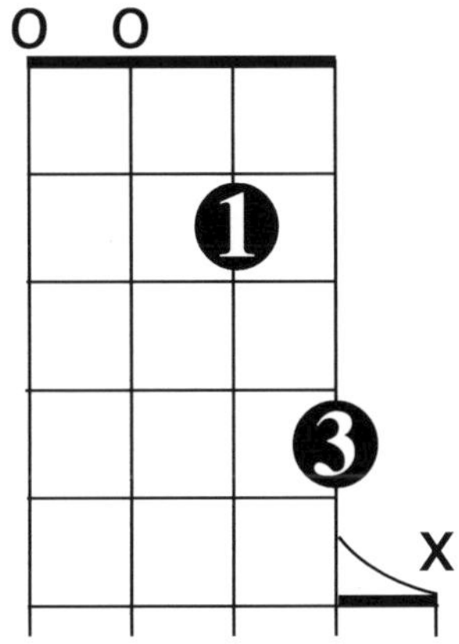

D Chords

D Minor Sixth

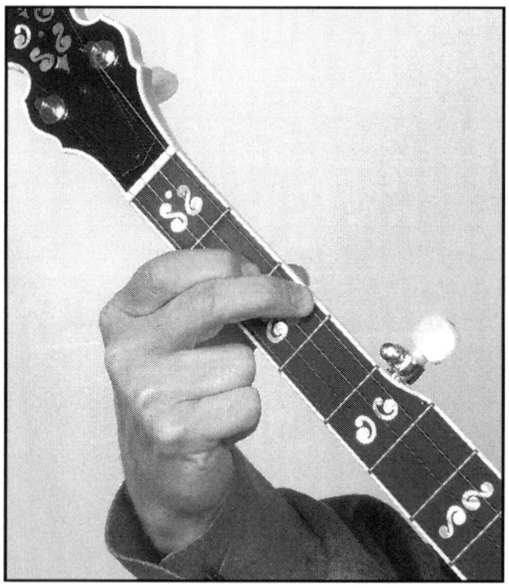

Root - ♭3rd - 5th - 6th
D - F♮ - A - B

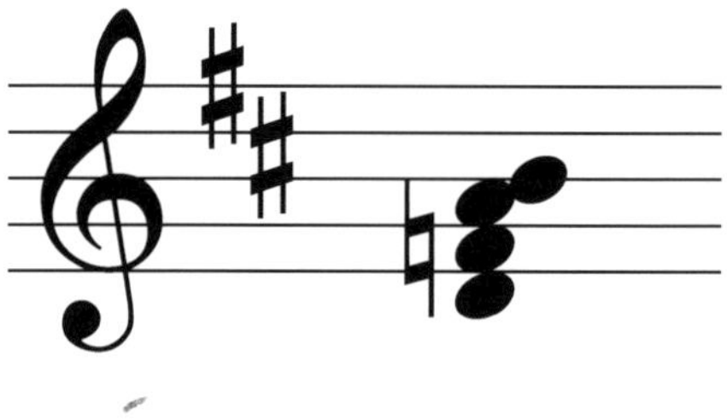

Dm6

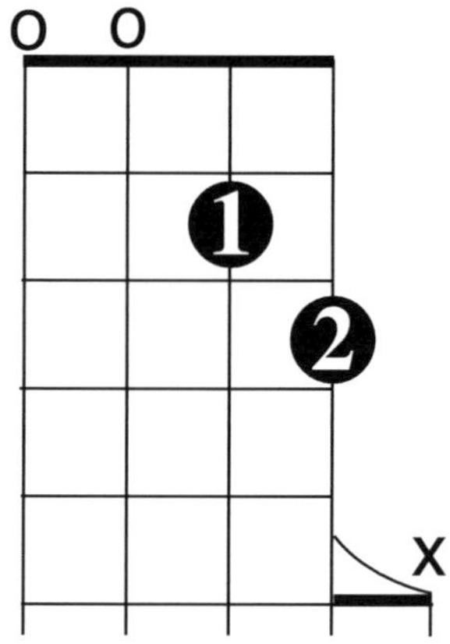

D Seven Flat Five

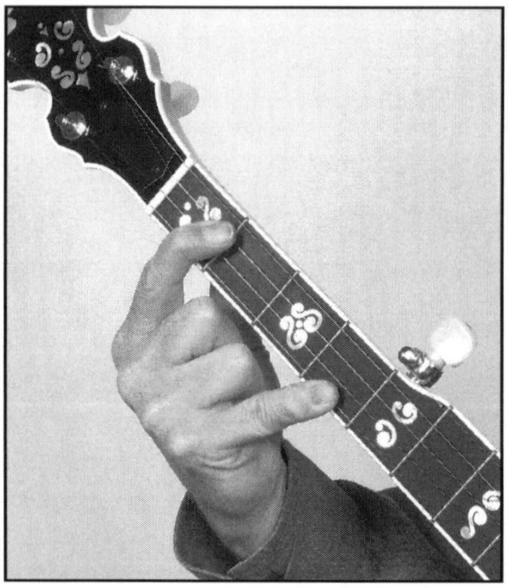

Root - 3rd - ♭5th - ♭7th
D - F♯ - A♭ - C♮

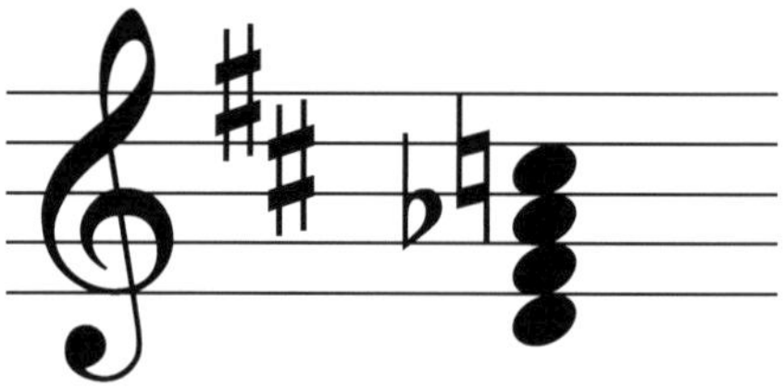

D7♭5

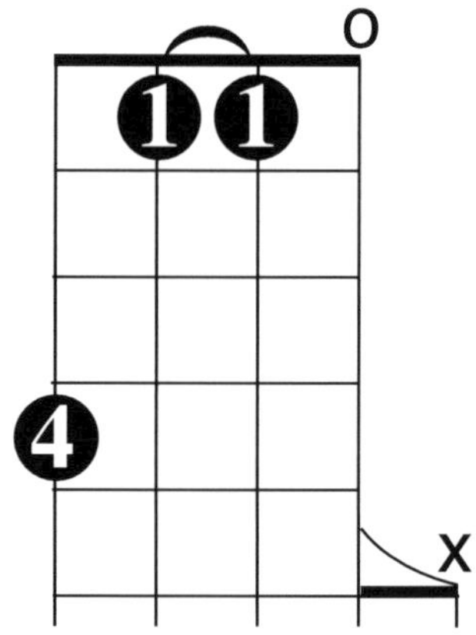

D Major Seventh

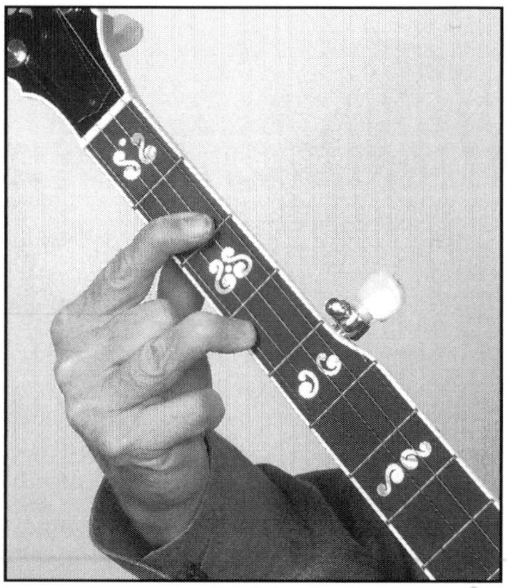

Root - 3rd - 5th - 7th
D - F♯ - A - C♯

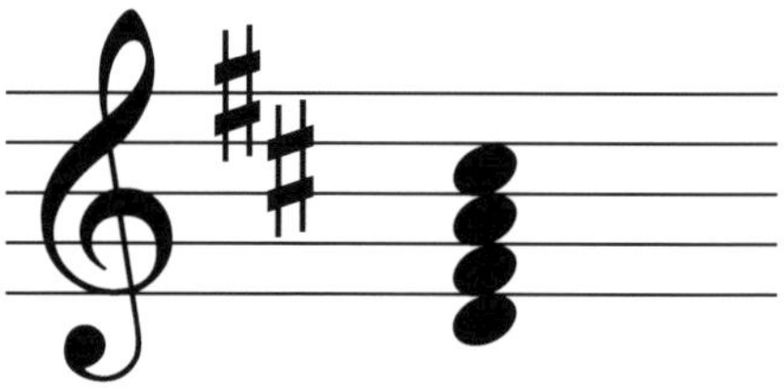

DMaj7

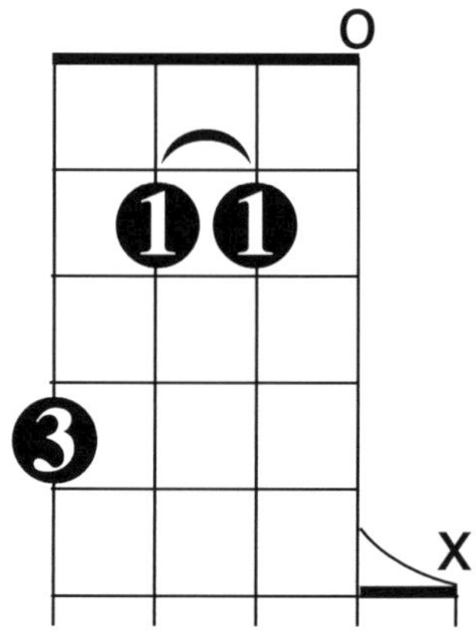

D Chords

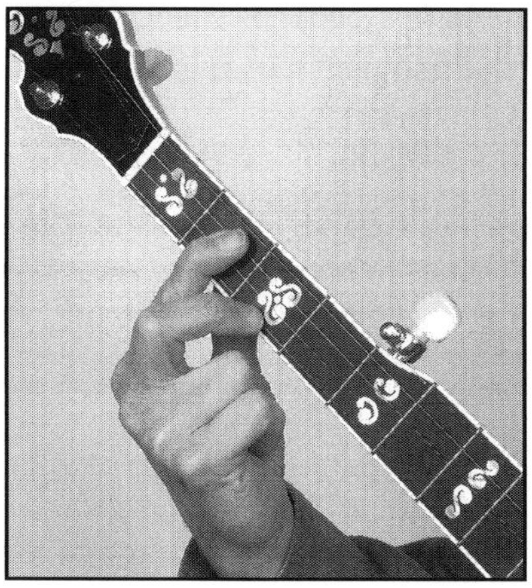

D Major Seventh Flat Third DMaj7♭3

Root - ♭3rd - 5th - 7th
D - F♮ - A - C♯

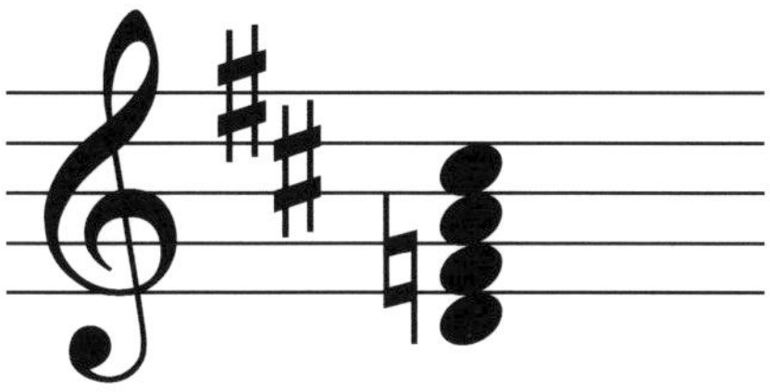

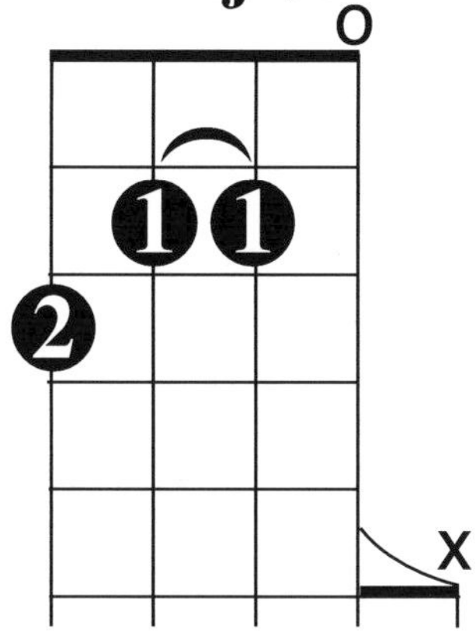

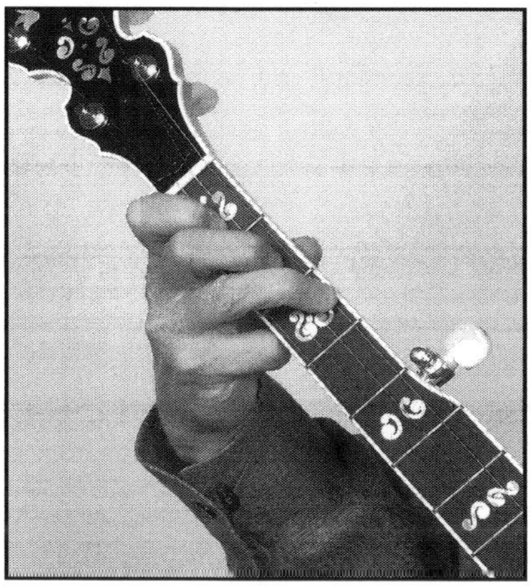

D Minor Seventh Dm7

Root - ♭3rd - 5th - ♭7th
D - F♮ - A - C♮

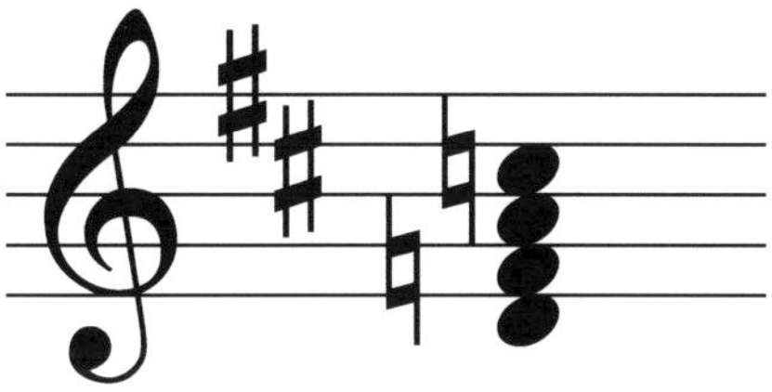

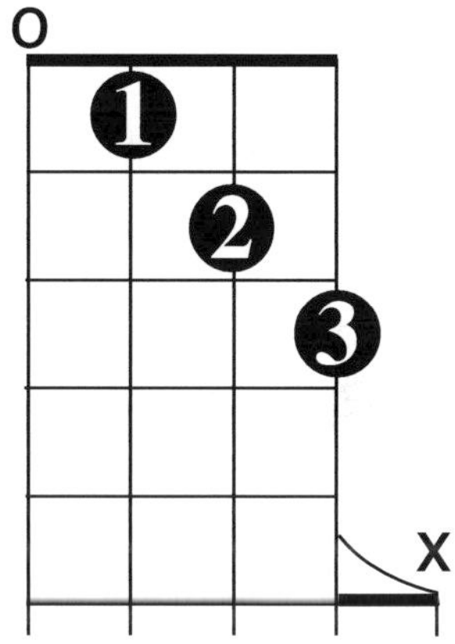

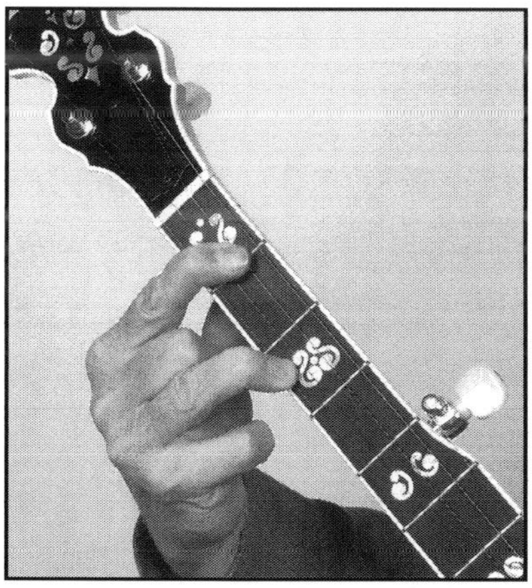

D Minor Seventh Flat Five Dm7♭5

Root - ♭3rd - ♭5th - ♭7th
D - F♮ - A♭ - C♮

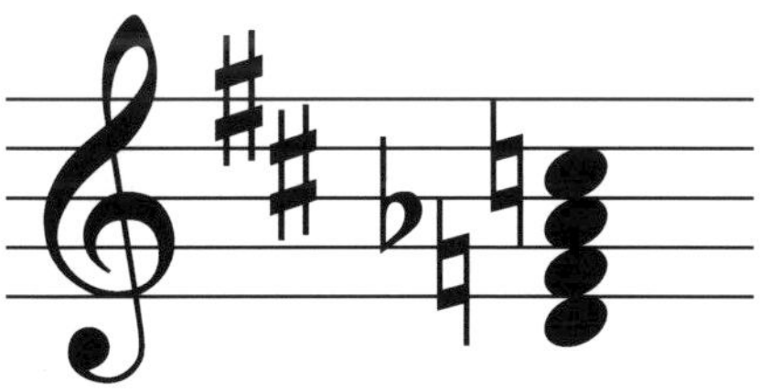

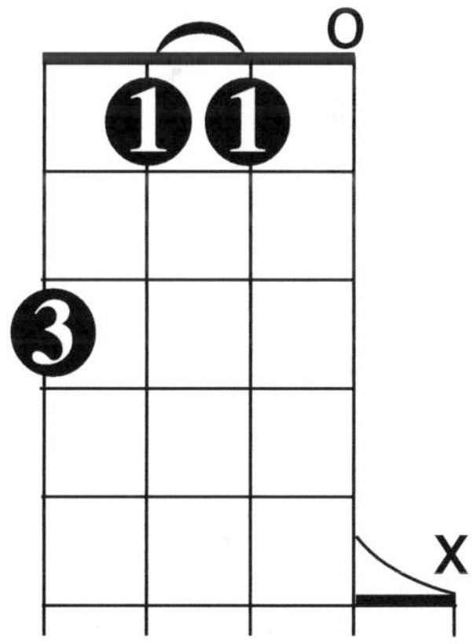

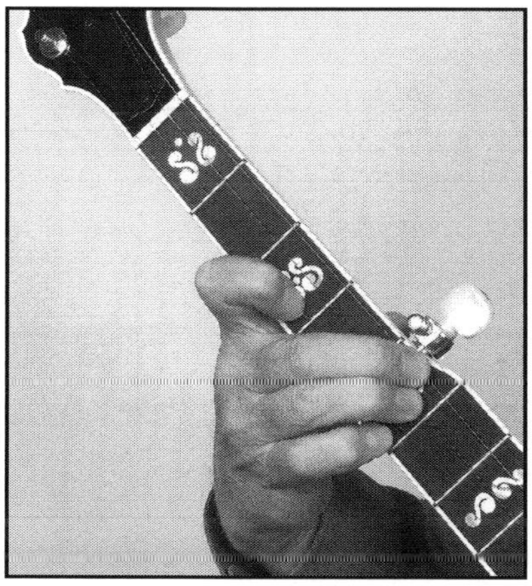

D Seventh Suspended Fourth D7sus4

Root - 4th - 5th - ♭7th
D - G - A - C♮

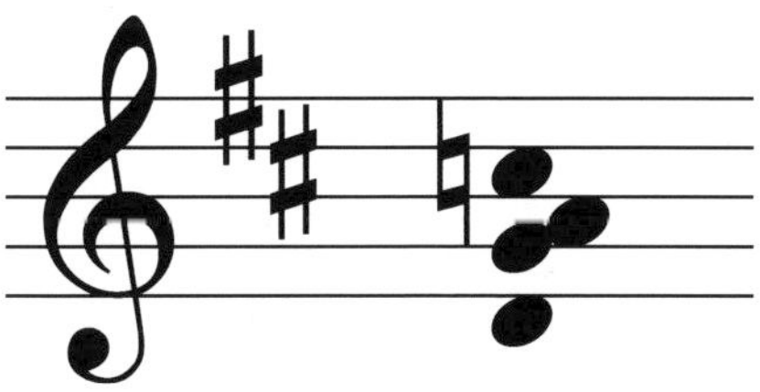

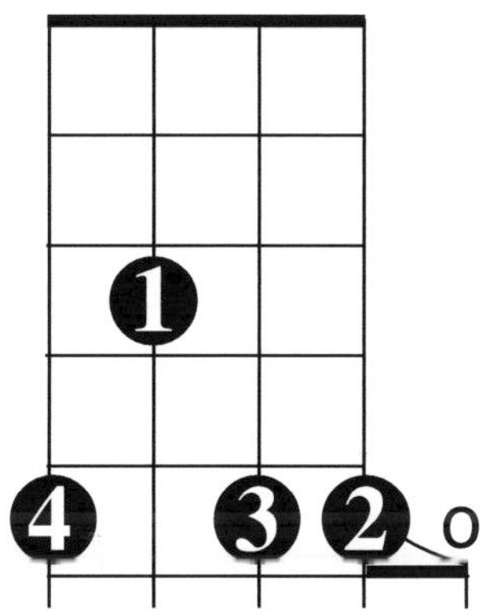

E♭/D♯ Chords

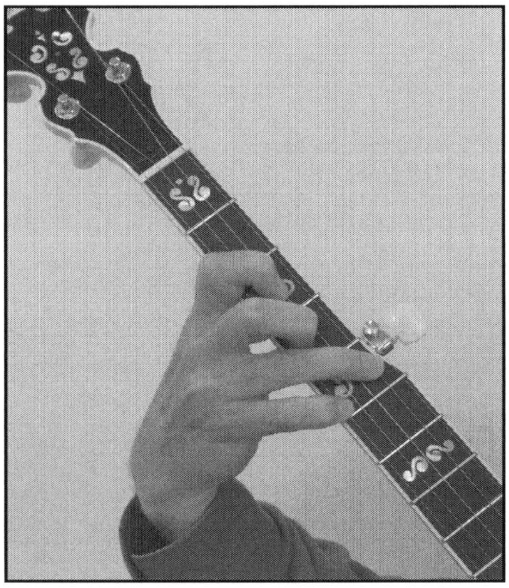

E♭ Major

Root - 3rd - 5th
E♭ - G - B♭

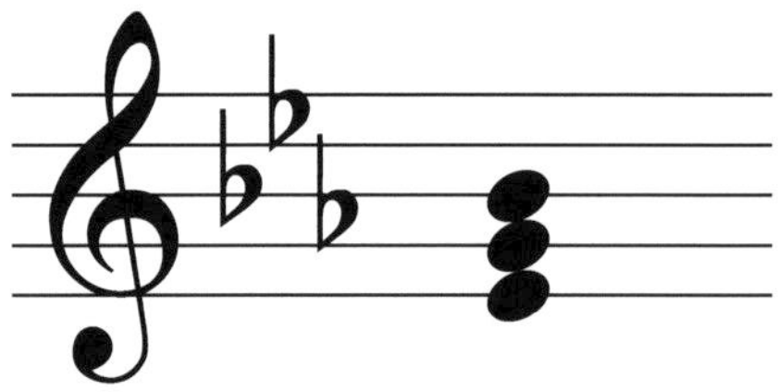

E♭

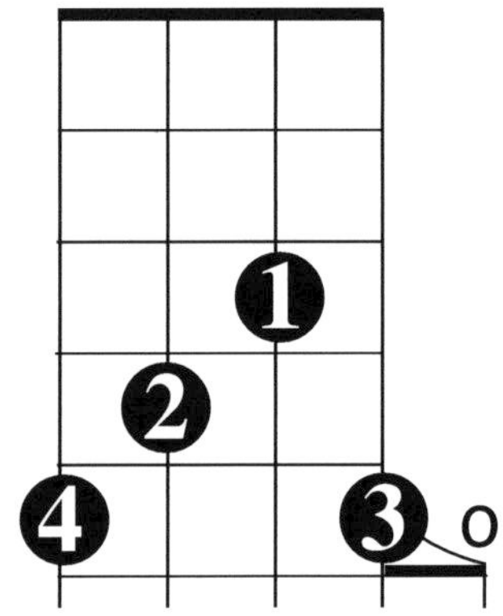

E♭ Minor

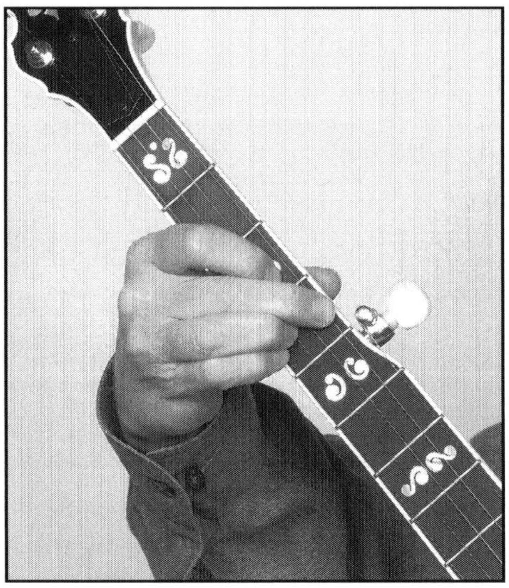

Root - ♭3rd - 5th
E♭ - G♭ - B♭

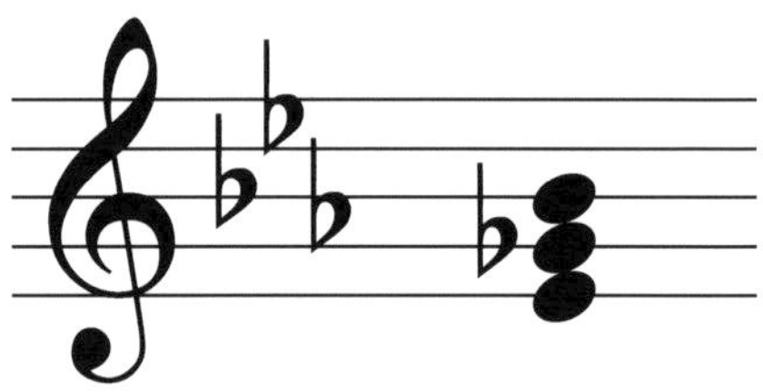

E♭m

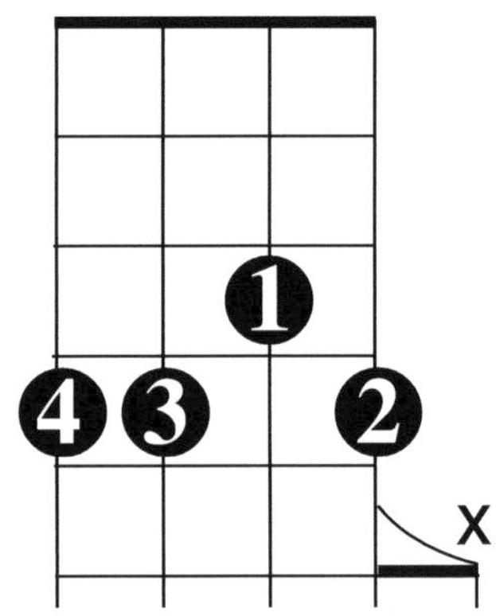

E♭ Seventh

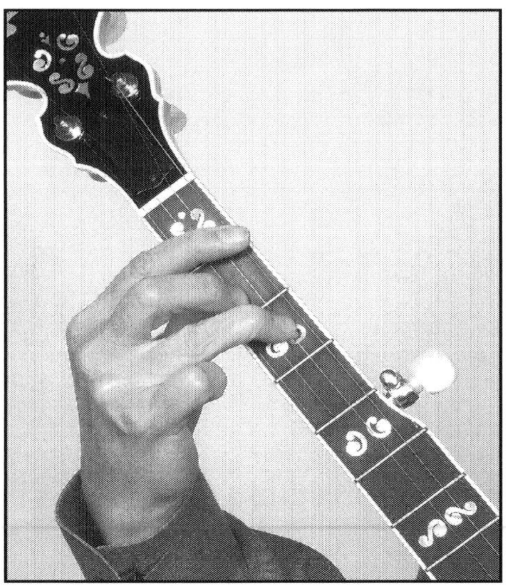

Root - 3rd - 5th - ♭7th
E♭ - G - B♭ - D♭

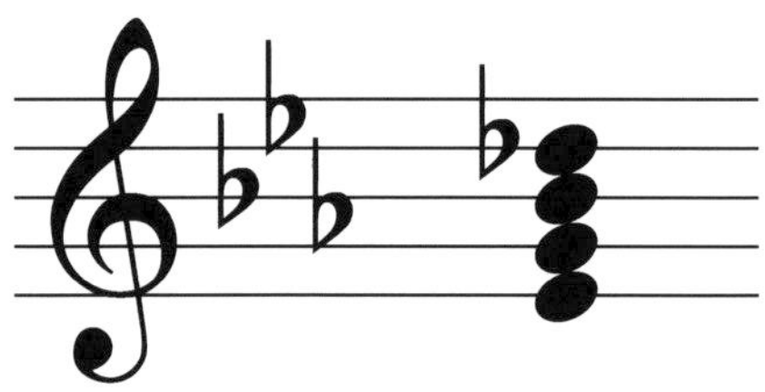

E♭7

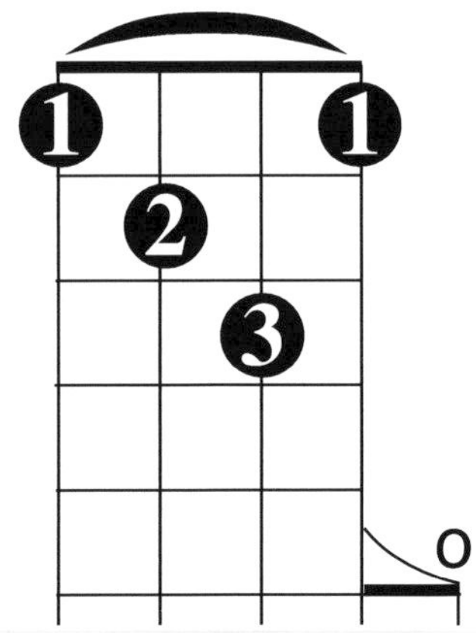

E♭/D♯ Chords

E♭ Diminished

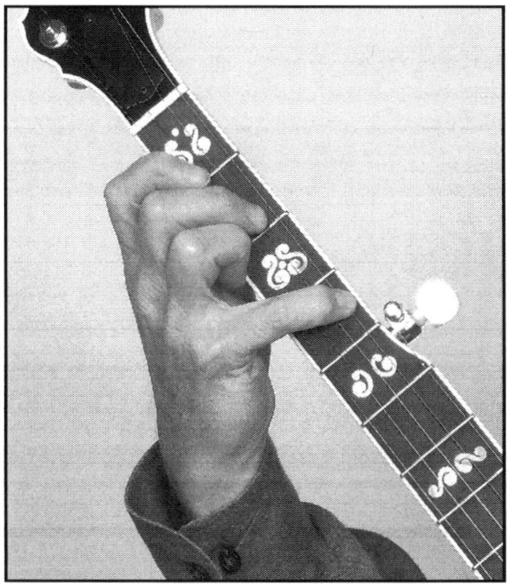

Root - ♭3rd - ♭5th - ♭♭7th
E♭ - G♭ - B♭♭ - D♭♭

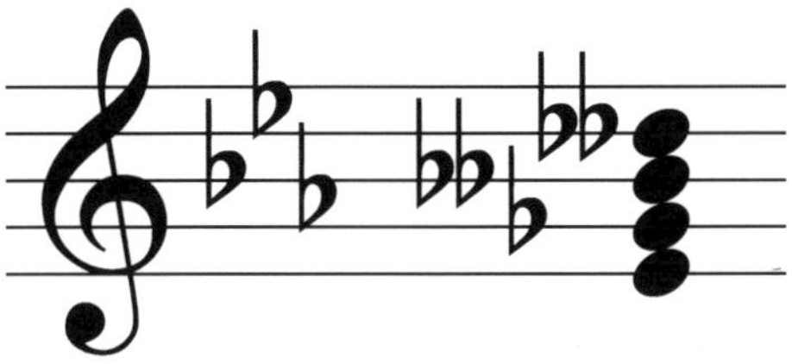

E♭o

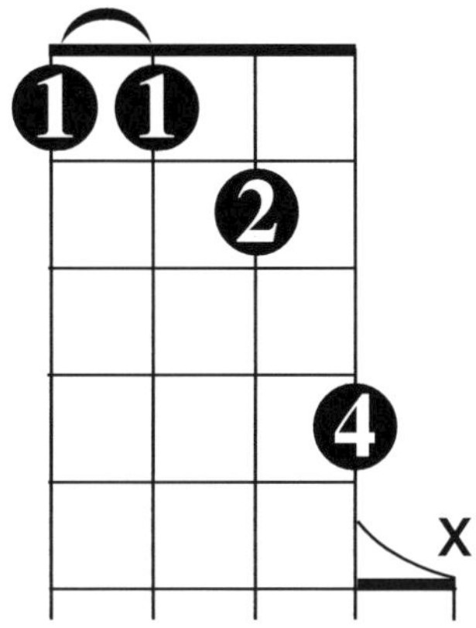

E♭ Augmented

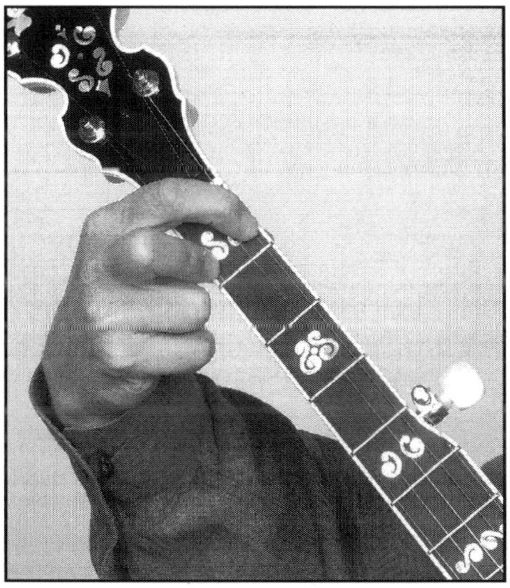

Root - 3rd - ♯5th
E♭ - G - B♮

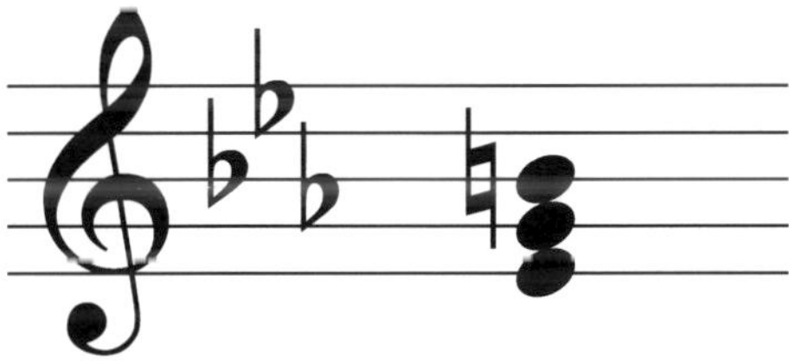

E♭+

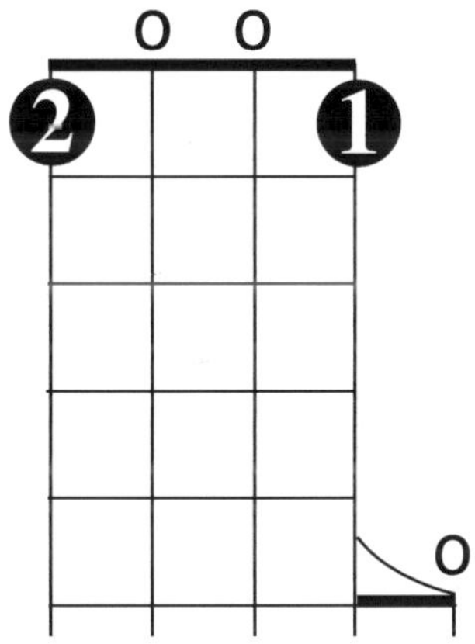

E♭ Sixth

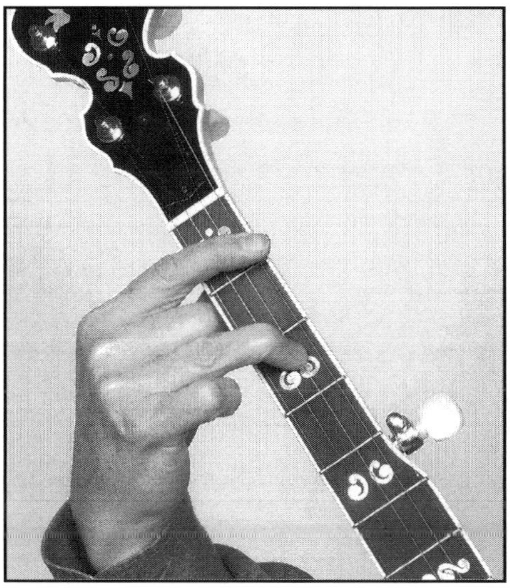

Root - 3rd - 5th - 6th
E♭ - G - B♭ - C

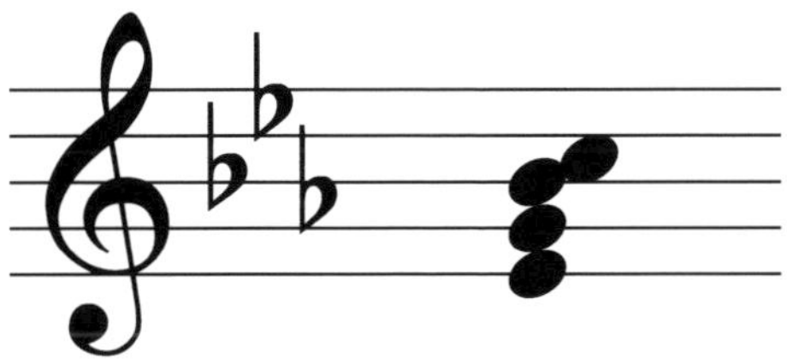

E♭6

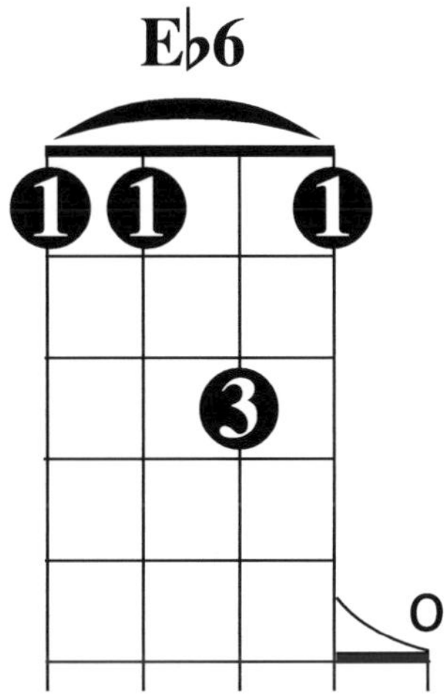

E♭/D♯ Chords

E♭ Minor Sixth

Root - ♭3rd - 5th - 6th
E♭ - G♭ - B♭ - C

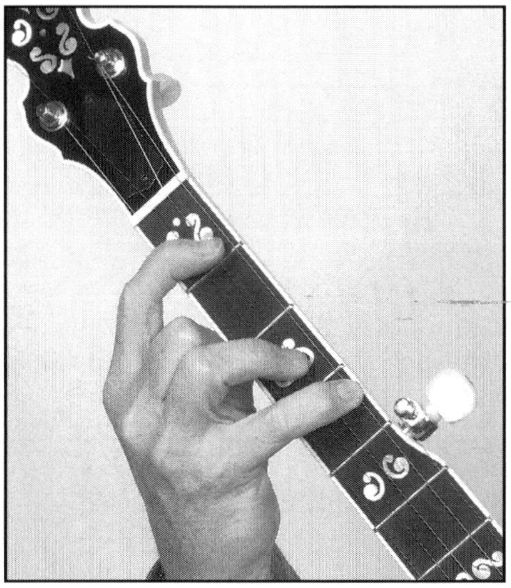

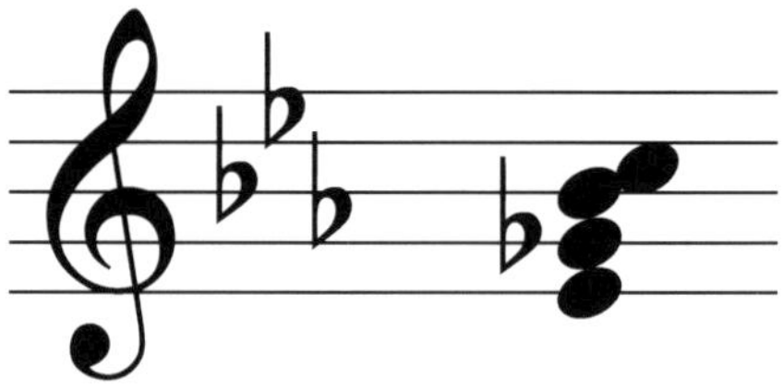

E♭m6

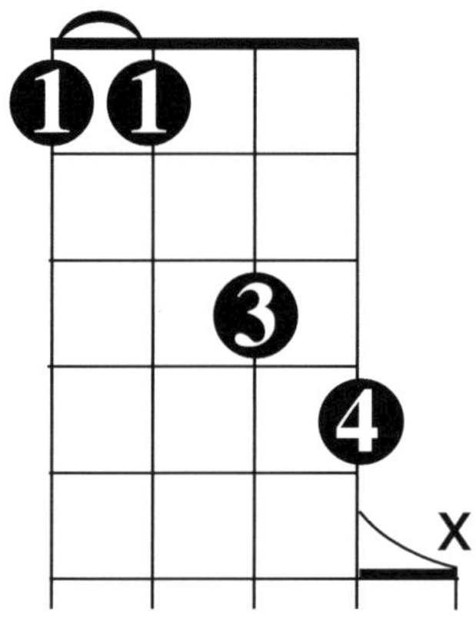

E♭ Seven Flat Five

Root - 3rd - ♭5th - ♭7th
E♭ - G - B♭♭ - D♭

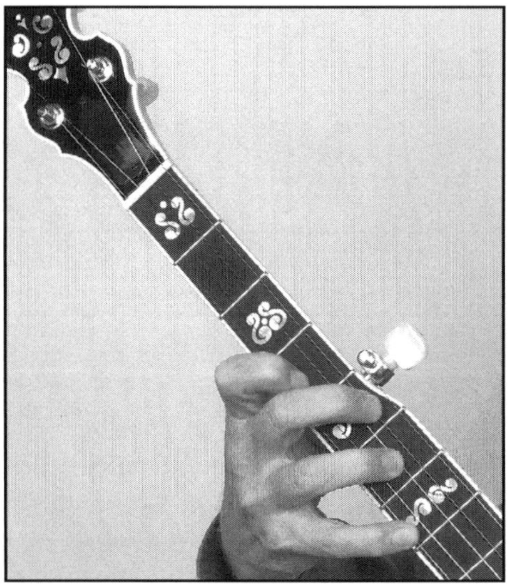

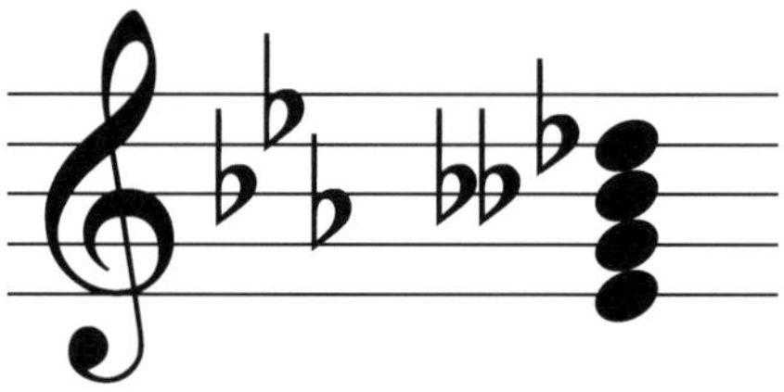

E♭7♭5

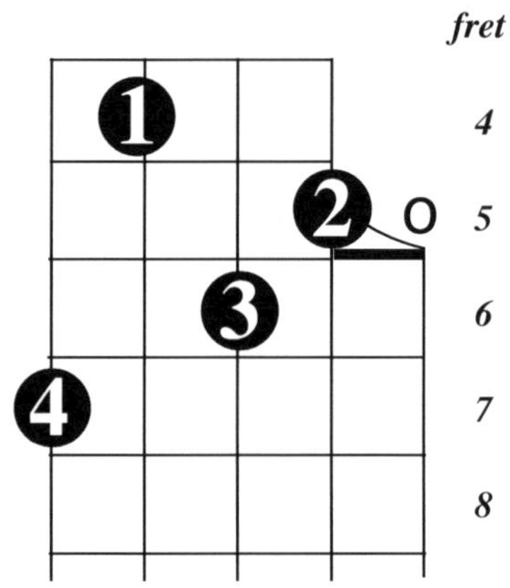

E♭ Major Seventh

Root - 3rd - 5th - 7th
E♭ - G - B♭ - D

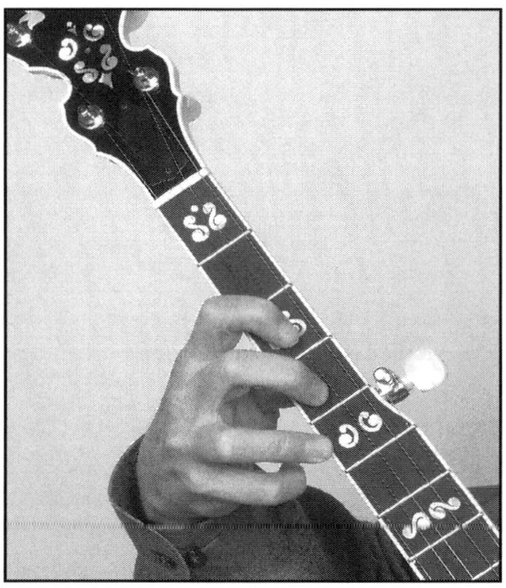

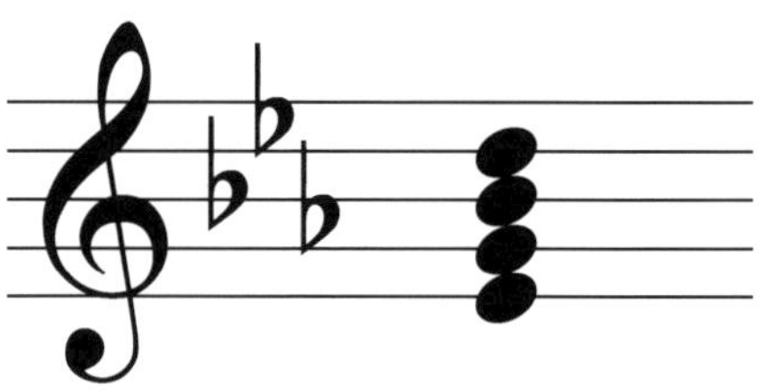

E♭Maj7

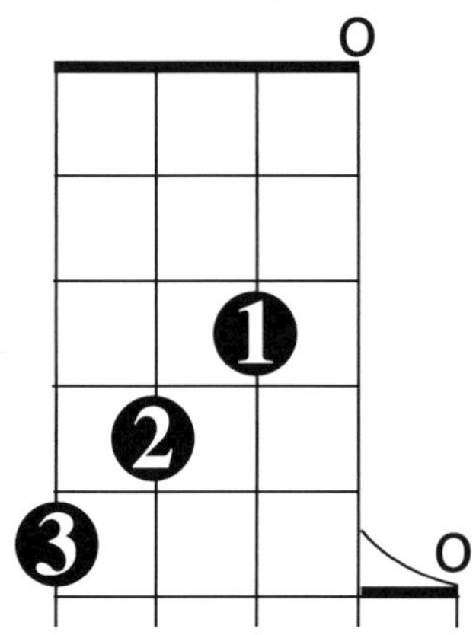

E♭/D♯ Chords

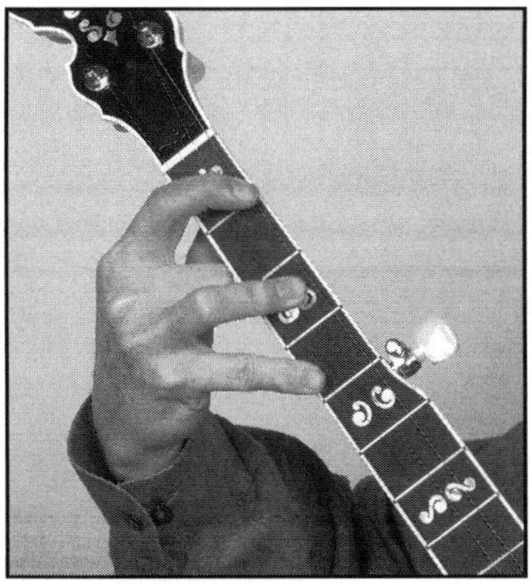

E♭ Major Seventh Flat Third E♭Maj7♭3

Root - ♭3rd - 5th - 7th
E♭ - G♭ - B♭ - D

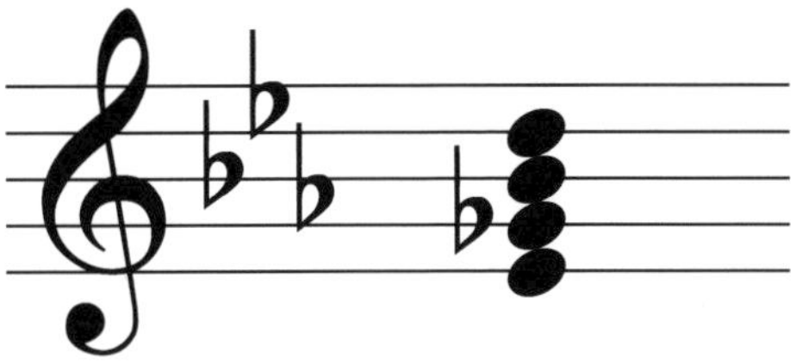

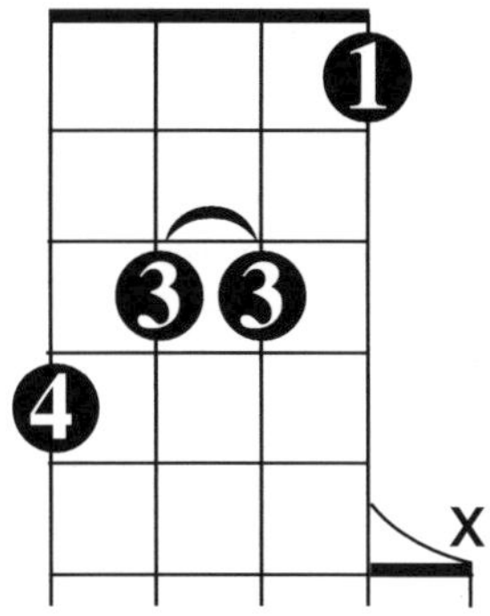

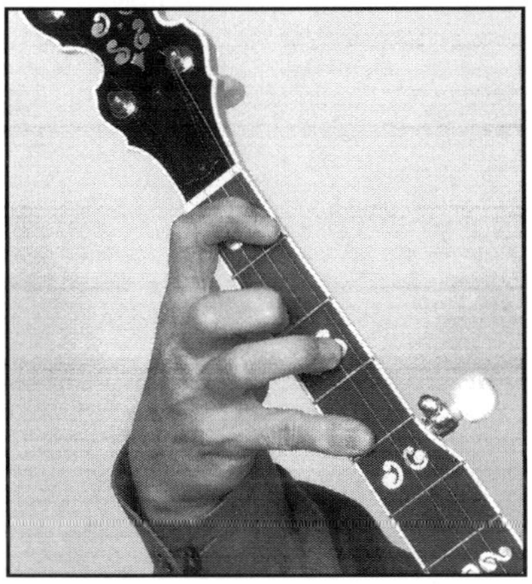

E♭ Minor Seventh E♭m7

Root - ♭3rd - 5th - ♭7th
E♭ - G♭ - B♭ - D♭

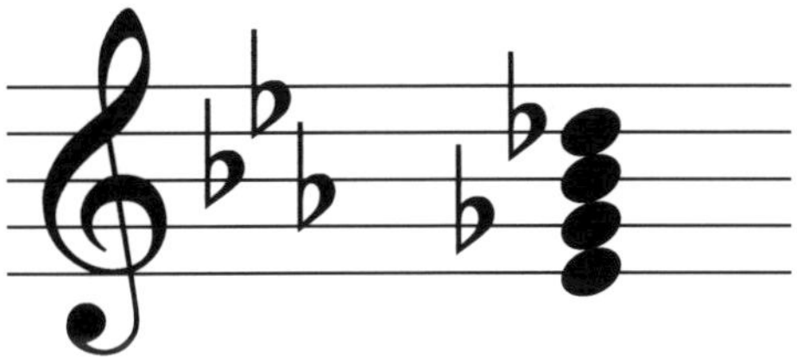

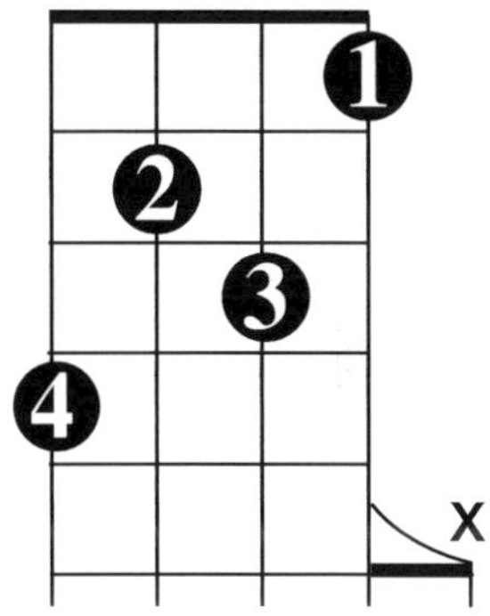

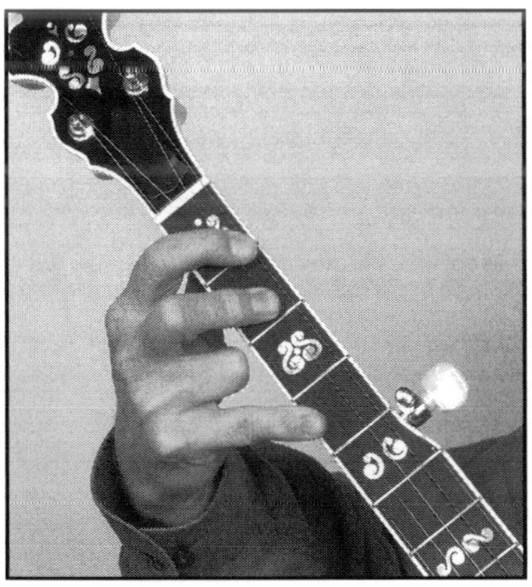

E♭ Minor Seventh Flat Five E♭m7♭5

Root - ♭3rd - ♭5th - ♭7th
E♭ - G♭ - B♭♭ - D♭

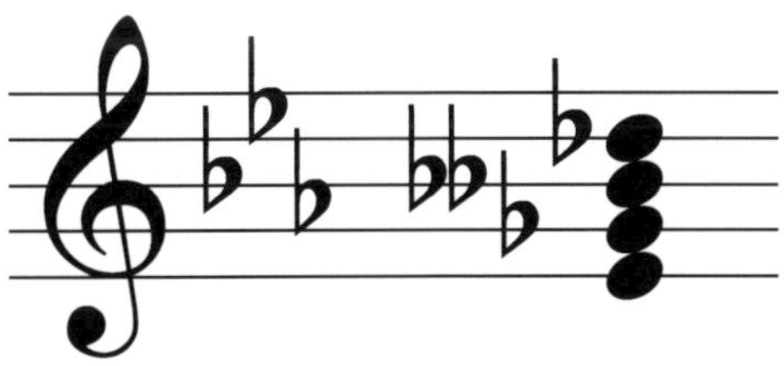

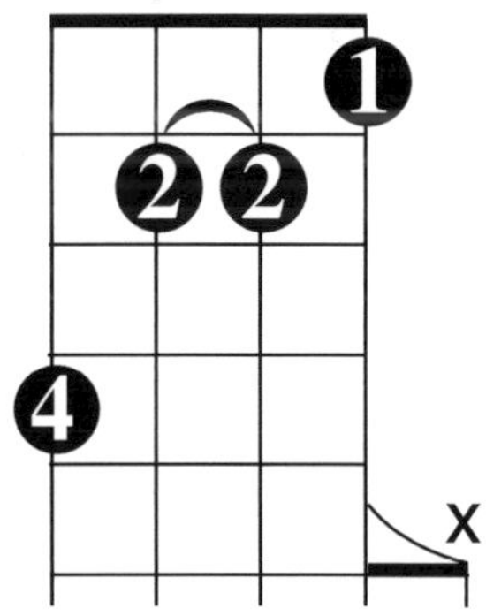

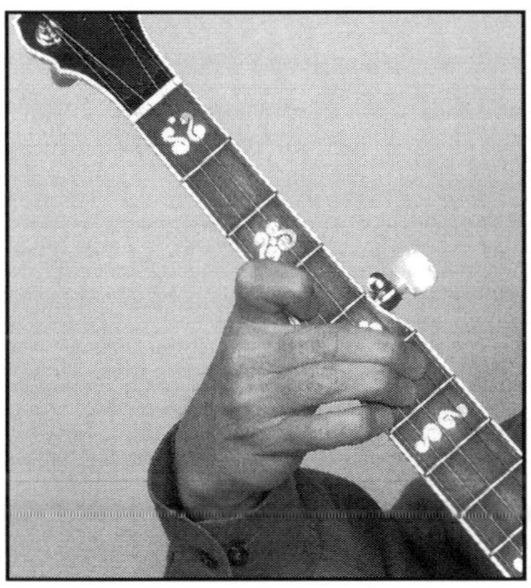

E♭ Seventh Suspended Fourth E♭7sus4

Root - 4th - 5th - ♭7th
E♭ - A♭ - B♭ - D♭

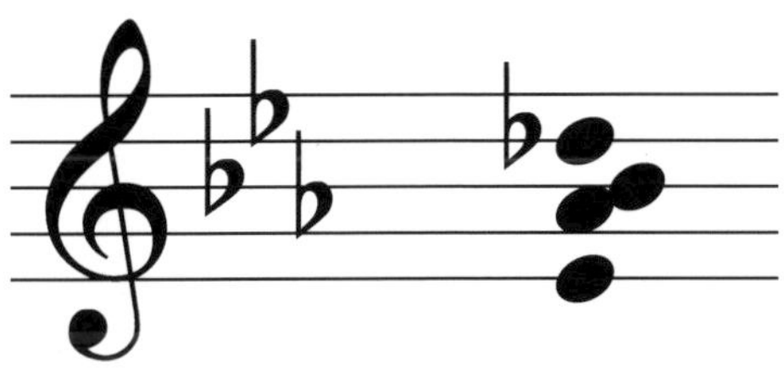

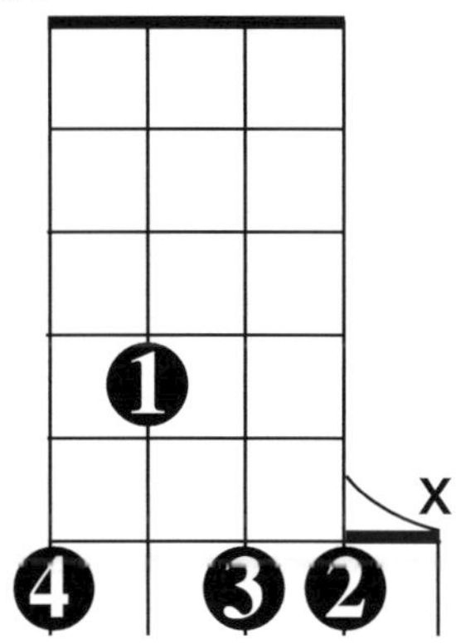

E Chords

E Major

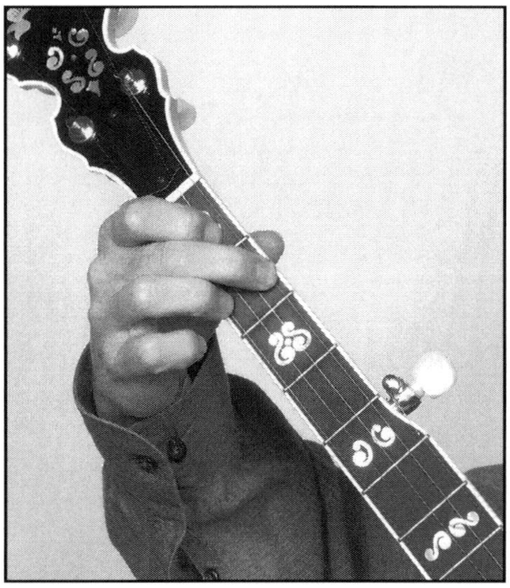

Root - 3rd - 5th
E - G♯ - B

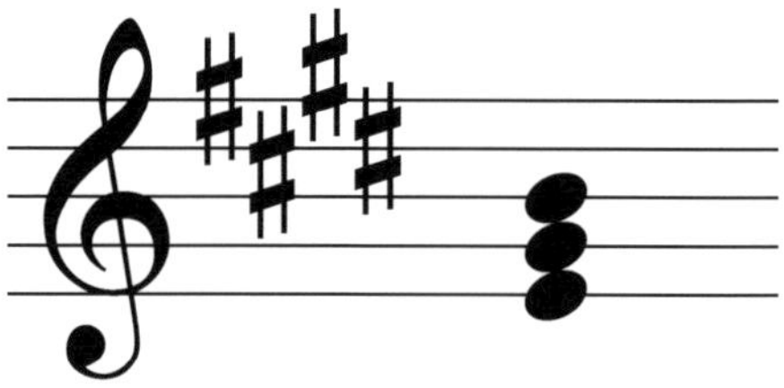

E

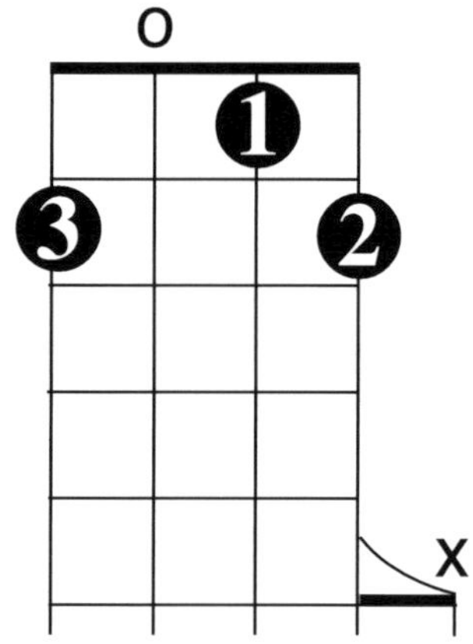

E Minor

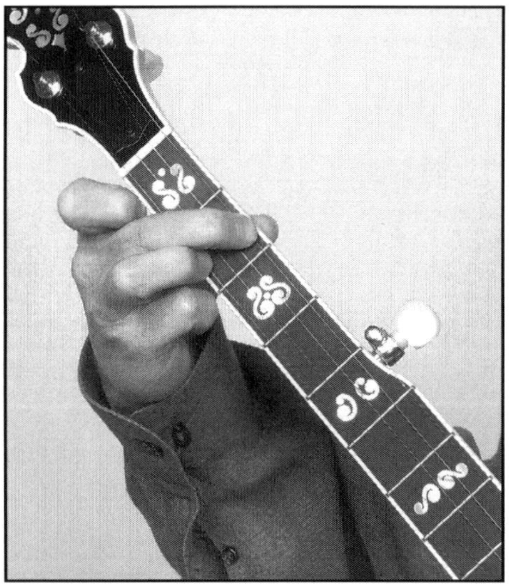

Root - ♭3rd - 5th
E - G♮ - B

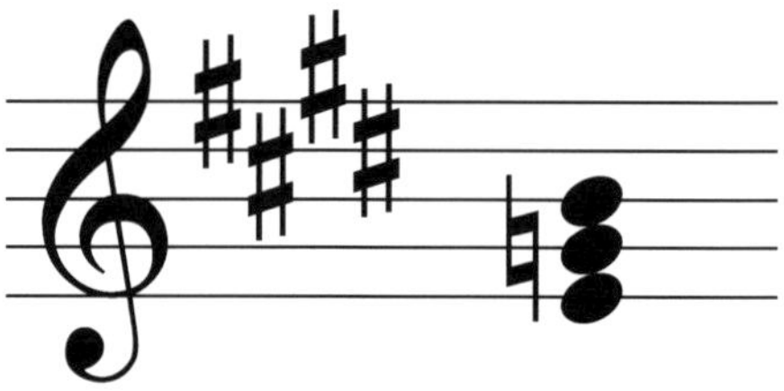

Em

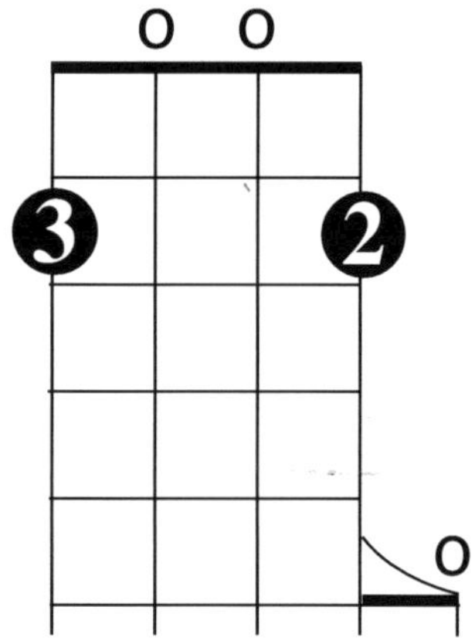

E Seventh

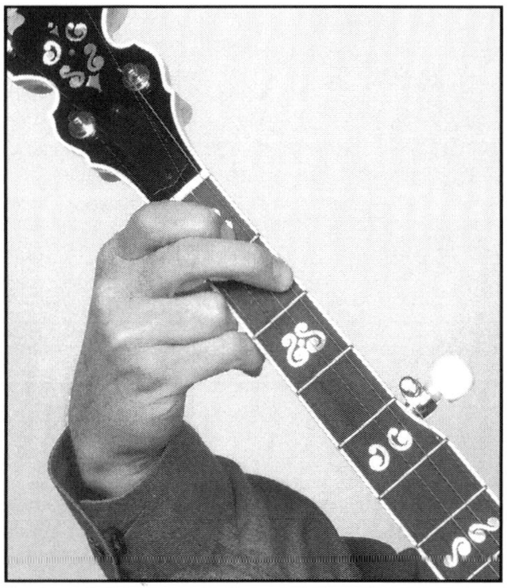

Root - 3rd - 5th - ♭7th
E - G♯ - B - D♮

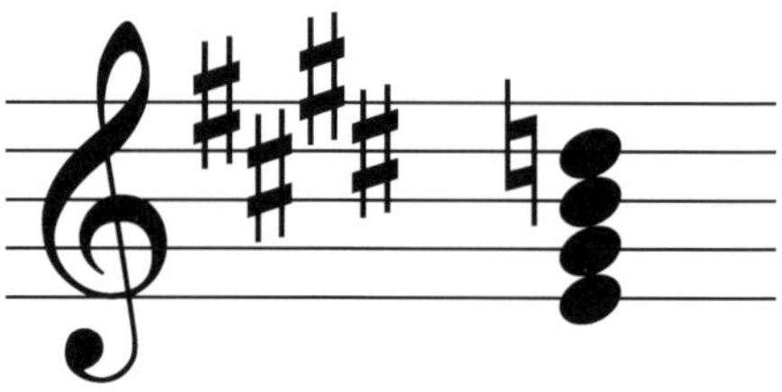

E7

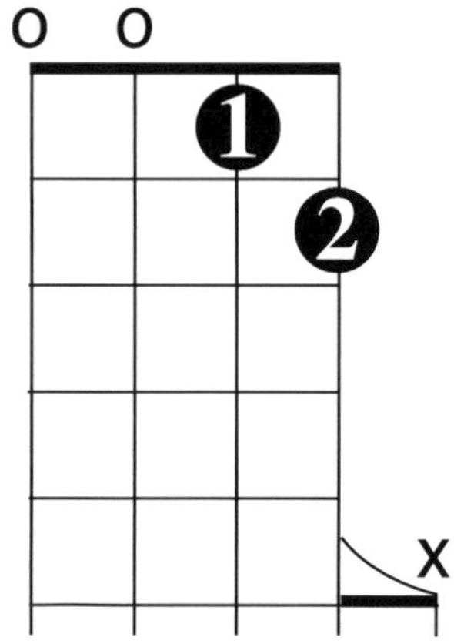

E Chords

E Diminished

Root - ♭3rd - ♭5th - ♭♭7th
E - G♮ - B♭ - D♭

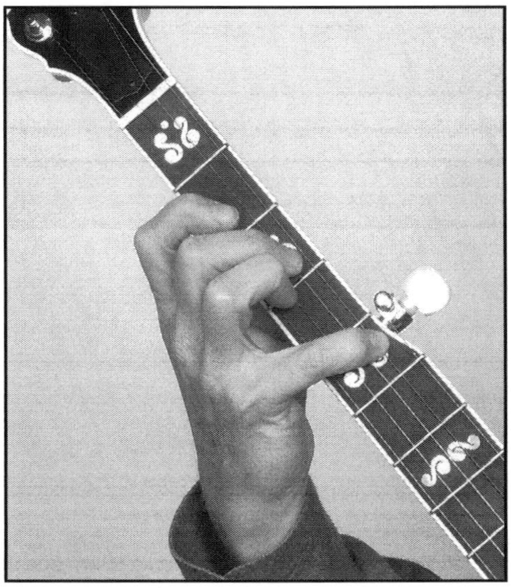

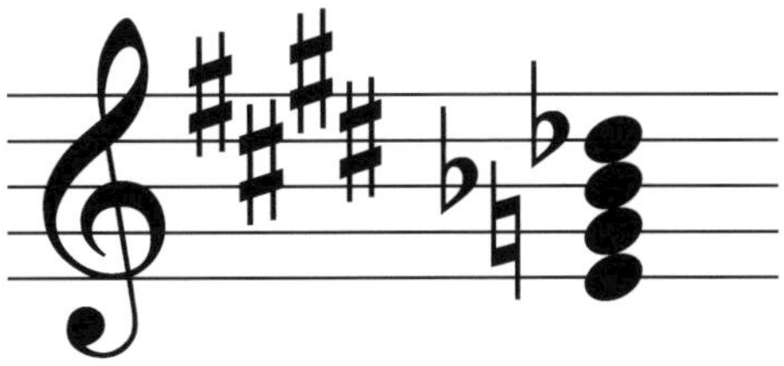

E°

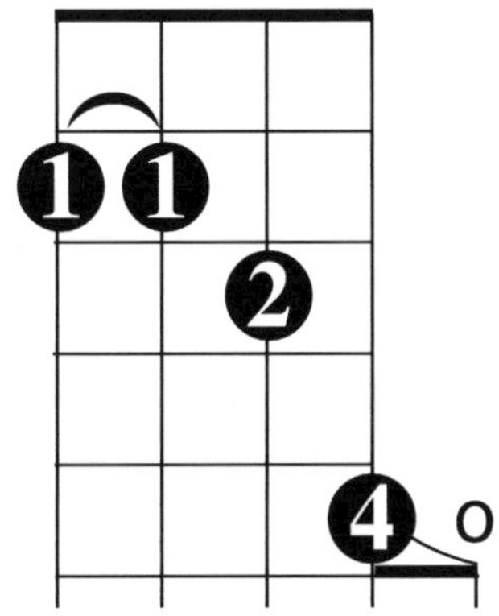

E Augmented

Root - 3rd - ♯5th
E - G♯ - B♯

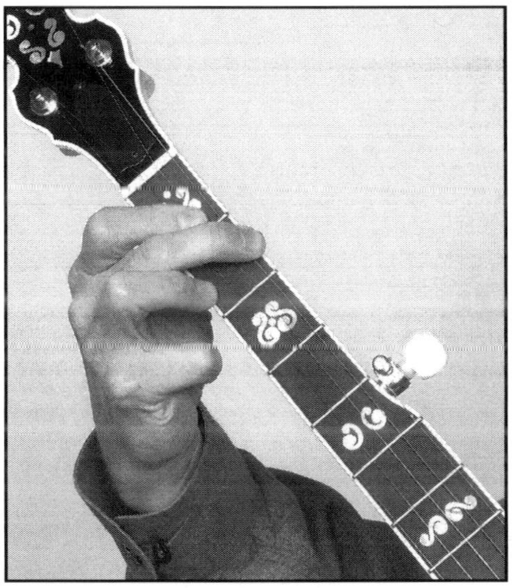

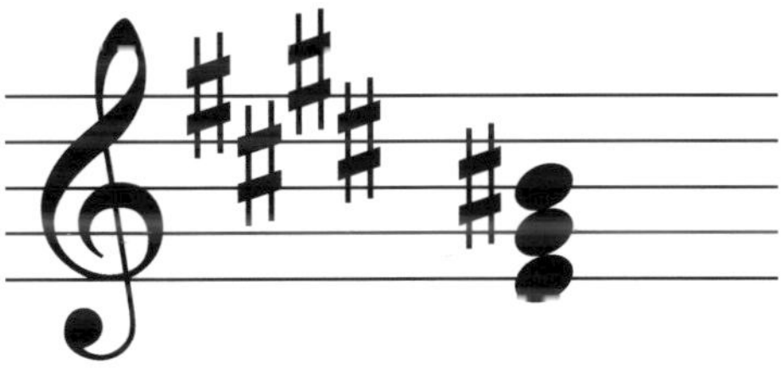

E+

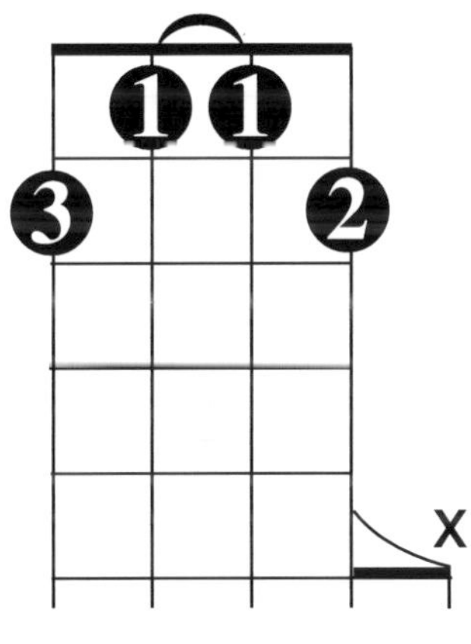

E Sixth

Root - 3rd - 5th - 6th
E - G♯ - B - C♯

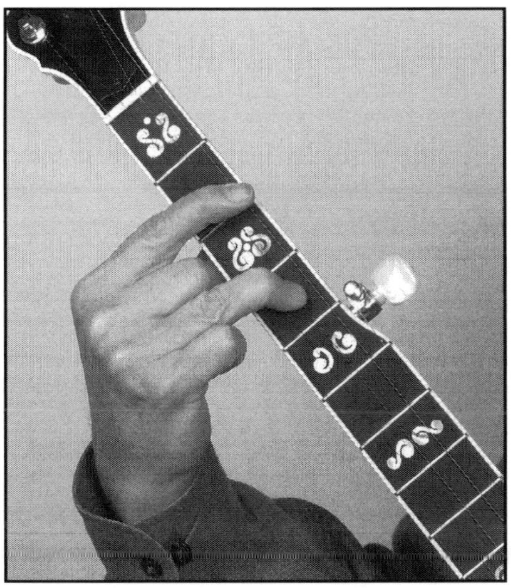

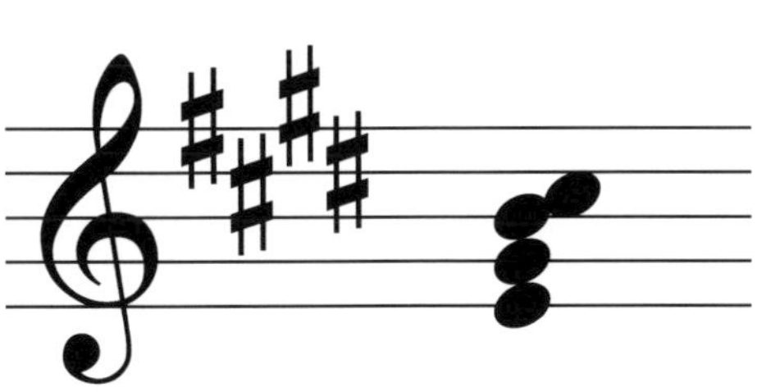

E6

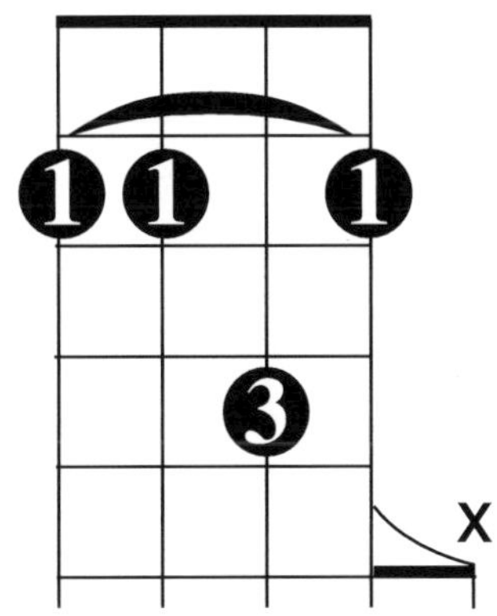

E Chords

E Minor Sixth

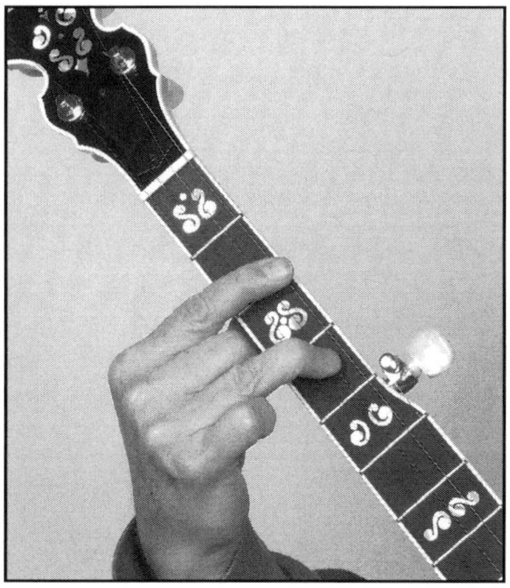

Root - ♭3rd - 5th - 6th
E - G♮ - B - C♯

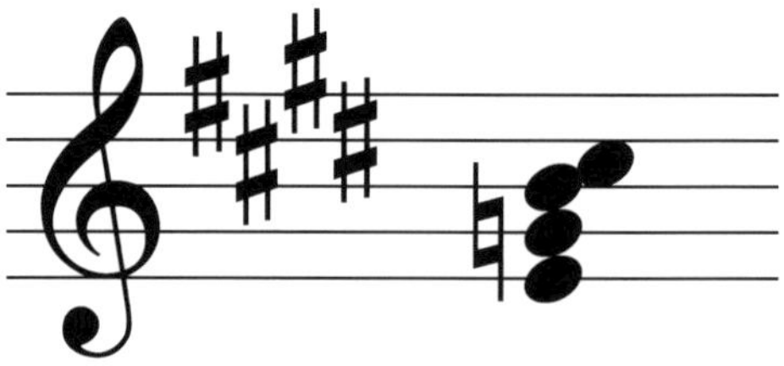

Em6

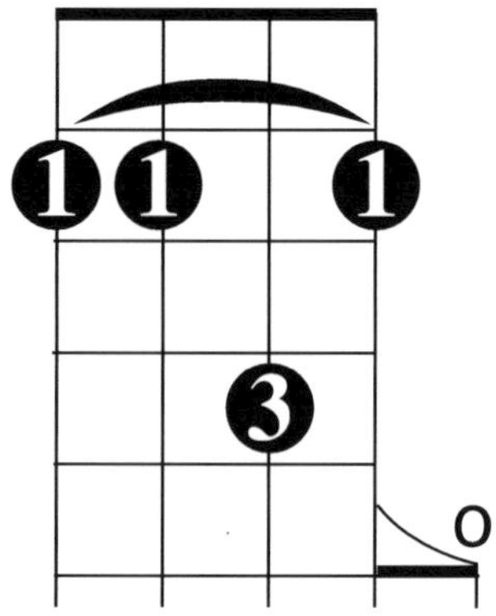

E Seven Flat Five

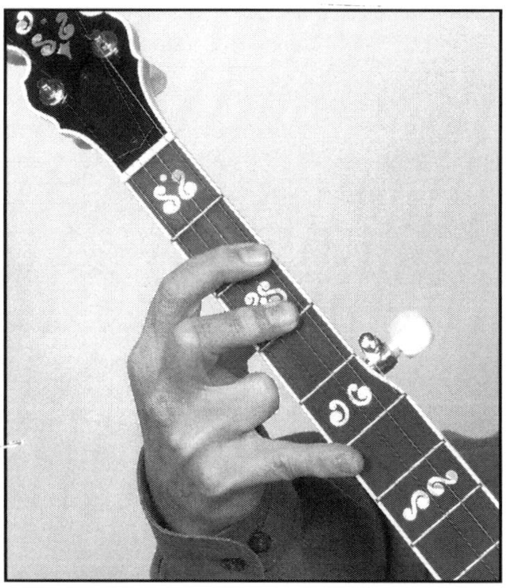

Root - 3rd - ♭5th - ♭7th
E - G♯ - B♭ - D♮

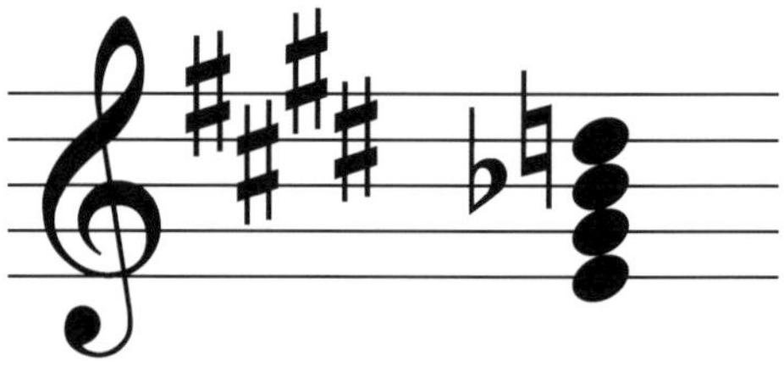

E7♭5

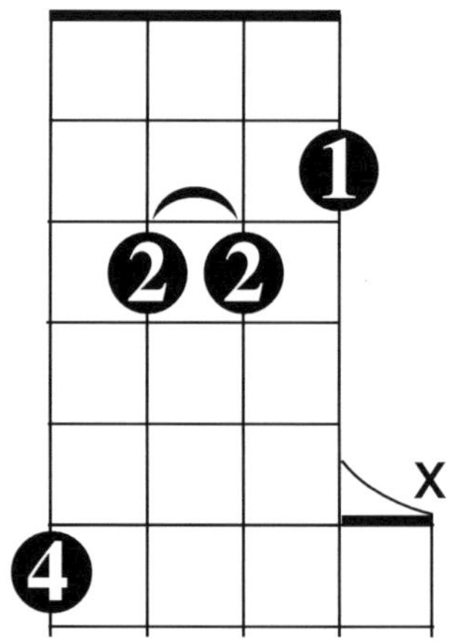

E Major Seventh

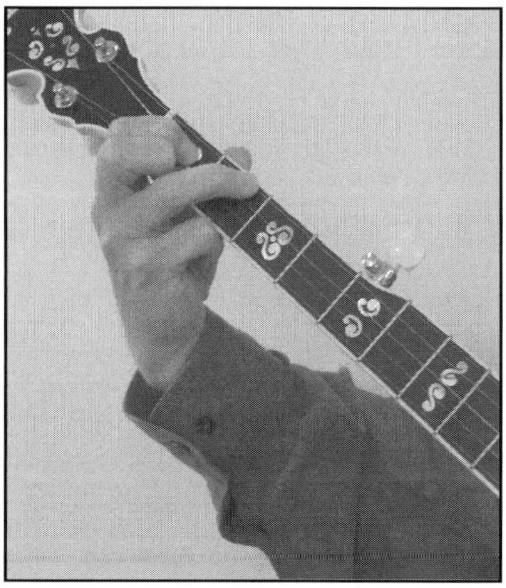

Root - 3rd - 5th - 7th
E - G♯ - B - D♯

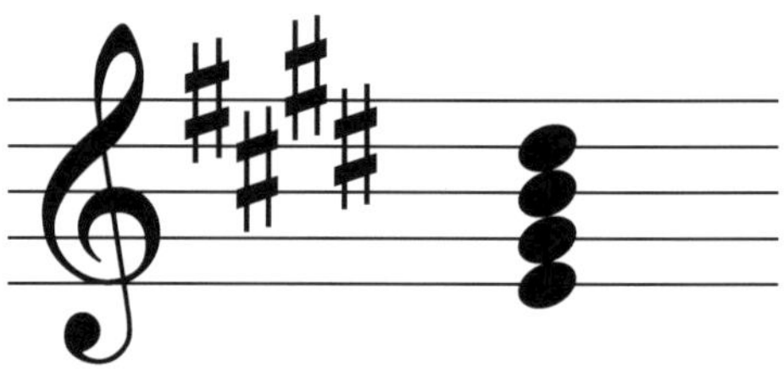

EMaj7

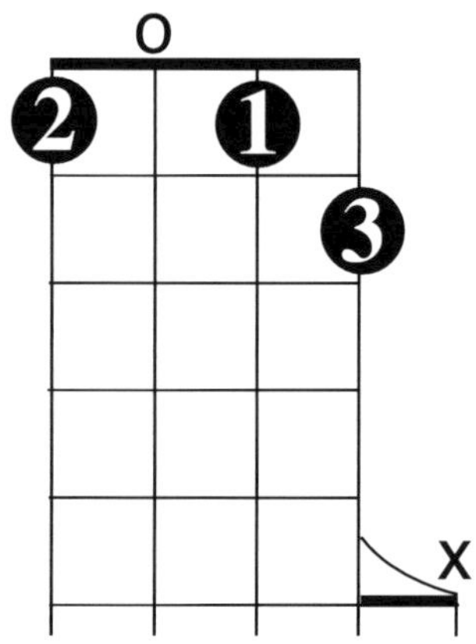

E Chords

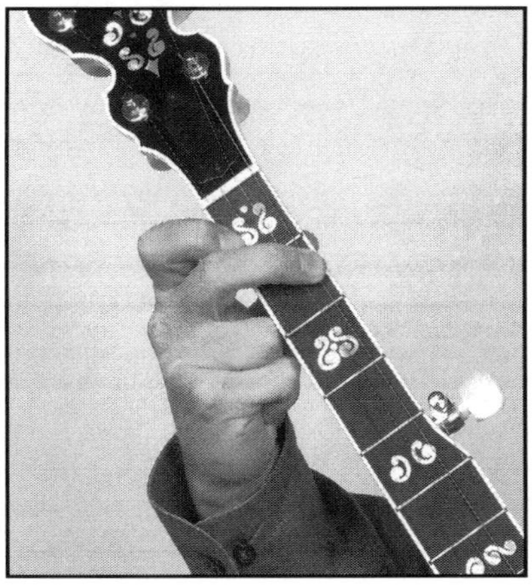

E Major Seventh Flat Third

EMaj7♭3

Root - ♭3rd - 5th - 7th
E - G♮ - B - D♯

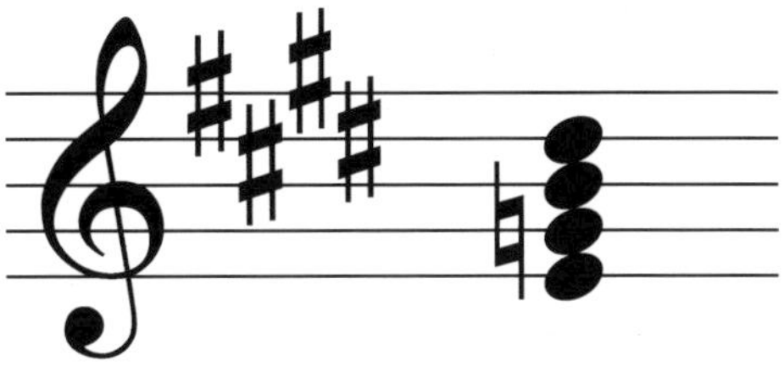

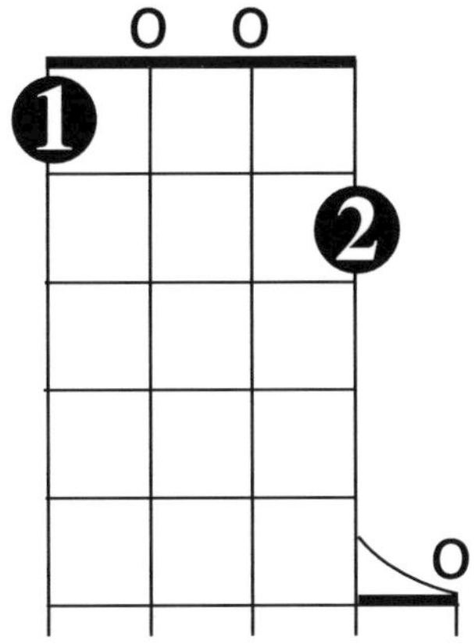

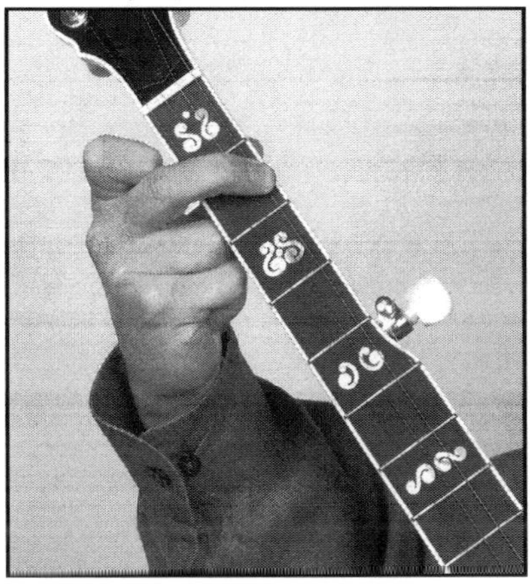

E Minor Seventh

Em7

Root - ♭3rd - 5th - ♭7th
E - G♮ - B - D♮

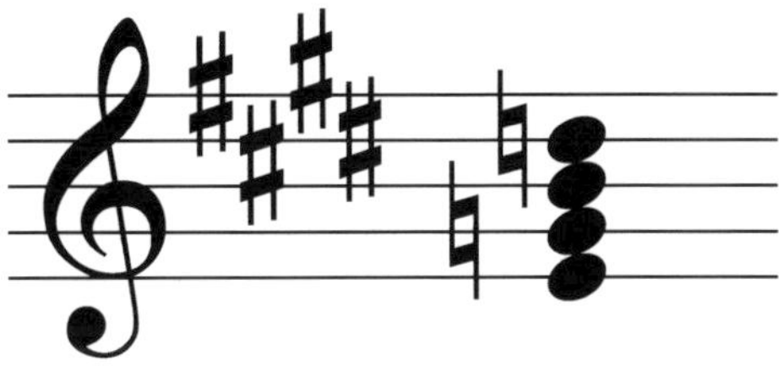

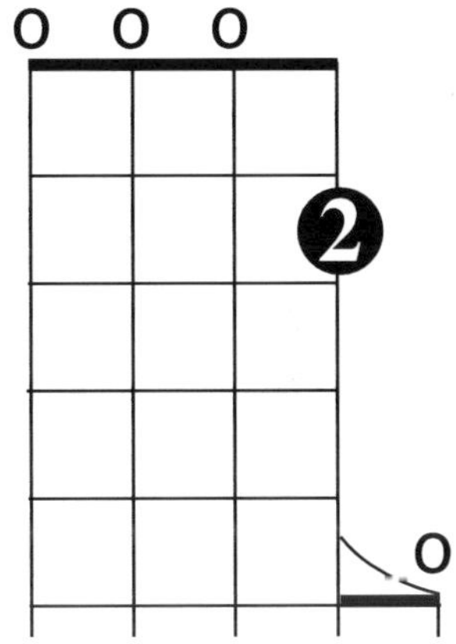

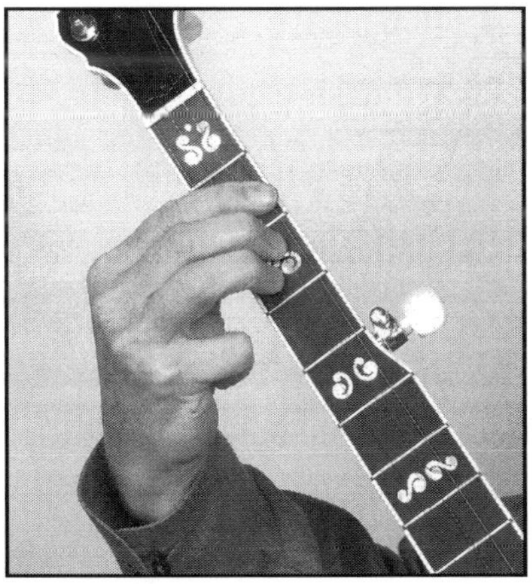

E Minor Seventh Flat Five

Em7♭5

Root - ♭3rd - ♭5th - ♭7th
E - G♮ - B♭ - D♮

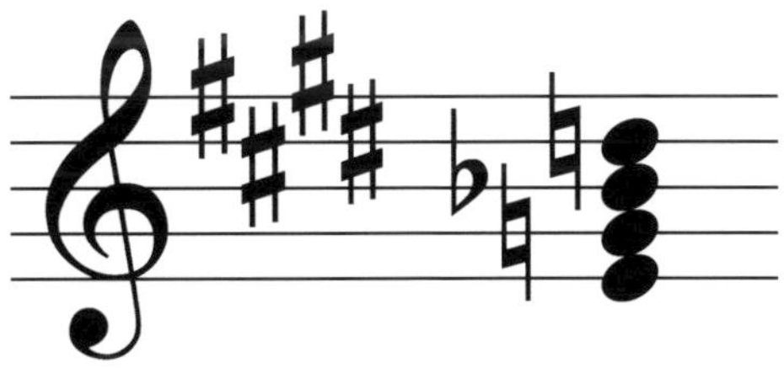

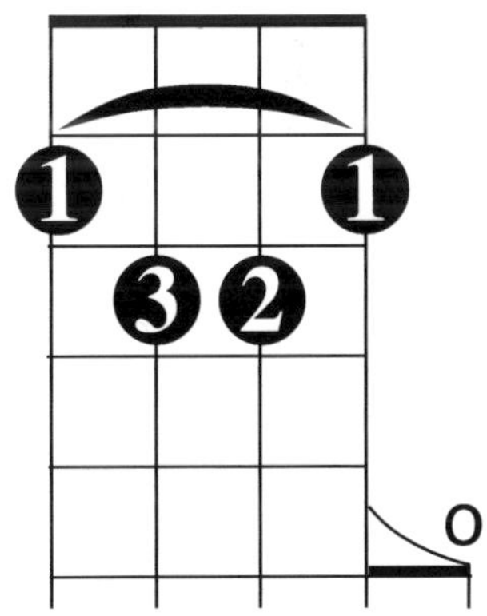

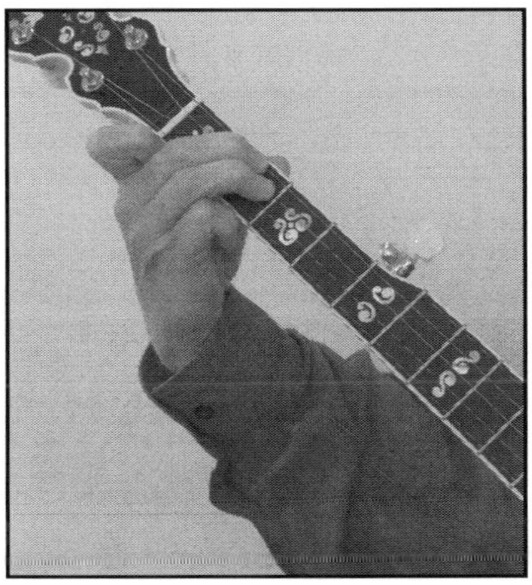

E Seventh Suspended Fourth

E7sus4

Root - 4th - 5th - ♭7th
E - A - B - D♮

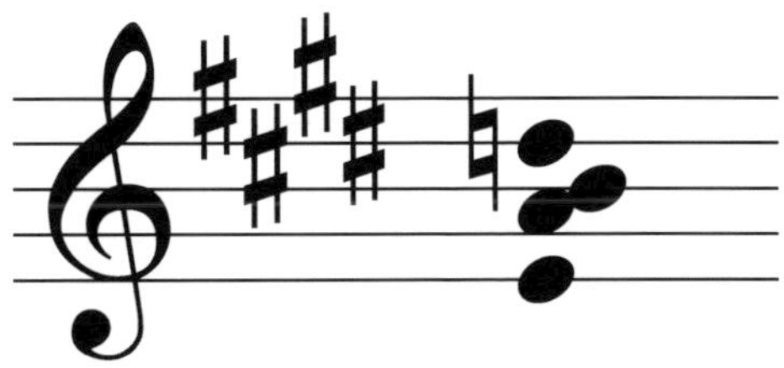

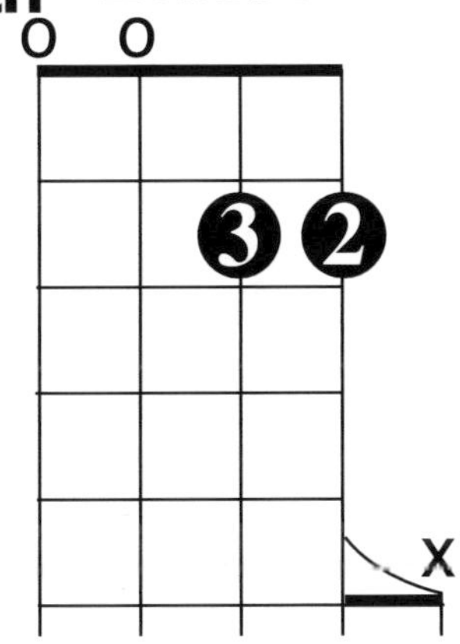

F Chords

F Major

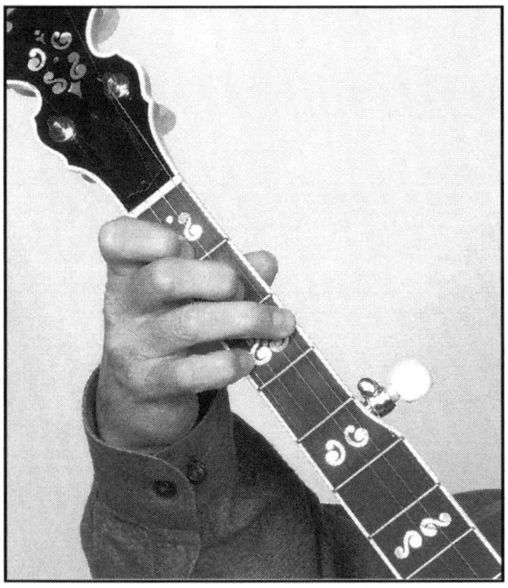

Root - 3rd - 5th
F - A - C

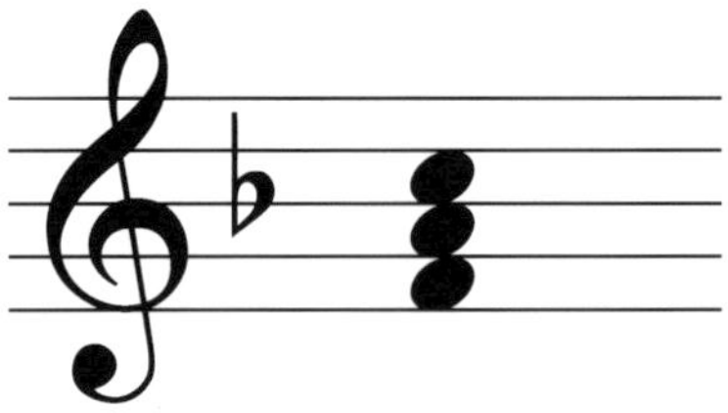

F

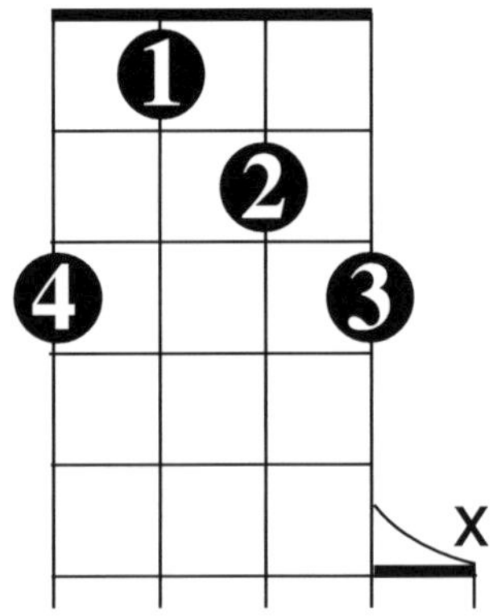

F Minor

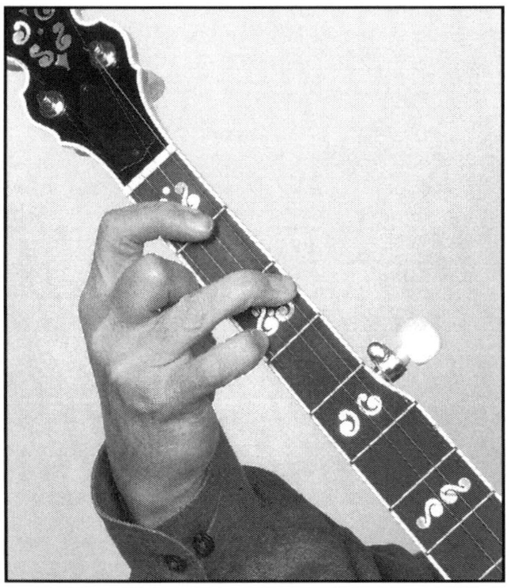

Root - ♭3rd - 5th
F - A♭ - C

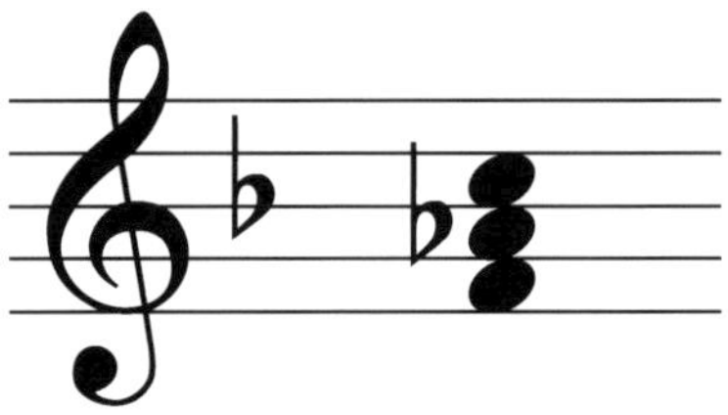

Fm

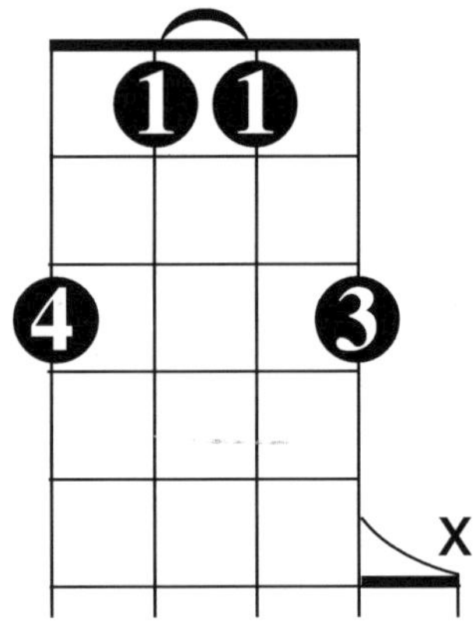

F Seventh

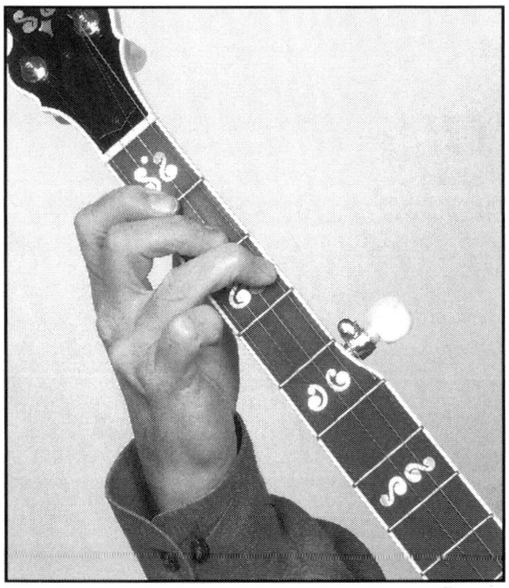

Root - 3rd - 5th - ♭7th
F - A - C - E♭

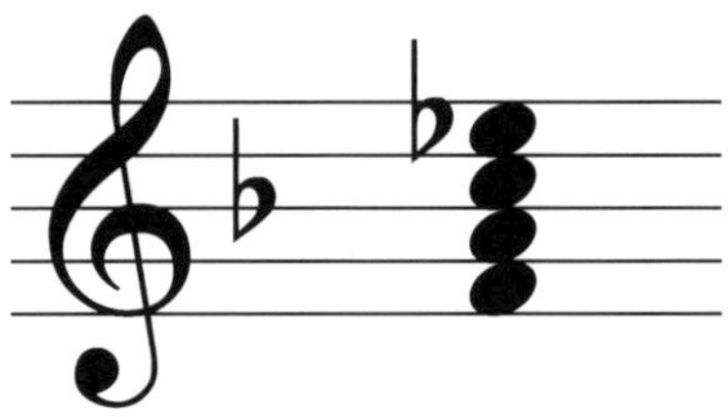

F7

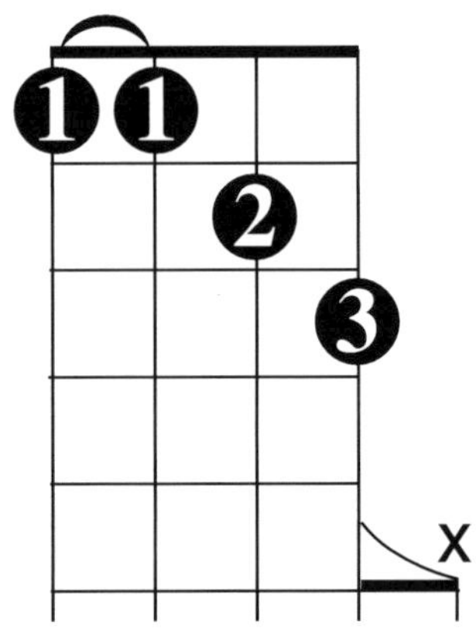

F Chords

F Diminished

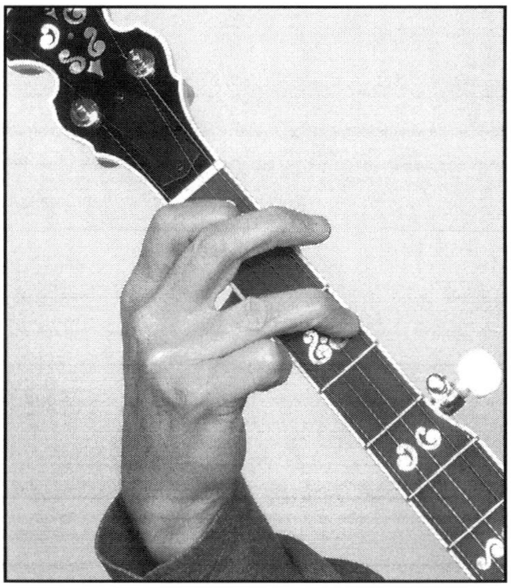

Root - ♭3rd - ♭5th - 𝄫7th
F - A♭ - C♭ - E𝄫

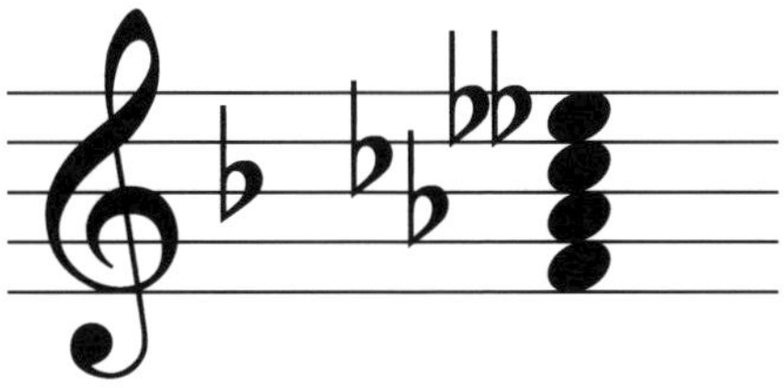

F°

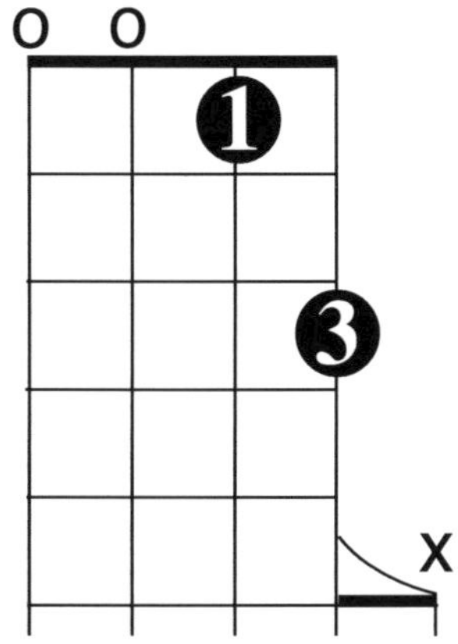

F Augmented

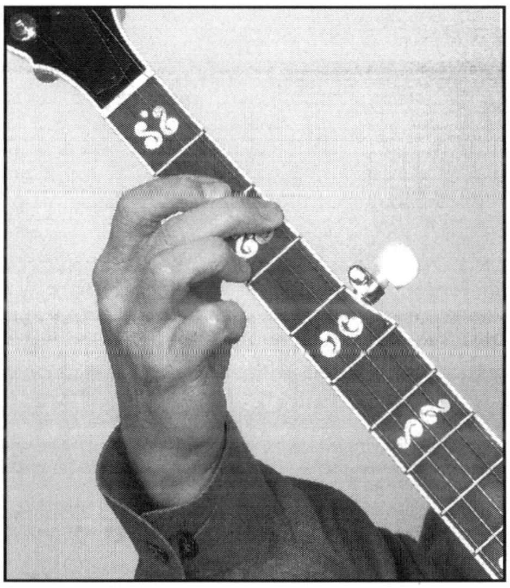

Root - 3rd - ♯5th
F - A - C♯

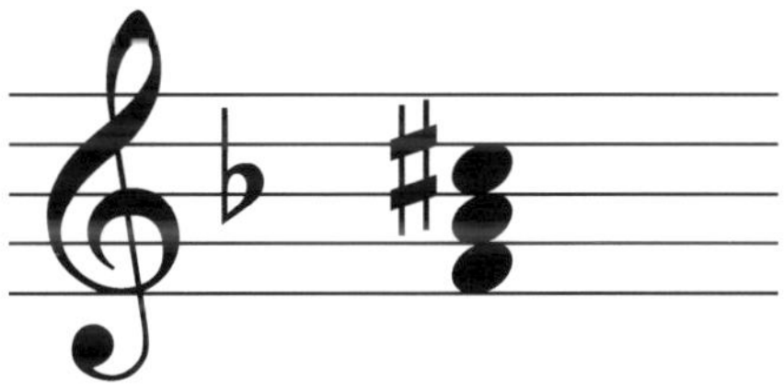

F+

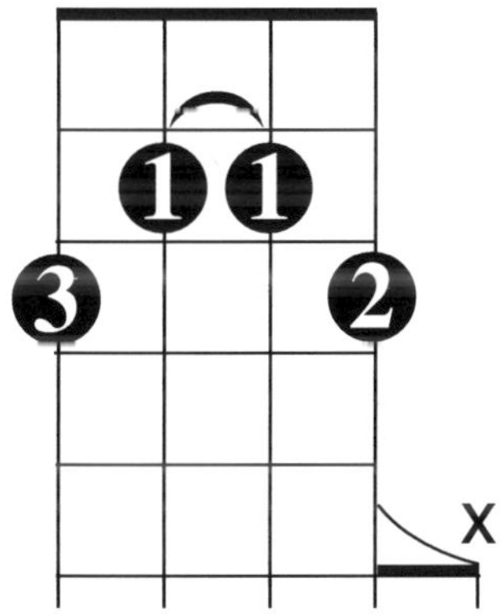

F Sixth

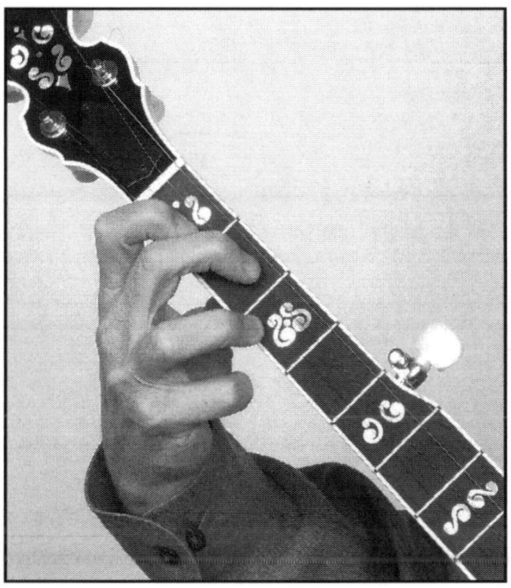

Root - 3rd - 5th - 6th
F - A - C - D

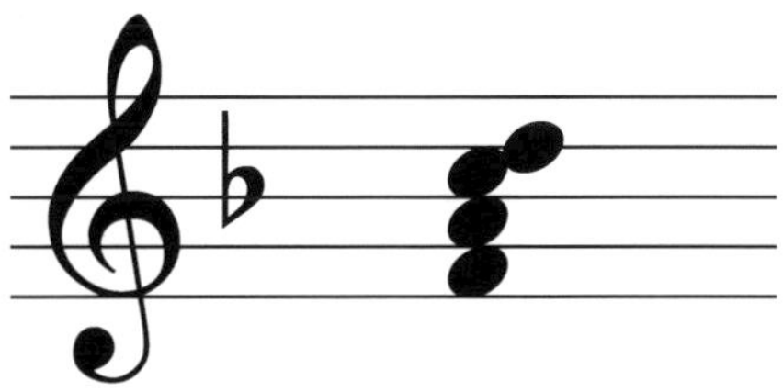

F6

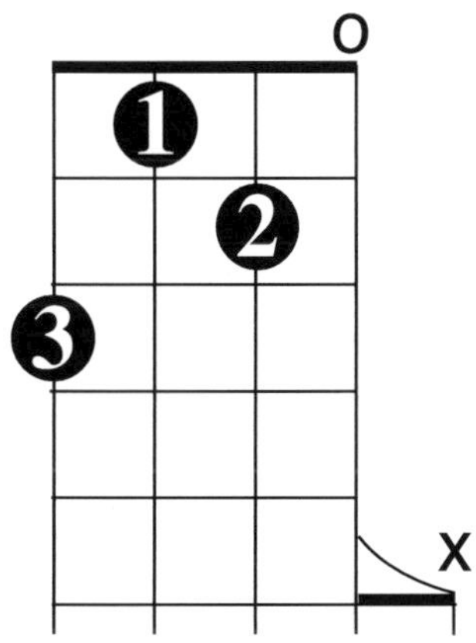

F Chords

F Minor Sixth

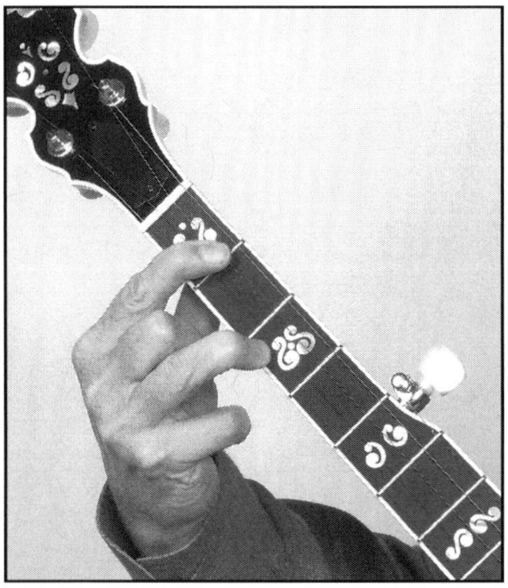

Root - ♭3rd - 5th - 6th
F - A♭ - C - D

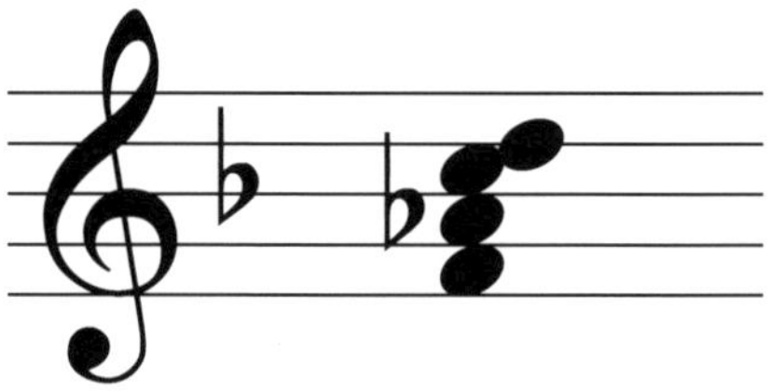

Fm6

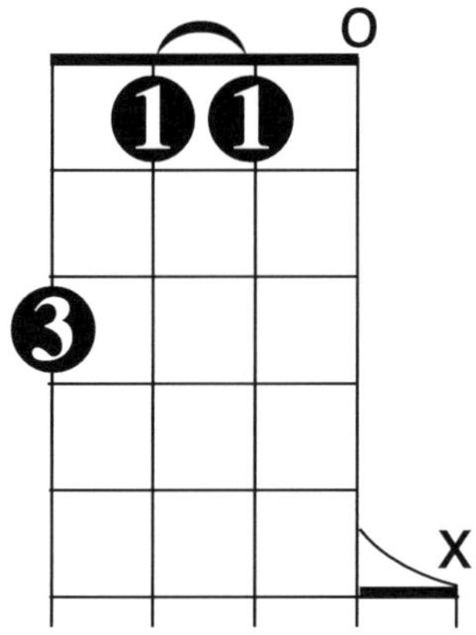

F Seven Flat Five

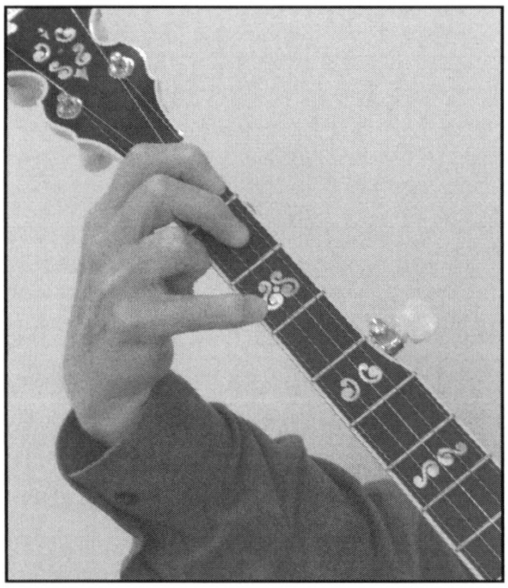

Root - 3rd - ♭5th - ♭7th
F - A - C♭ - E♭

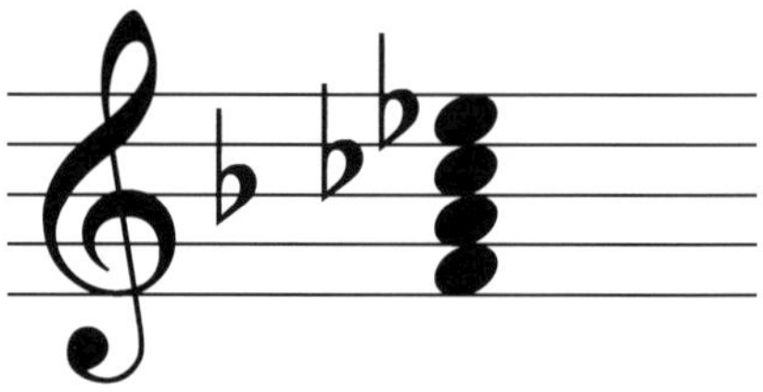

F7♭5

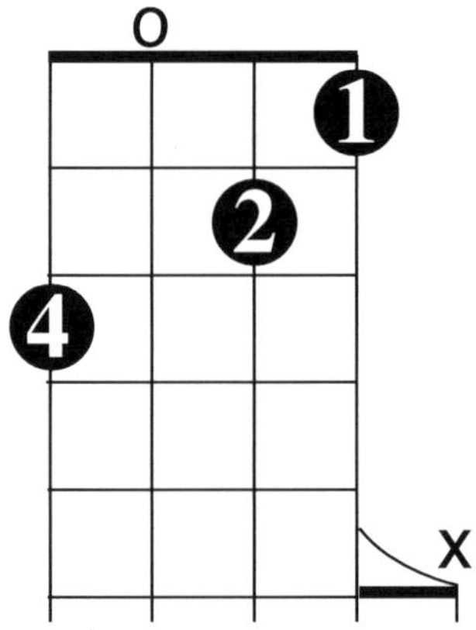

F Major Seventh

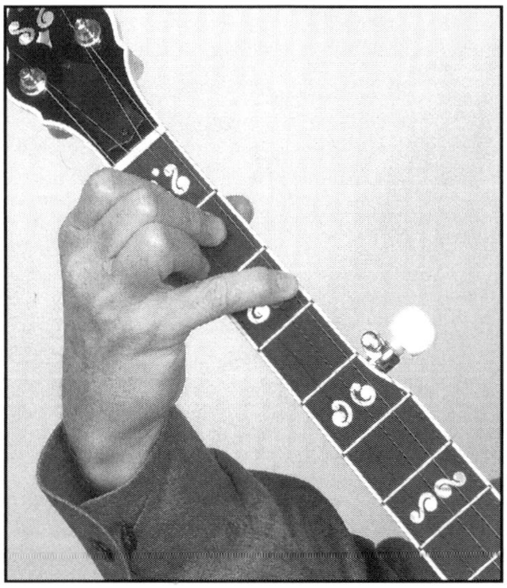

Root - 3rd - 5th - 7th
F - A - C - E

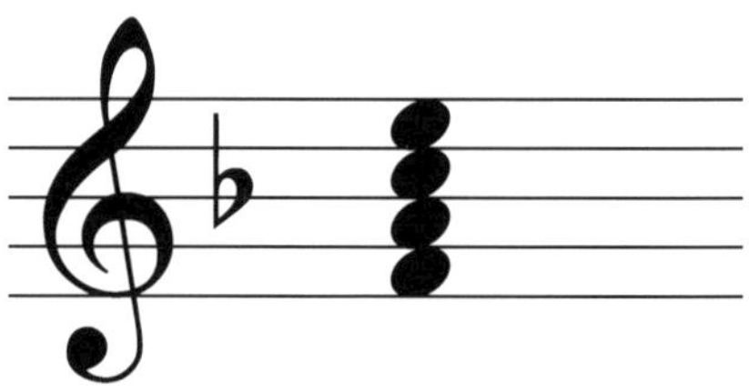

FMaj7

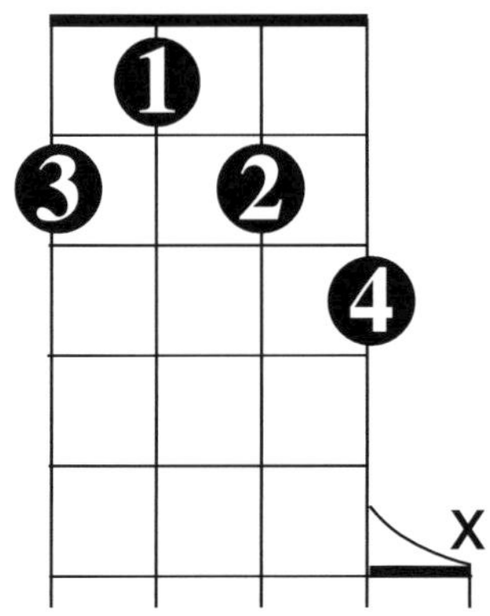

F Chords

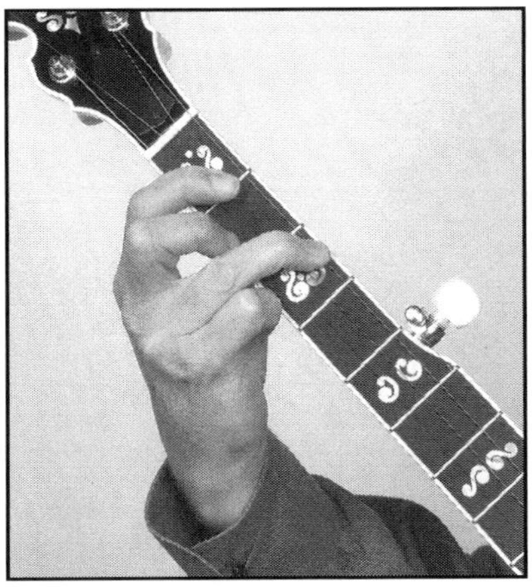

F Major Seventh Flat Third

FMaj7♭3

Root - ♭3rd - 5th - 7th
F - A♭ - C - E

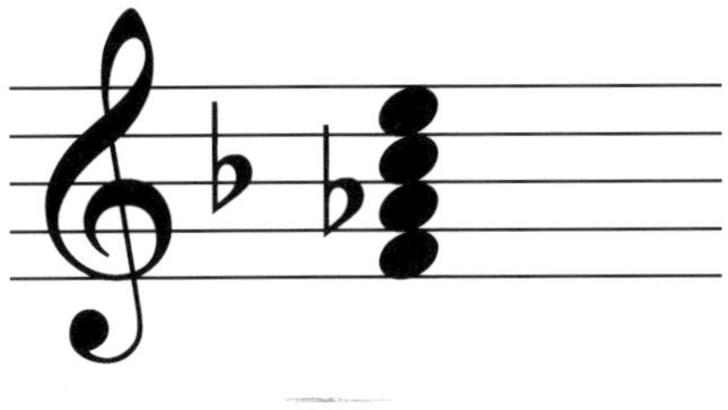

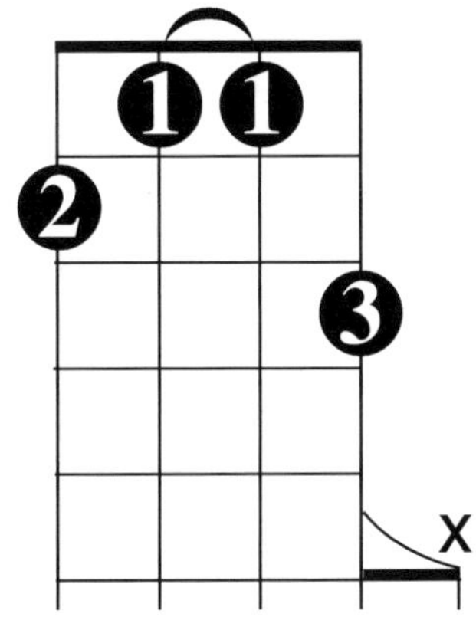

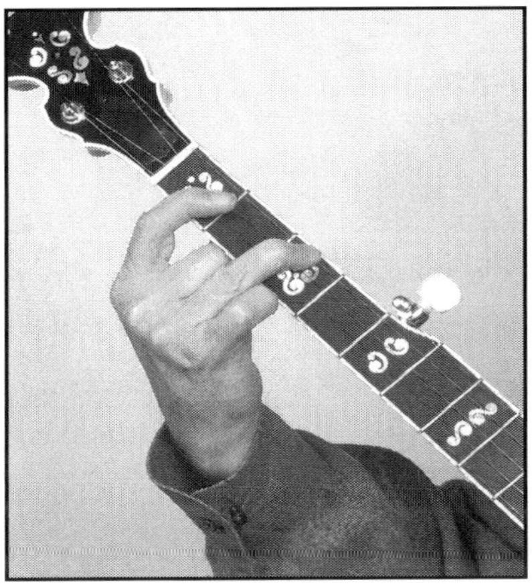

F Minor Seventh

Fm7

Root - ♭3rd - 5th - ♭7th
F - A♭ - C - E♭

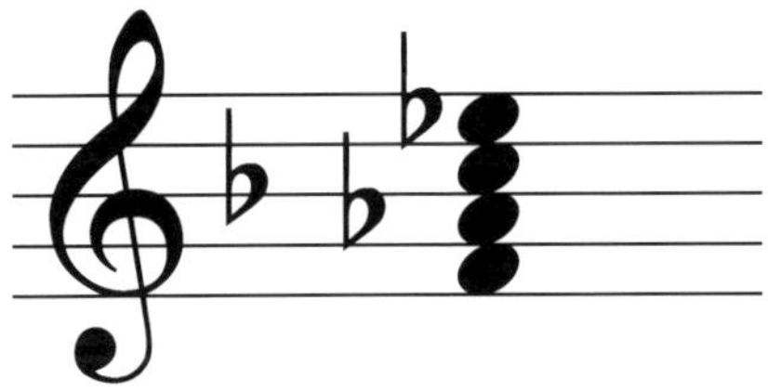

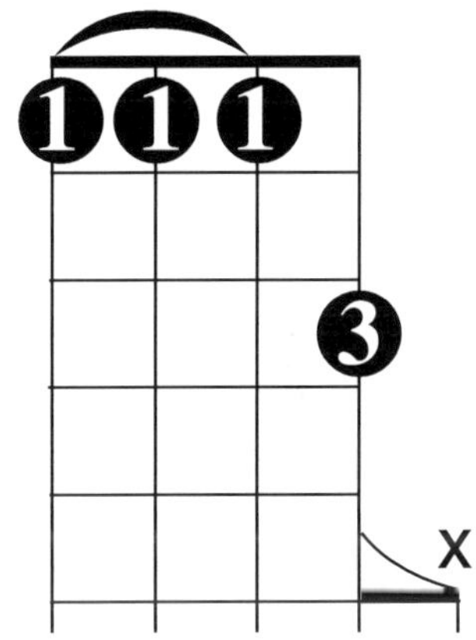

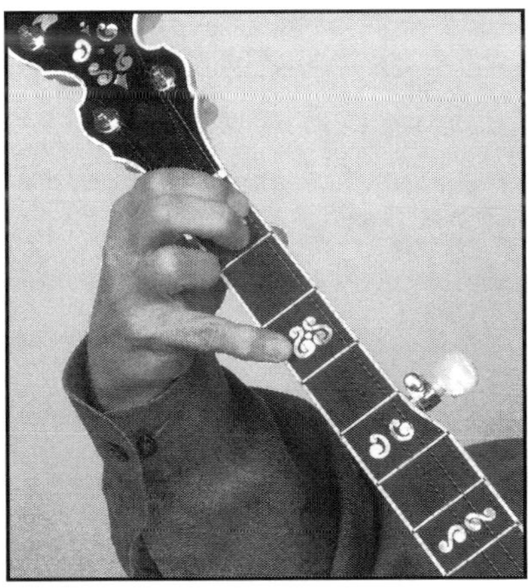

F Minor Seventh Flat Five

Fm7♭5

Root - ♭3rd - ♭5th - ♭7th
F - A♭ - C♭ - E♭

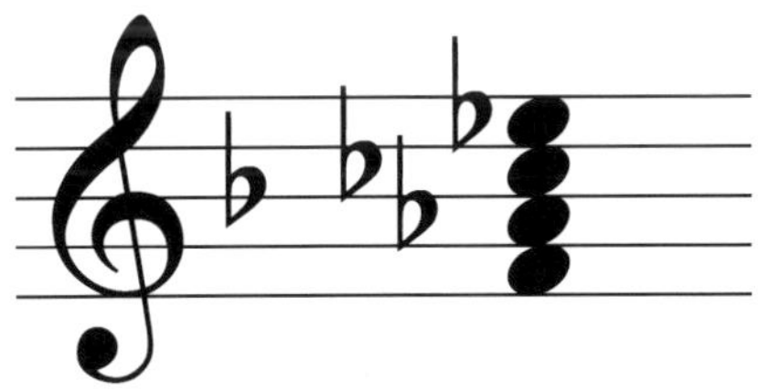

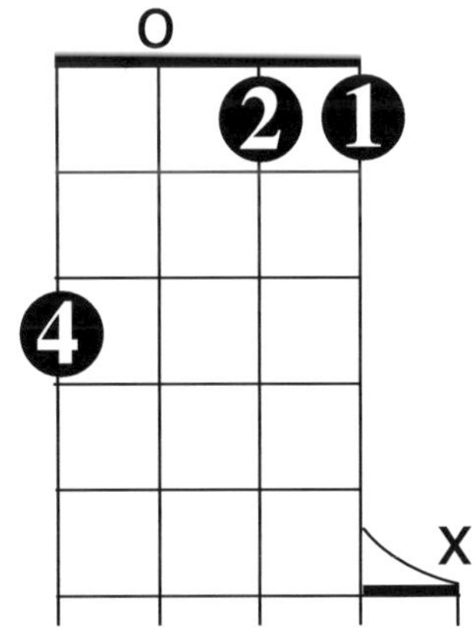

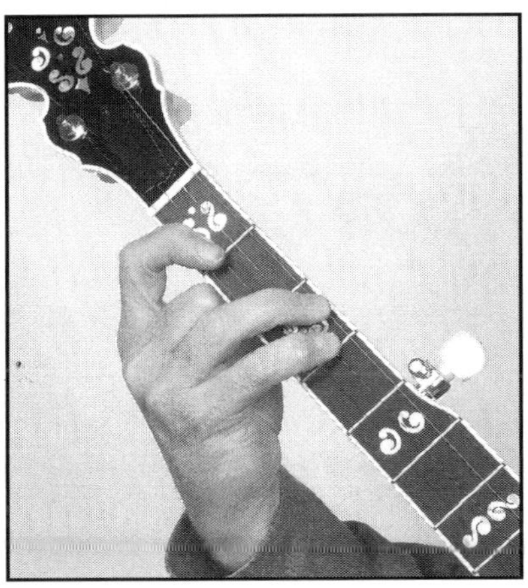

F Seventh Suspended Fourth

F7sus4

Root - 4th - 5th - ♭7th
F - B♭ - C - E♭

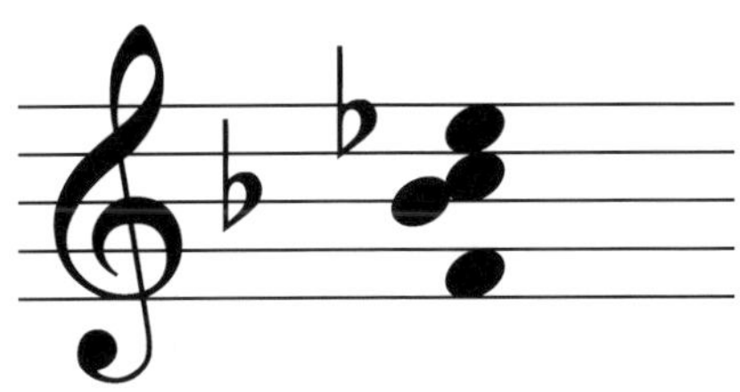

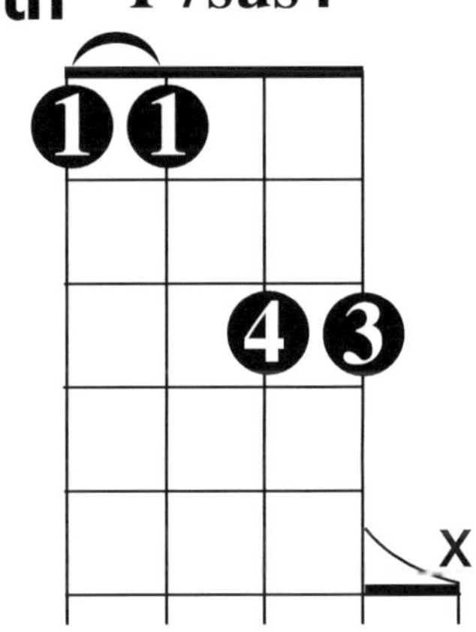

G♭/F♯ Chords

G♭ Major

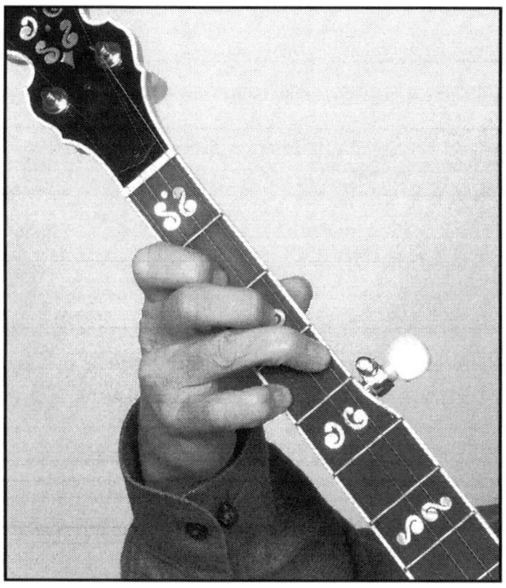

Root - 3rd - 5th
G♭ - B♭ - D♭
F♯ - A♯ - C♯

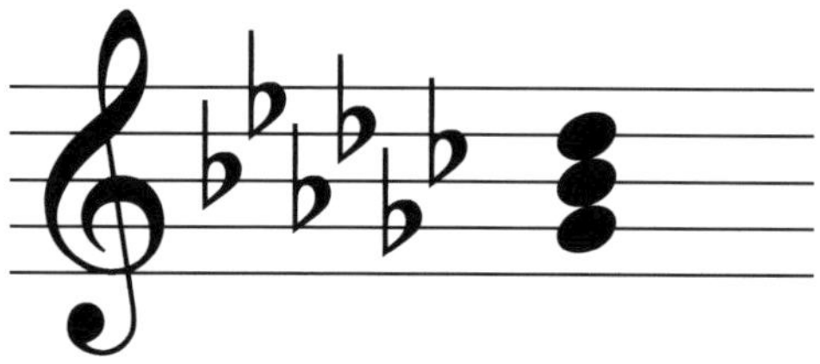

G♭

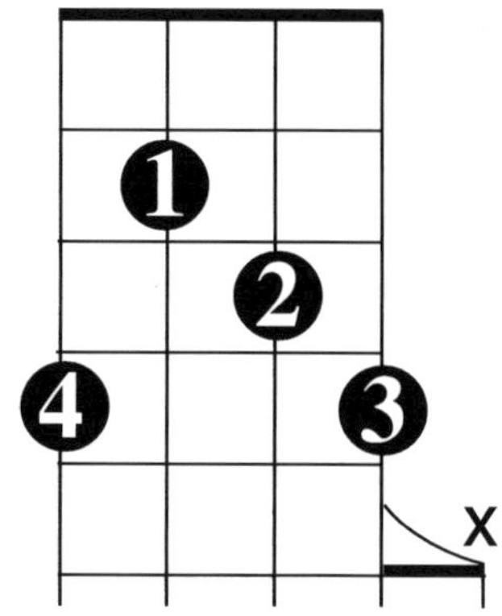

G♭ Minor

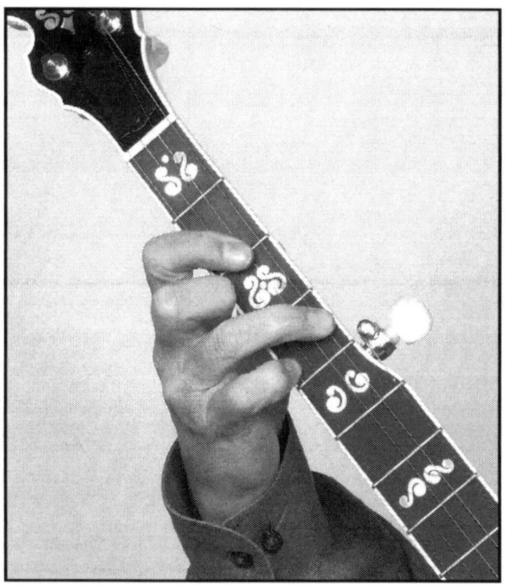

Root - ♭3rd - 5th
G♭ - B♭♭ - D♭
F♯ - A♮ - C♯

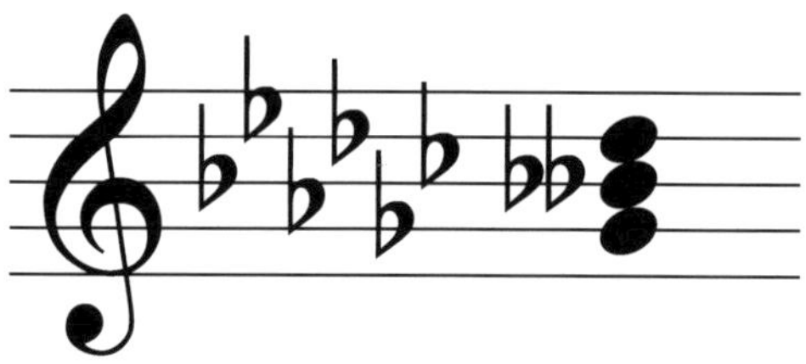

G♭m

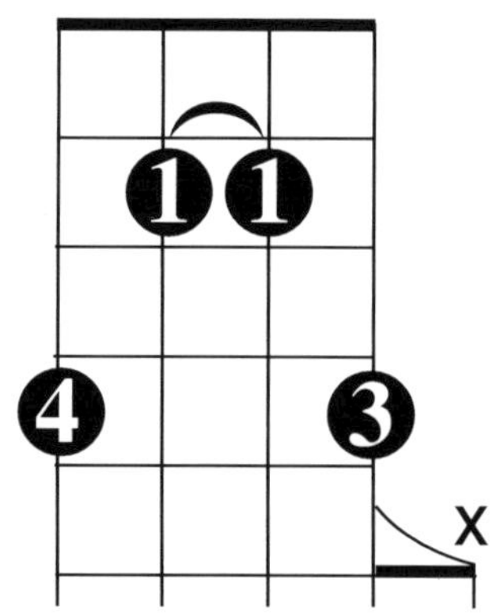

G♭ Seventh

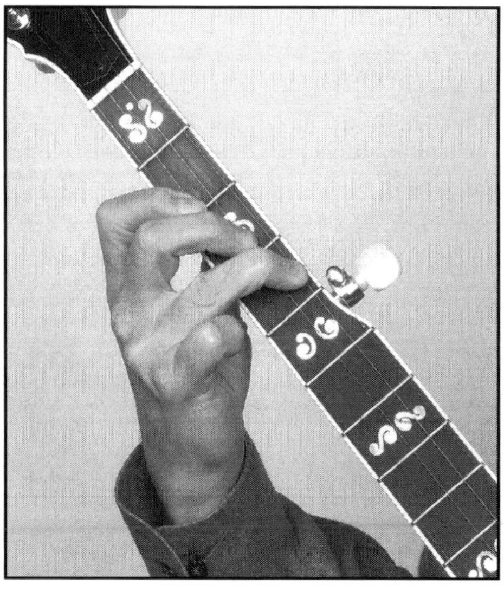

Root - 3rd - 5th - ♭7th
G♭ - B♭ - D♭ - F♭
F♯ - A♯ - C♯ - E♮

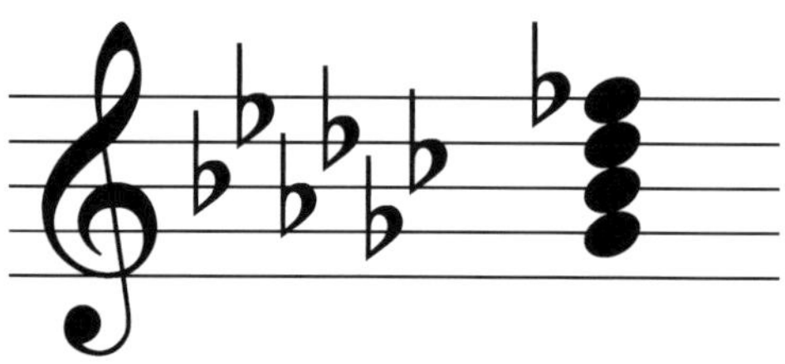

G♭7

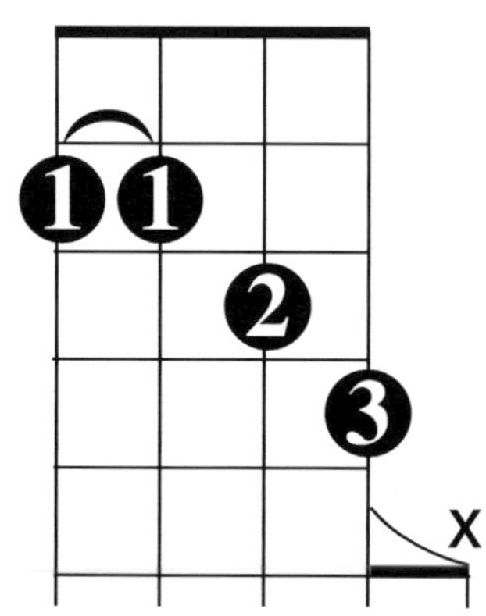

G♭/F♯ Chords

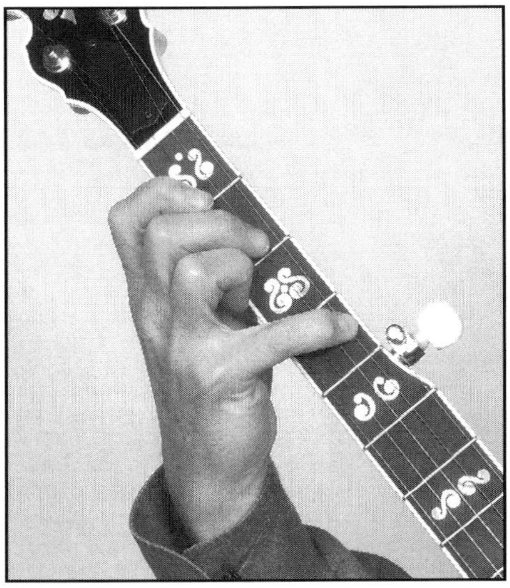

G♭ Diminished

Root - ♭3rd - ♭5th - 𝄫7th
G♭ - B𝄫 - D𝄫 - F𝄫
F♯ - A - C - E♭

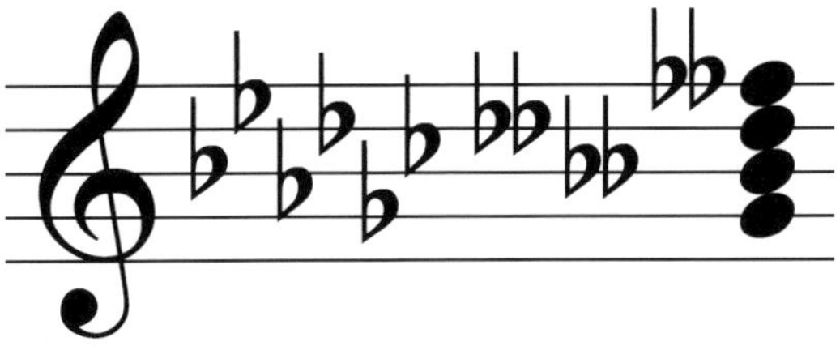

G♭o

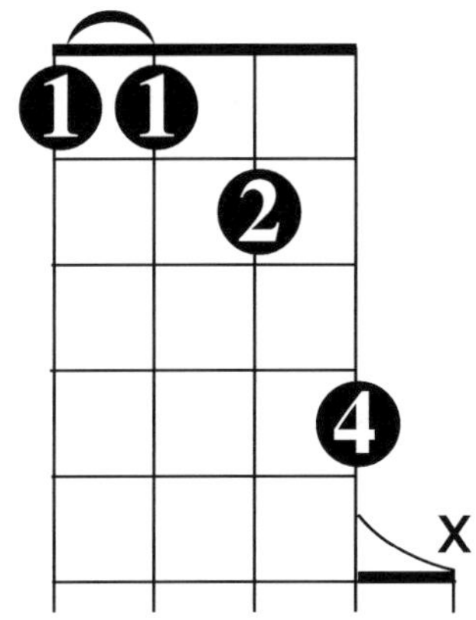

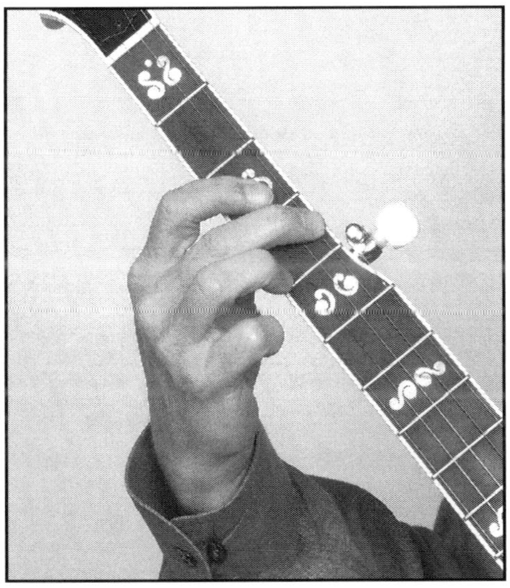

G♭ Augmented

Root - 3rd - ♯5th
G♭ - B♭ - D♮
F♯ - A♯ - C𝄪

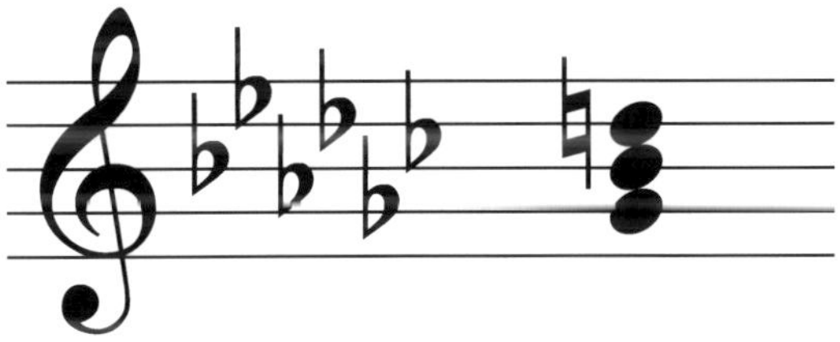

G♭+

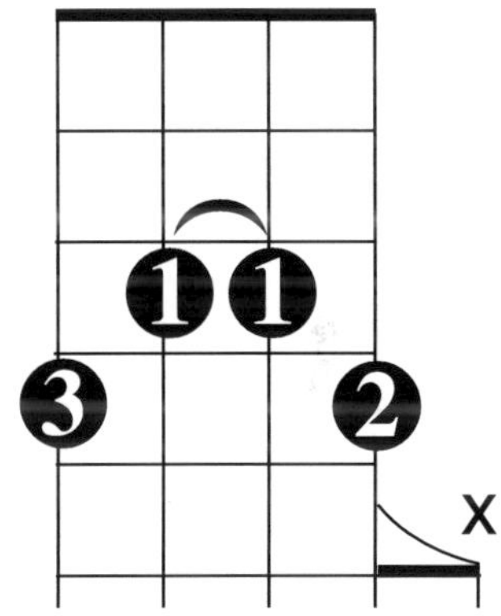

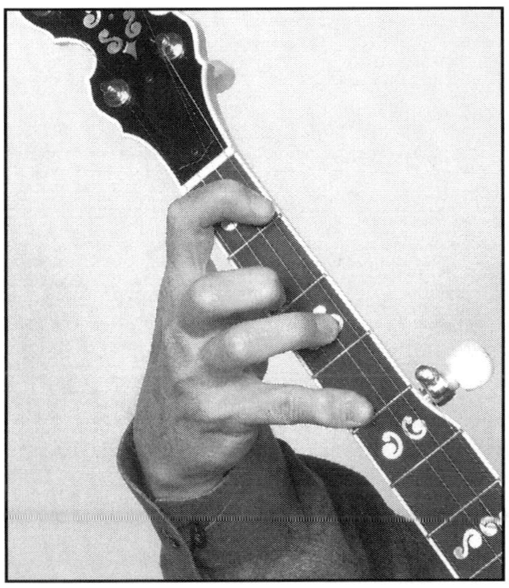

G♭ Sixth

Root - 3rd - 5th - 6th
G♭ - B♭ - D♭ - E♭
F♯ - A♯ - C♯ - D♯

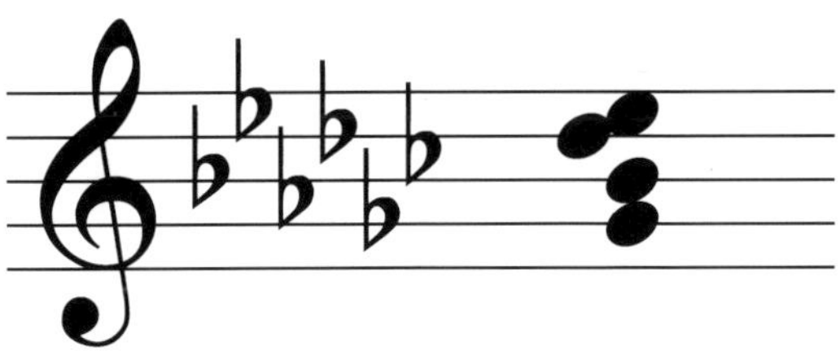

G♭6

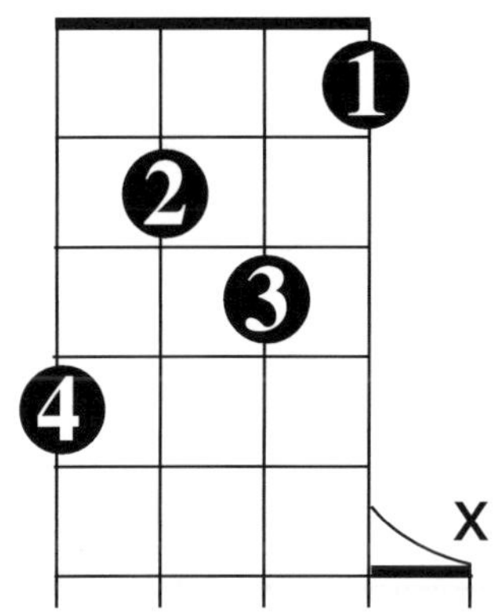

G♭/F♯ Chords

G♭ Minor Sixth

Root - ♭3rd - 5th - 6th
G♭ - B♭♭ - D♭ - E♭
F♯ - A - C♯ - D♯

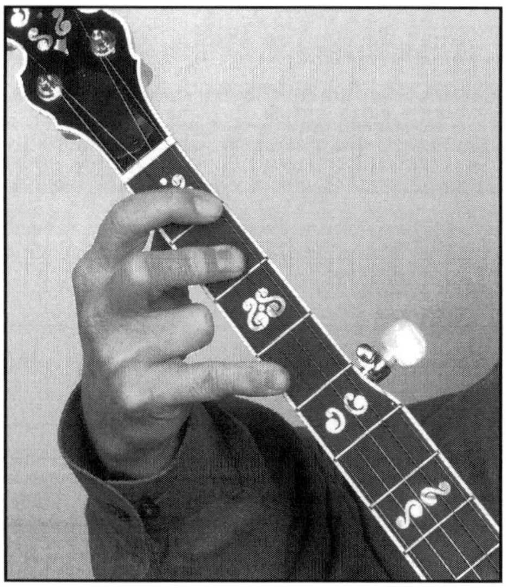

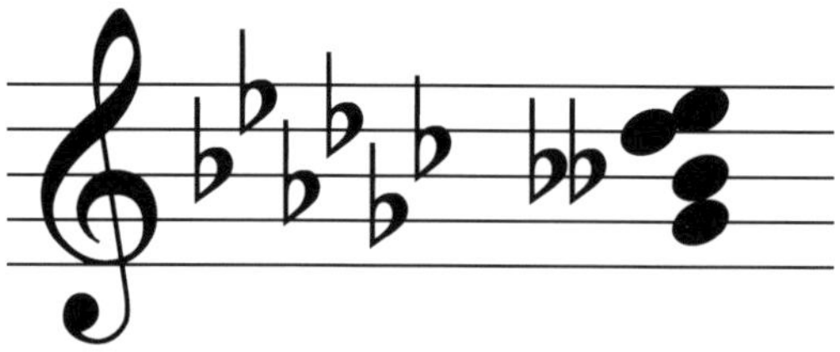

G♭m6

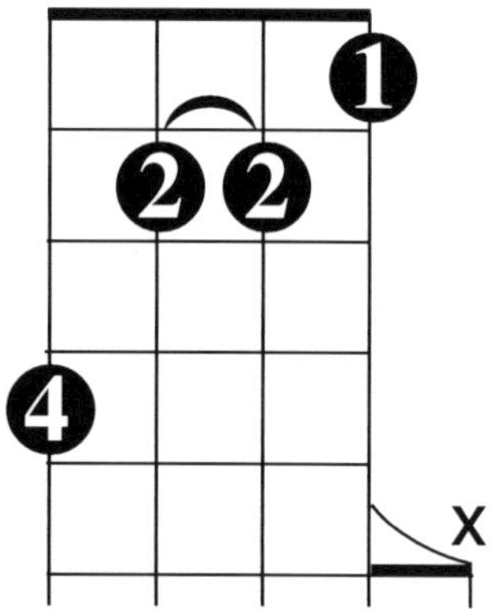

G♭ Seven Flat Five

Root - 3rd - ♭5th - ♭7th
G♭ - B♭ - D♭♭ - F♭
F♯ - A♯ - C - E

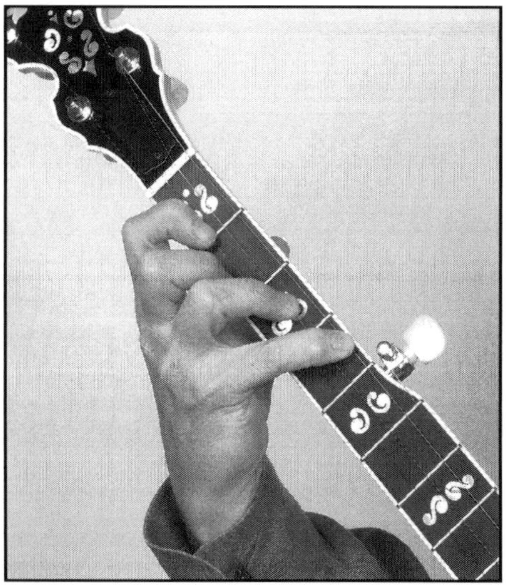

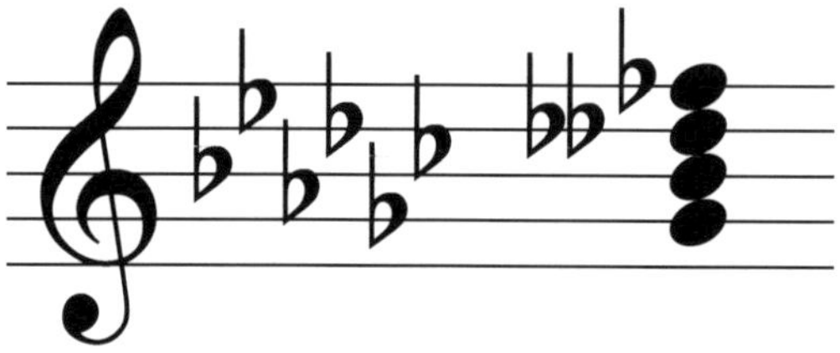

G♭7♭5

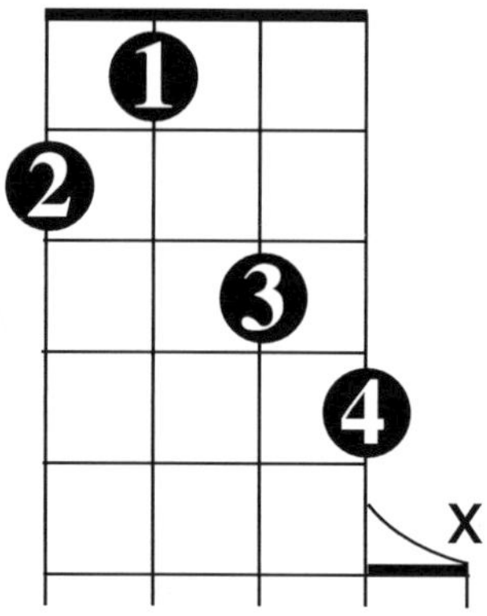

G♭ Major Seventh

Root - 3rd - 5th - 7th
G♭ - B♭ - D♭ - F
F♯ - A♯ - C♯ - E♯

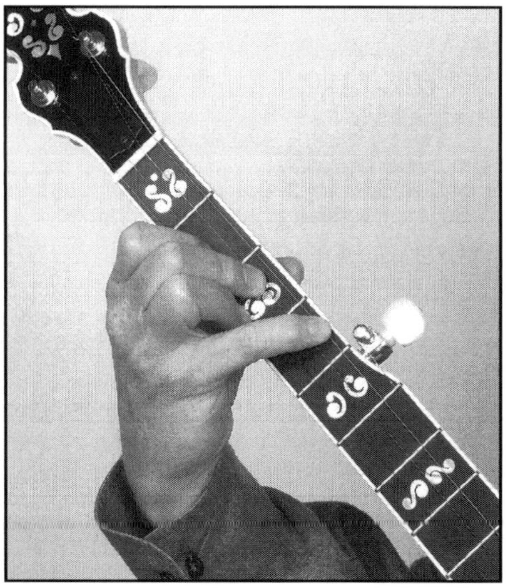

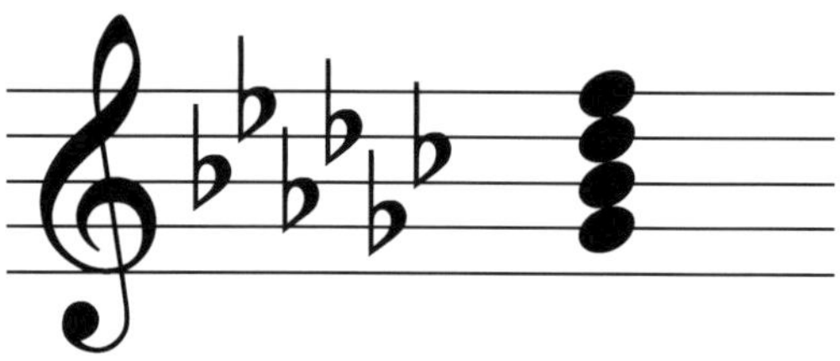

G♭Maj7

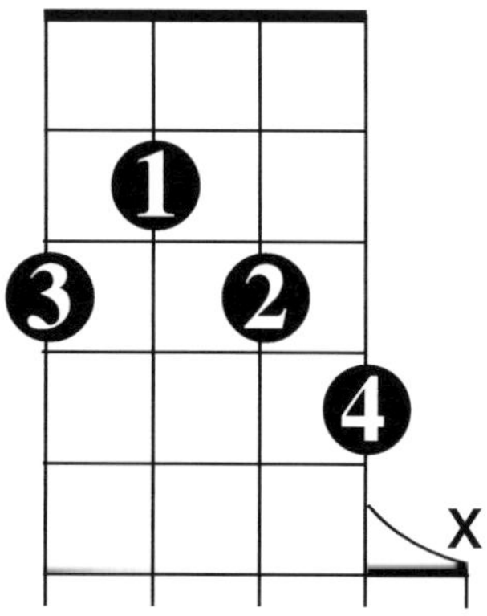

G♭/F♯ Chords

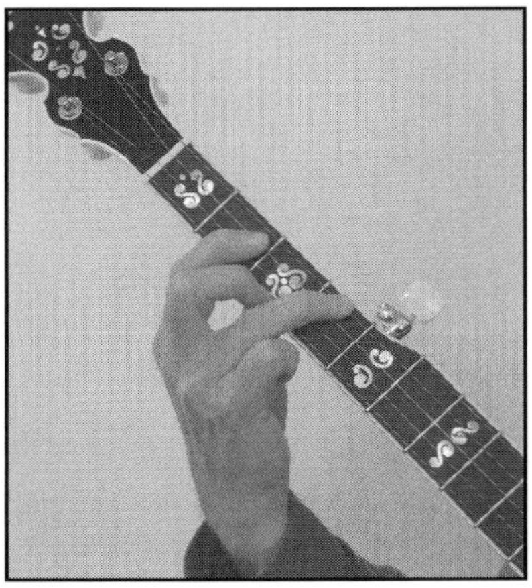

G♭ Major Seventh Flat Third

Root - ♭3rd - 5th - 7th
G♭ - B♭♭ - D♭ - F
F♯ - A - C♯ - E♯

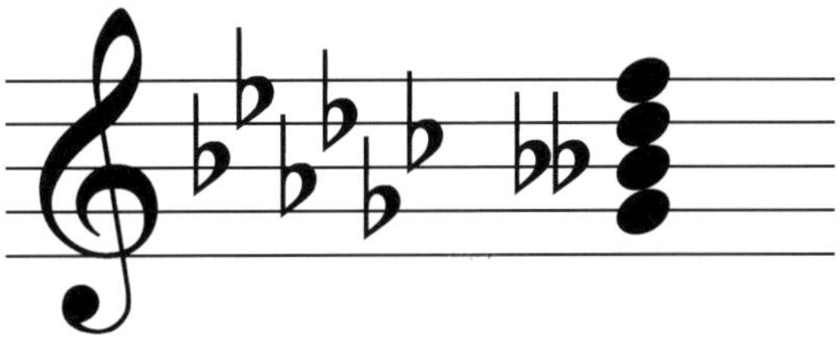

G♭Maj7♭3

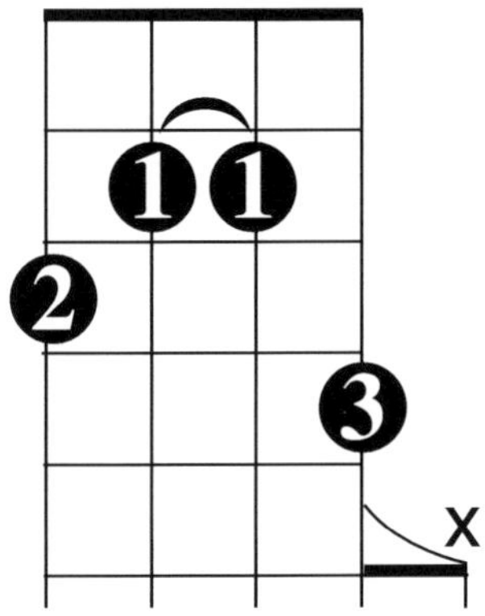

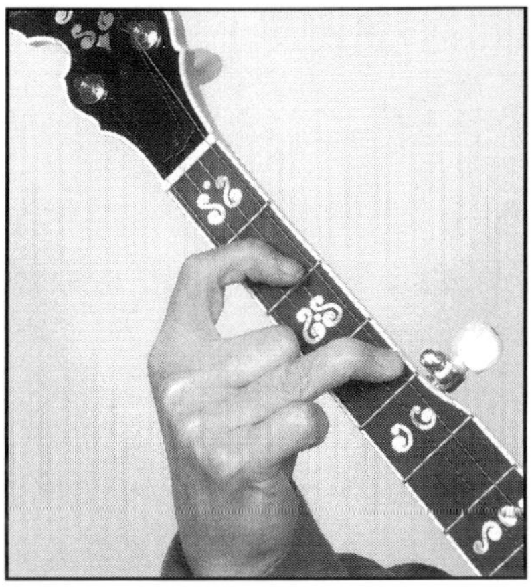

G♭ Minor Seventh

Root - ♭3rd - 5th - ♭7th
G♭ - B♭♭ - D♭ - F♭
F♯ - A - C♯ - E

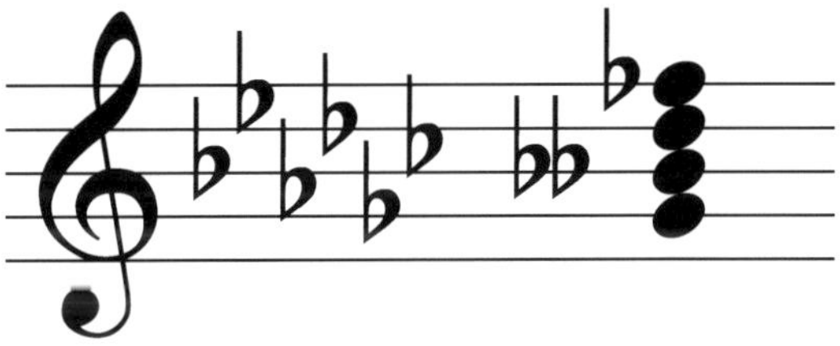

G♭m7

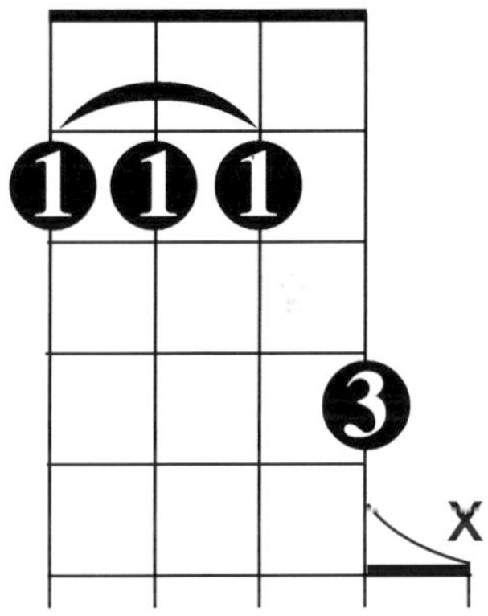

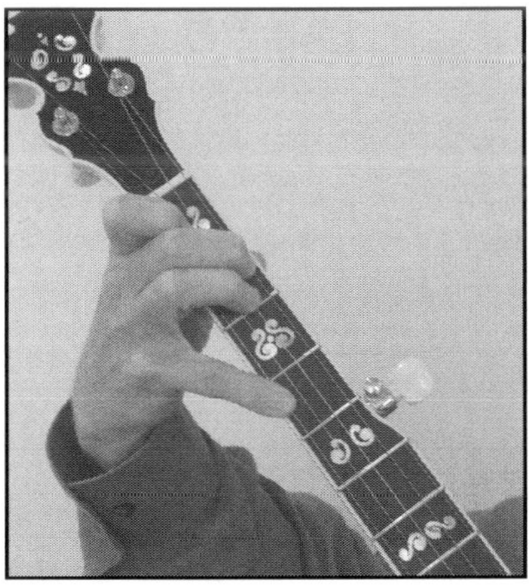

G♭ Minor Seventh Flat Five

G♭m7♭5

Root - ♭3rd - ♭5th - ♭7th
G♭ - B♭♭ - D♭♭ - F♭
F♯ - A - C - E

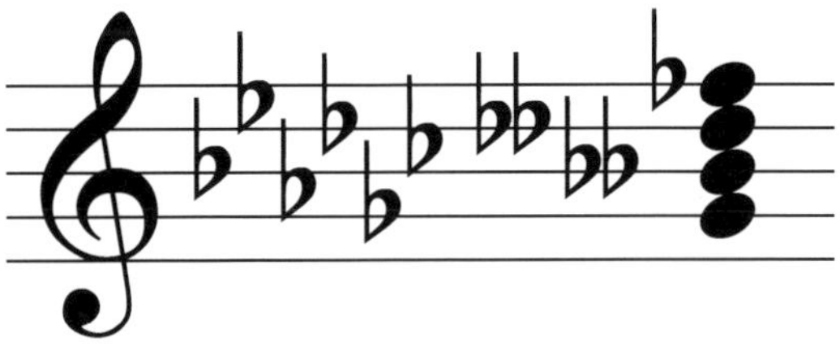

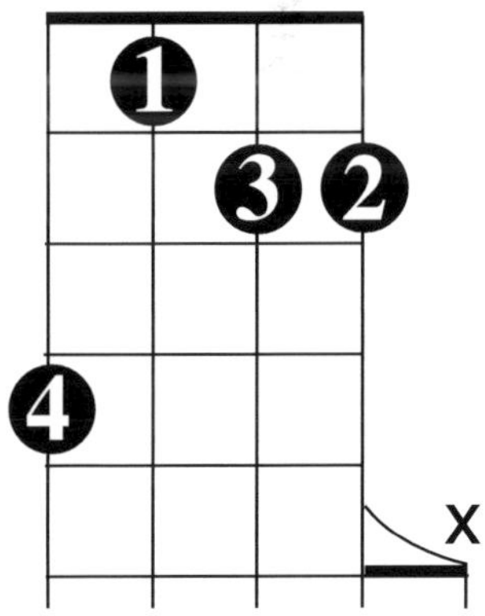

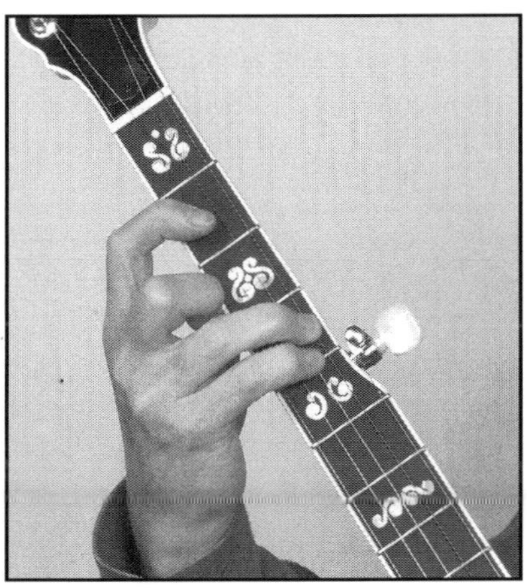

G♭ Seventh Suspended Fourth

Root - 4th - 5th - ♭7th
G♭ - C♭ - D♭ - F♭
F♯ - B - C♯ - E

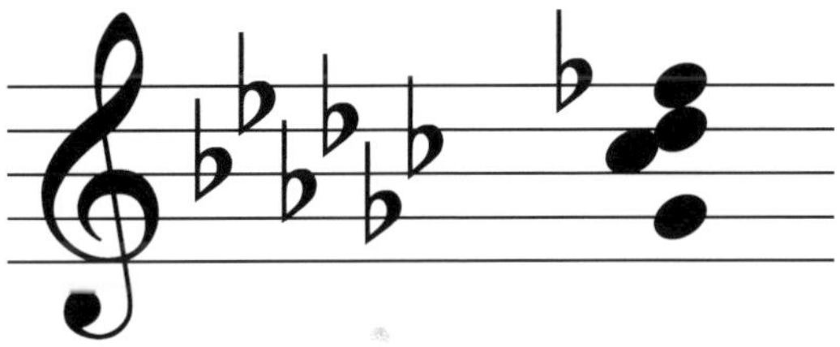

G♭7sus4

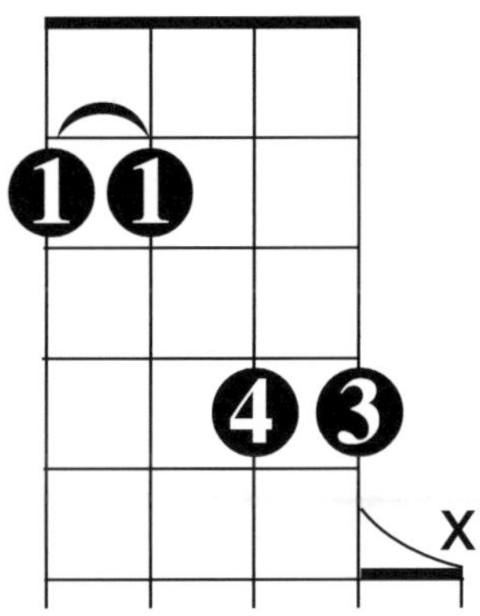

G Chords

G Major

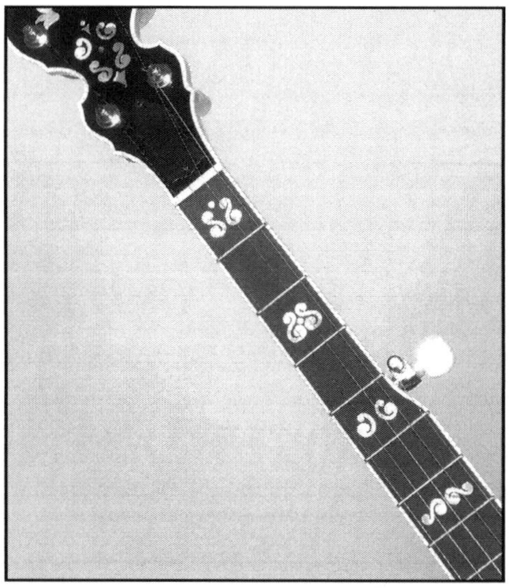

Root - 3rd - 5th
G - B - D

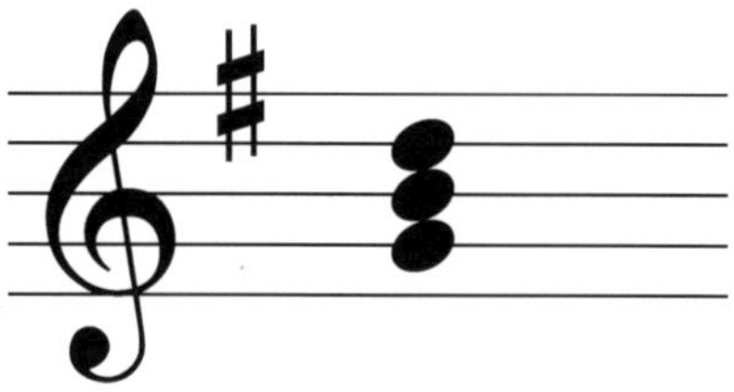

G

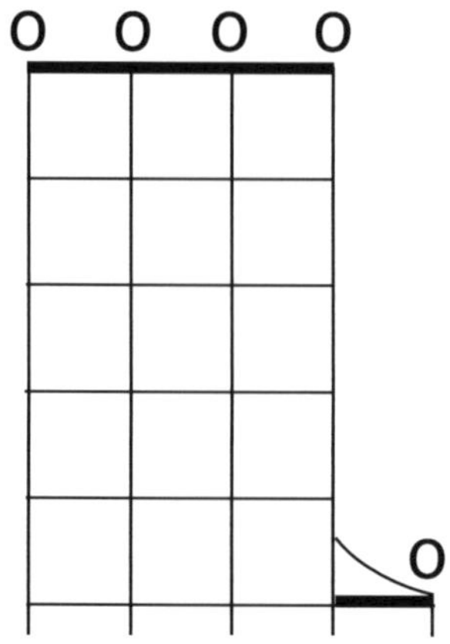

G Minor

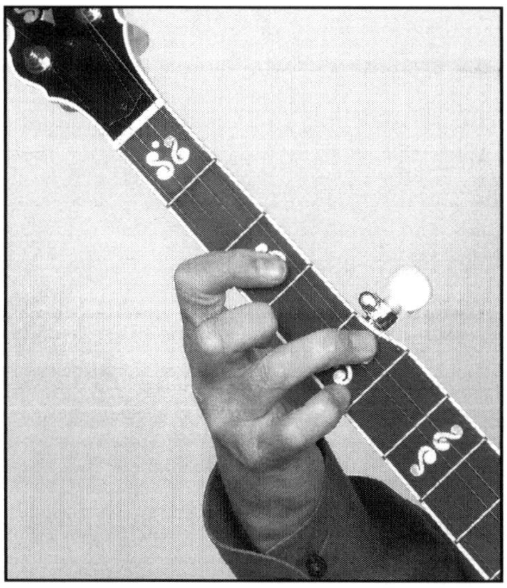

Root - ♭3rd - 5th
G - B♭ - D

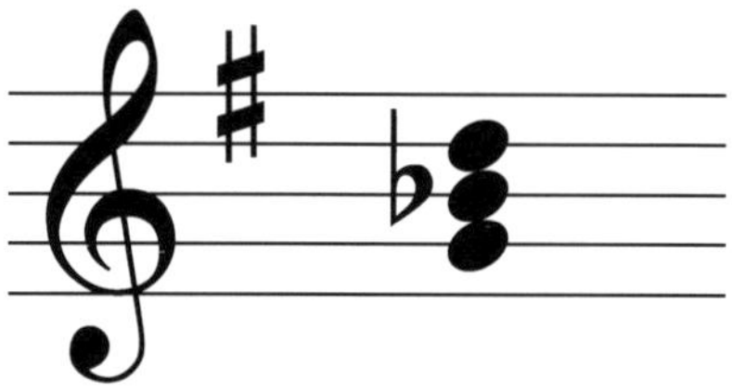

Gm

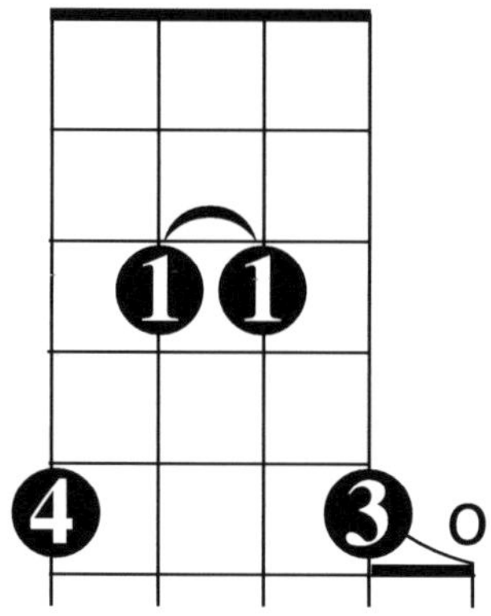

G Seventh

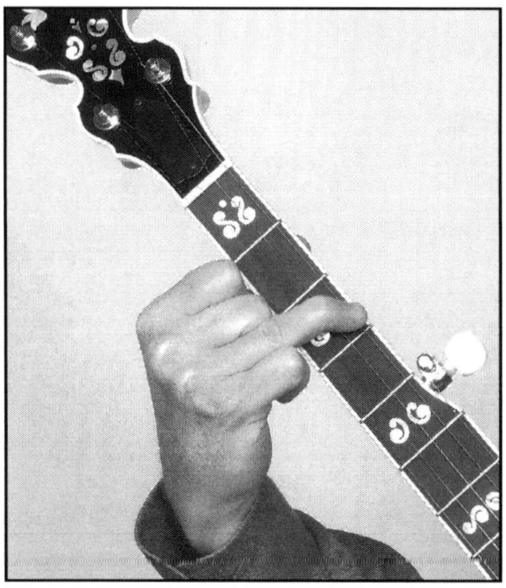

Root - 3rd - 5th - ♭7th
G - B - D - F♮

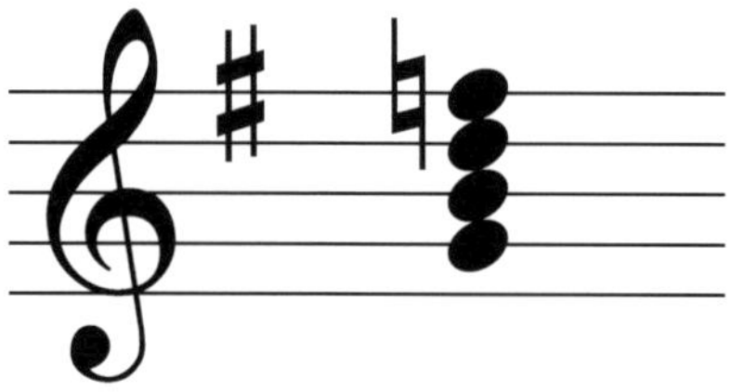

G7

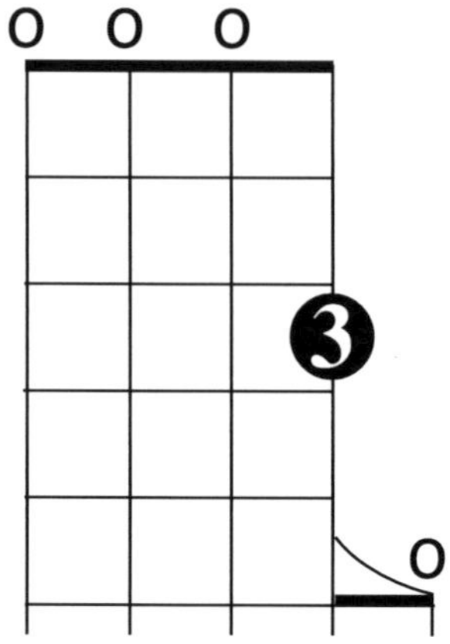

G Chords

G Diminished

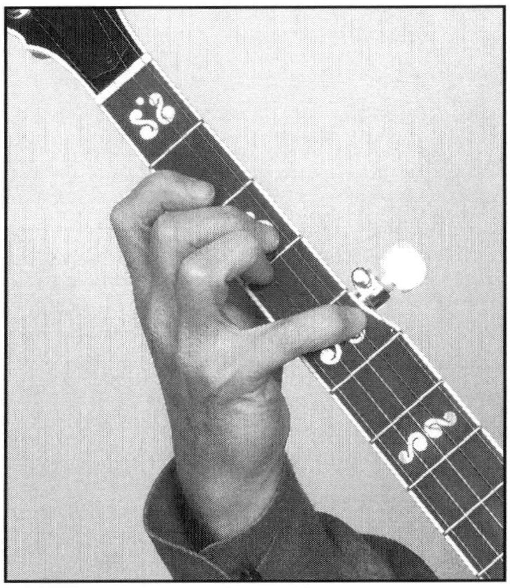

Root - ♭3rd - ♭5th - ♭♭7th
G - B♭ - D♭ - F♭

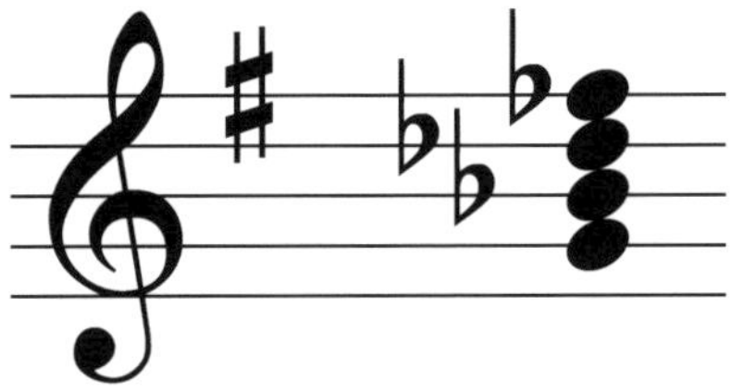

G°

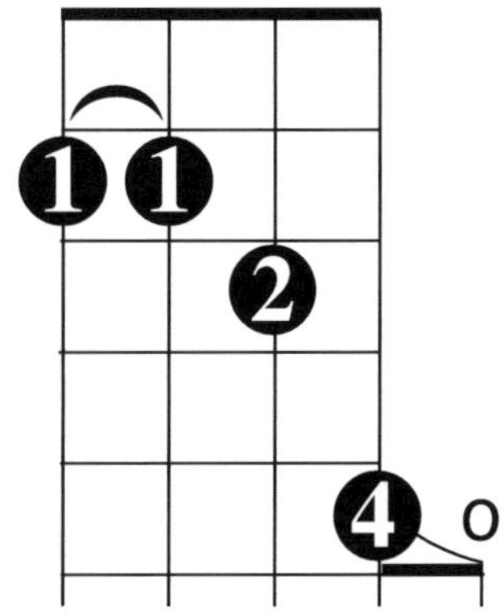

G Augmented

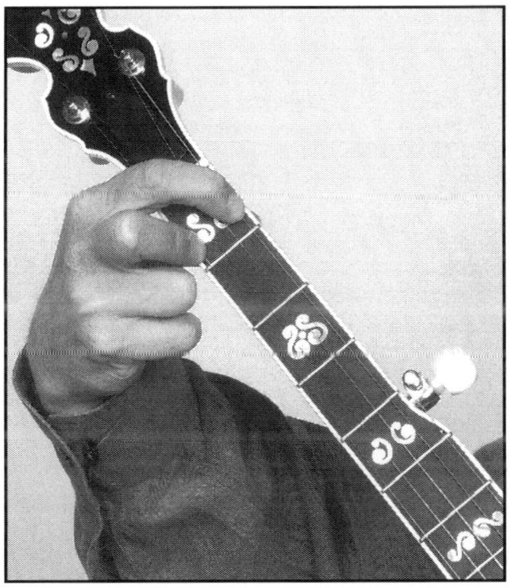

Root - 3rd - ♯5th
G - B - D♯

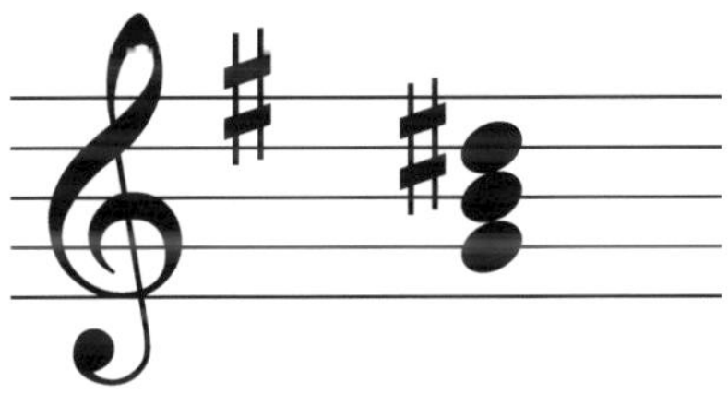

G+

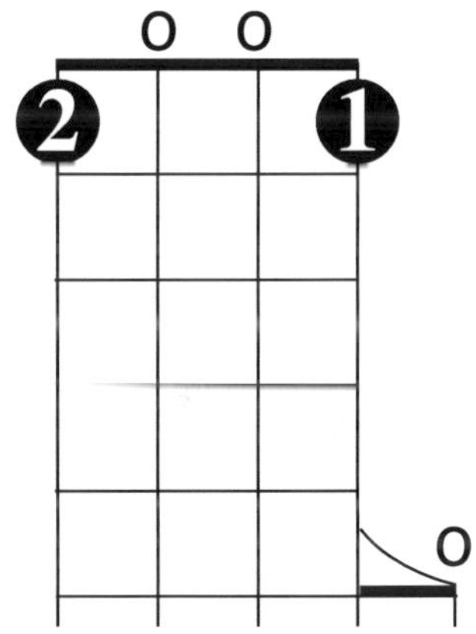

G Sixth

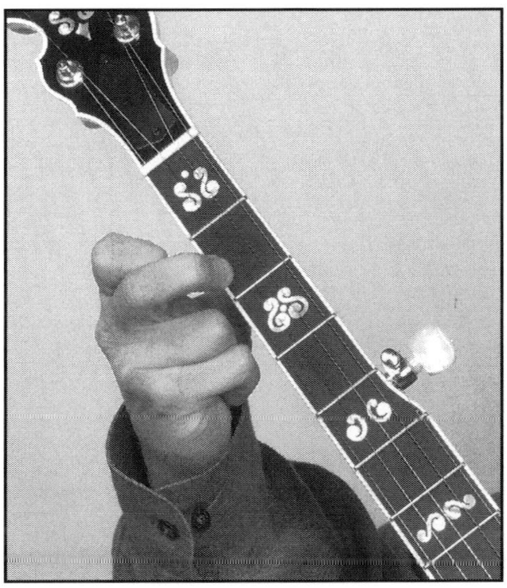

Root - 3rd - 5th - 6th
G - B - D - E

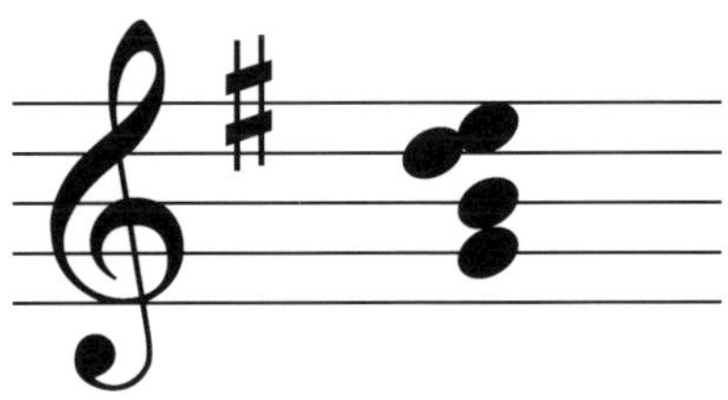

G6

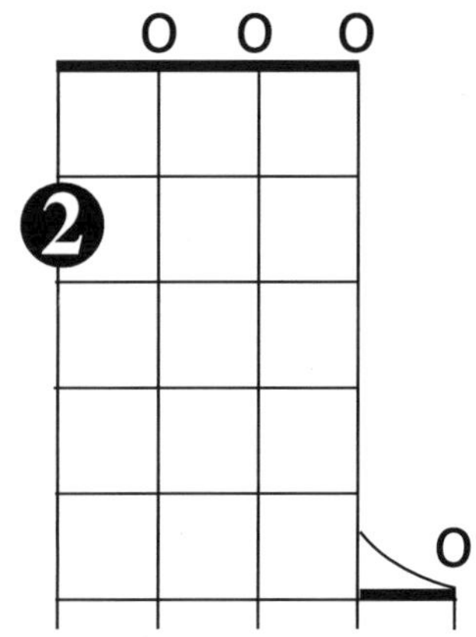

G Chords

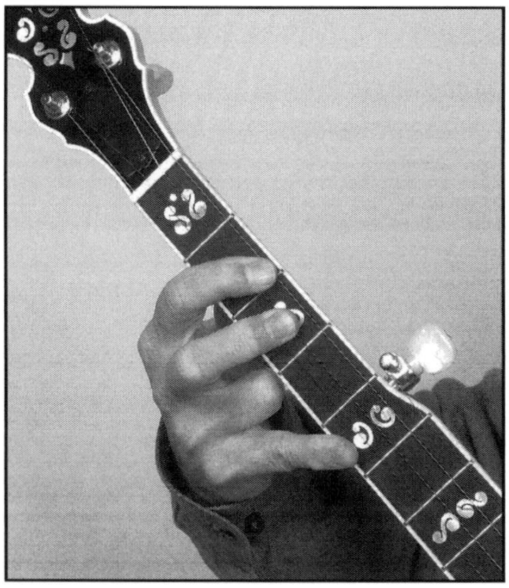

G Minor Sixth

Root - ♭3rd - 5th - 6th
G - B♭ - D - E

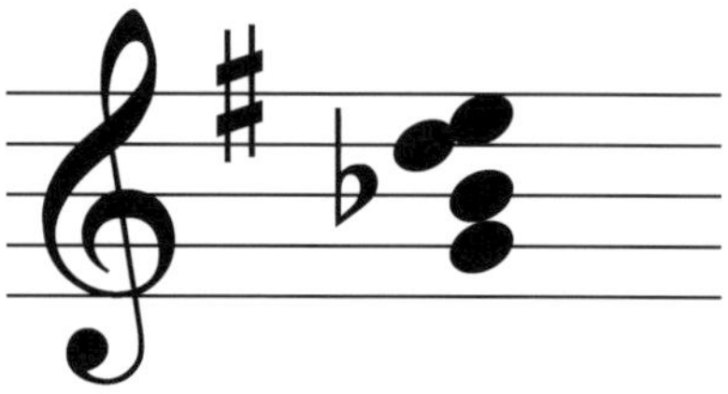

Gm6

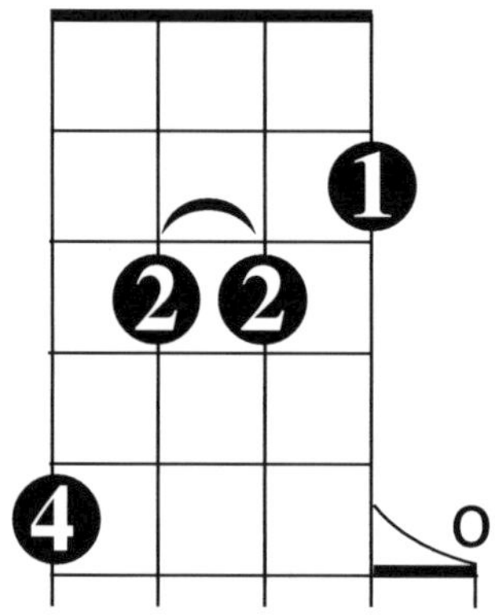

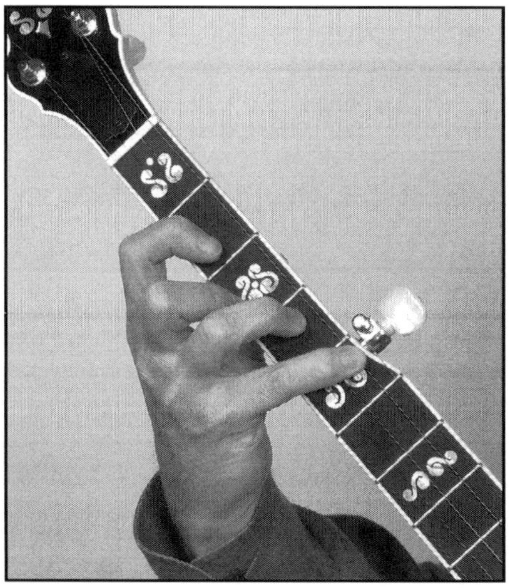

G Seven Flat Five

Root - 3rd - ♭5th - ♭7th
G - B - D♭ - F♮

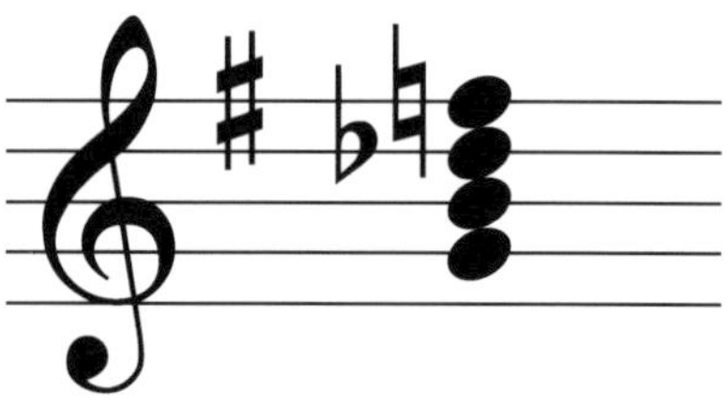

G7♭5

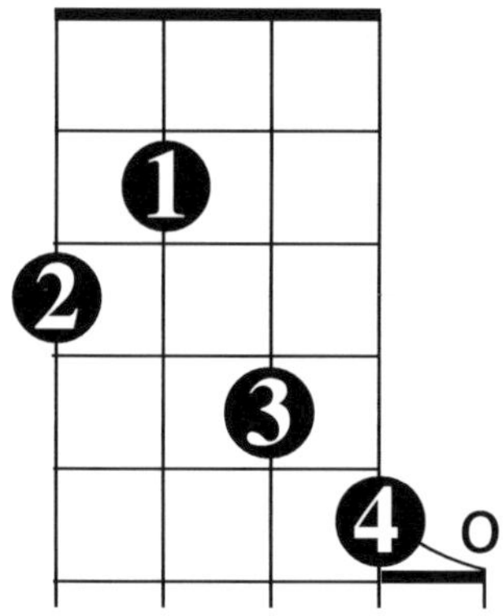

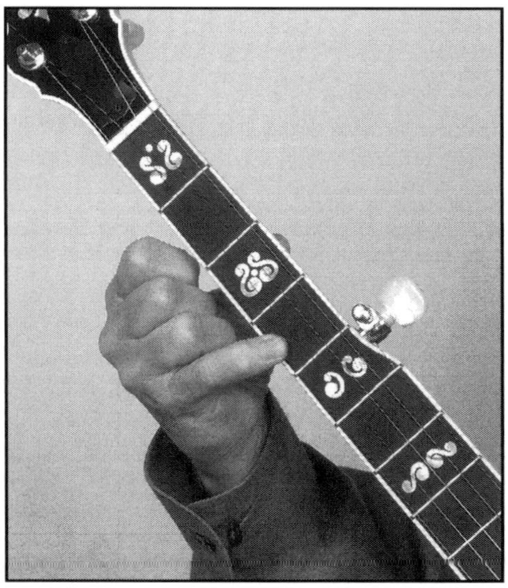

G Major Seventh

Root - 3rd - 5th - 7th
G - B - D - F♯

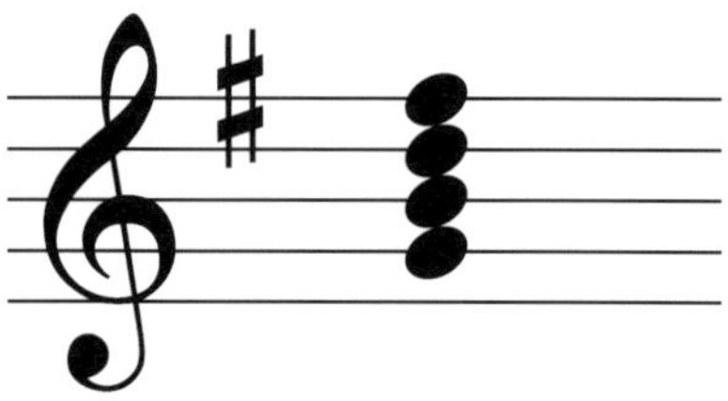

GMaj7

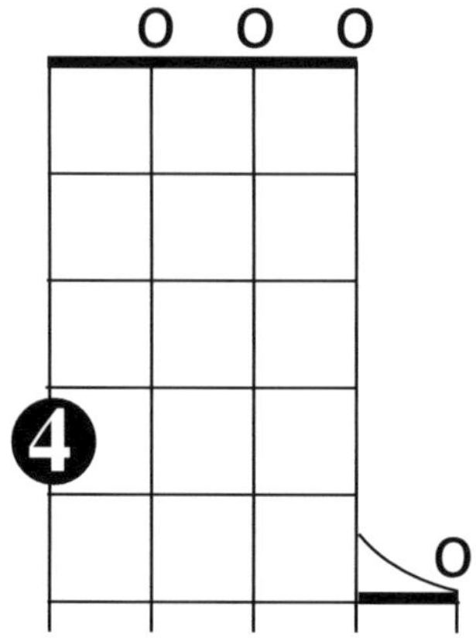

G Chords

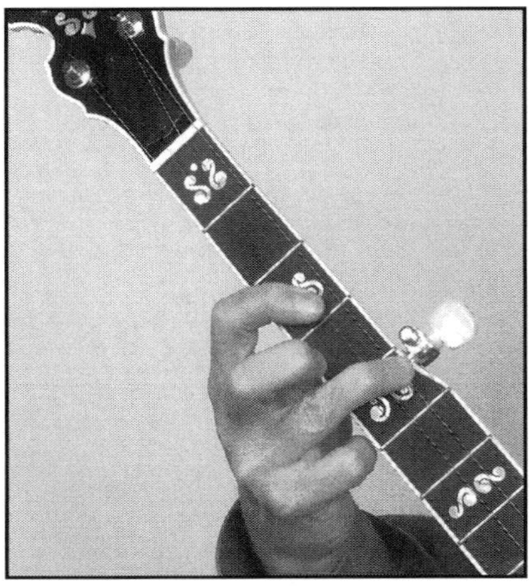

G Major Seventh Flat Third

GMaj7♭3

Root - ♭3rd - 5th - 7th
G - B♭ - D - F♯

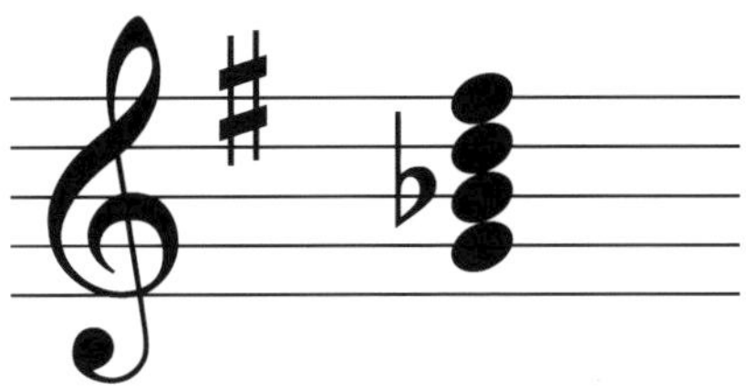

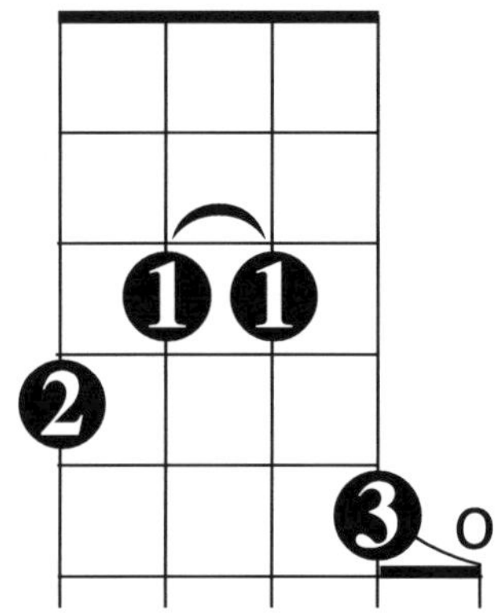

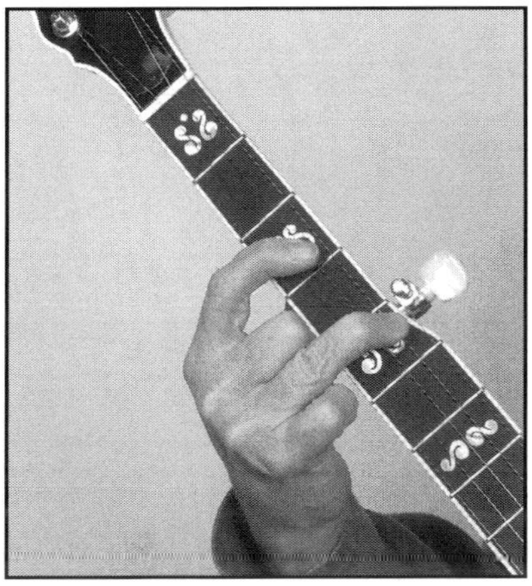

G Minor Seventh

Gm7

Root - ♭3rd - 5th - ♭7th
G - B♭ - D - F♮

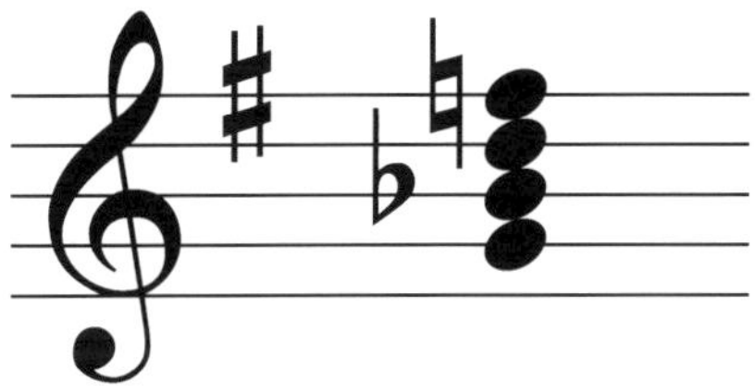

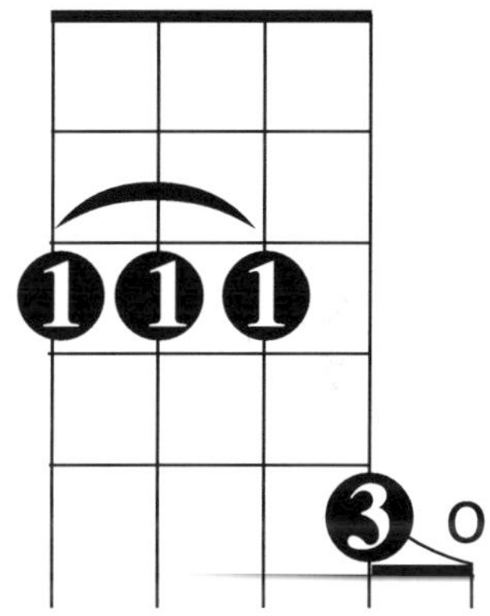

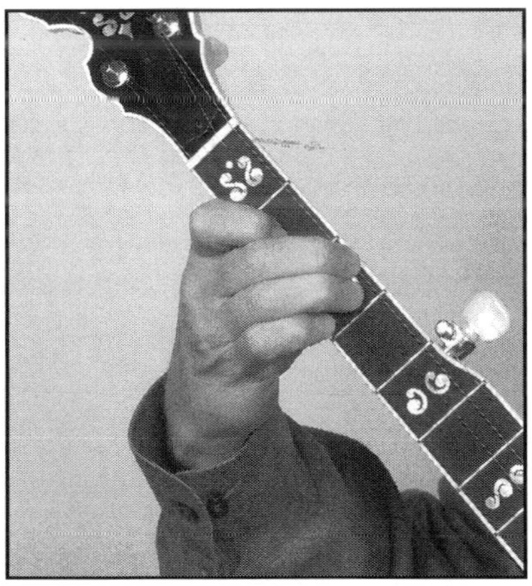

G Minor Seventh Flat Five

Gm7♭5

Root - ♭3rd - ♭5th - ♭7th
G - B♭ - D♭ - F♮

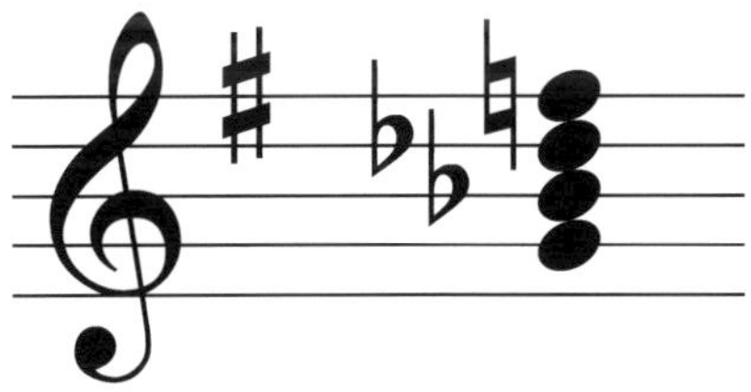

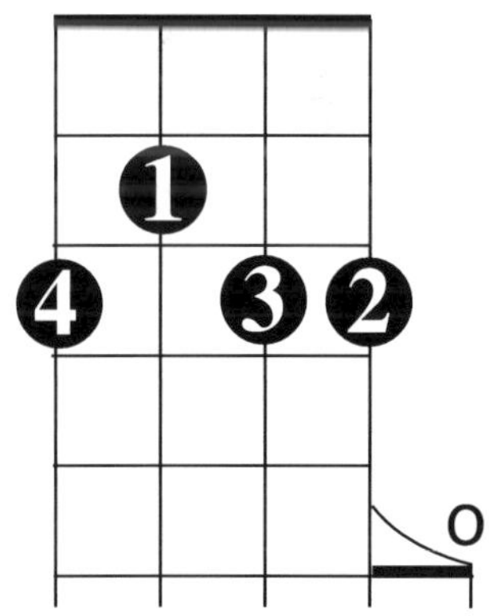

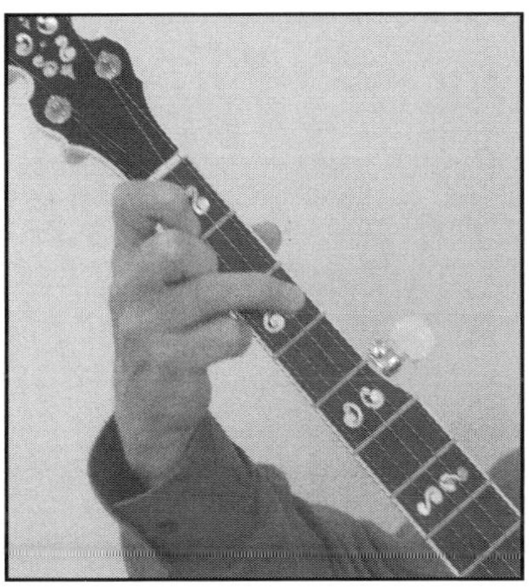

G Seventh Suspended Fourth

G7sus4

Root - 4th - 5th - ♭7th
G - C - D - F♮

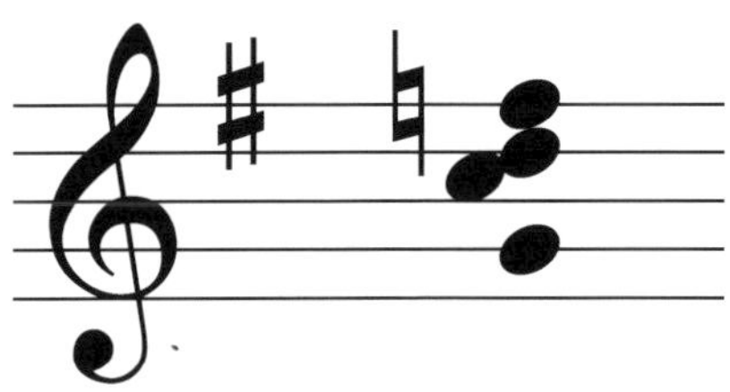

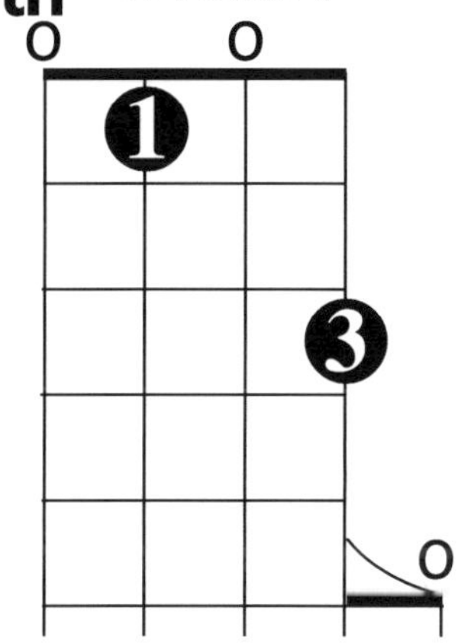

A♭/G♯ Chords

A♭ Major

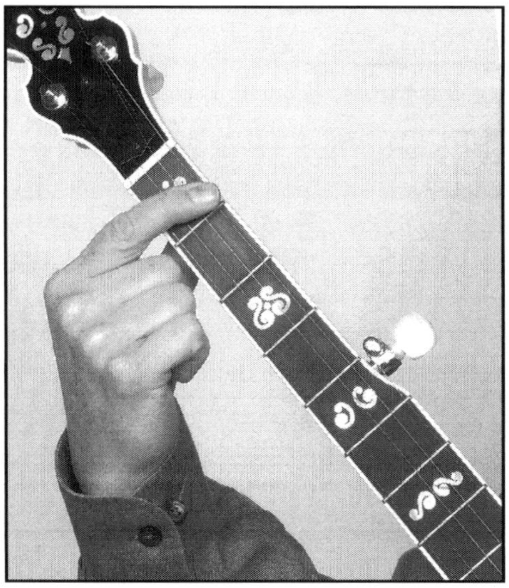

Root - 3rd - 5th
A♭ - C - E♭

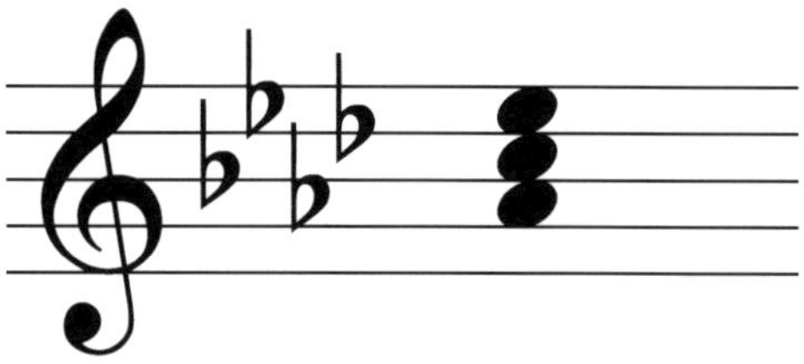

A♭

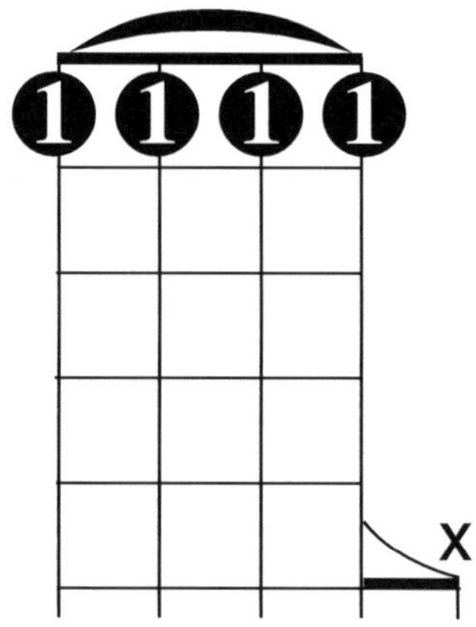

A♭ Minor

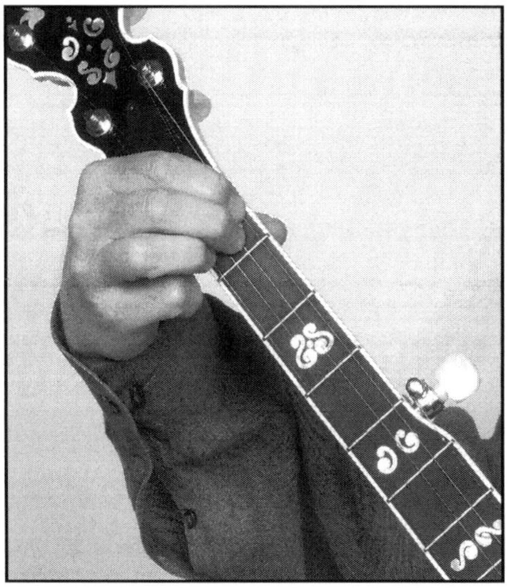

Root - ♭3rd - 5th
A♭ - C♭ - E♭

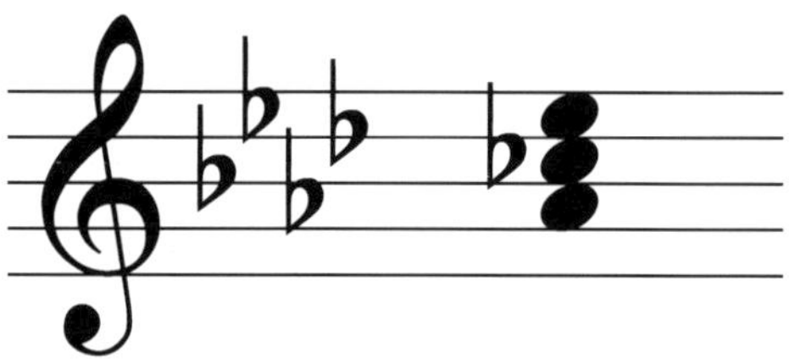

A♭m

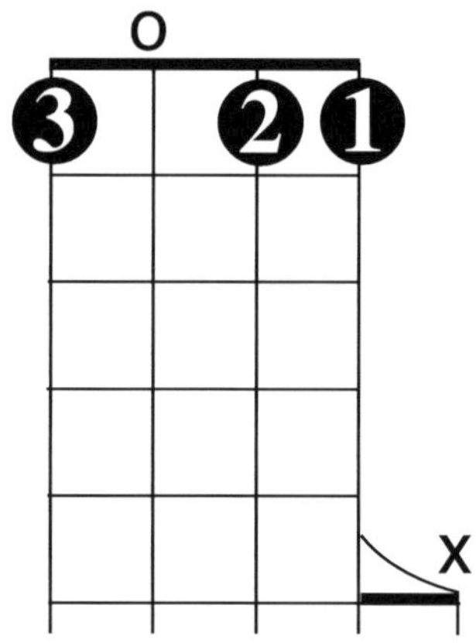

A♭ Seventh

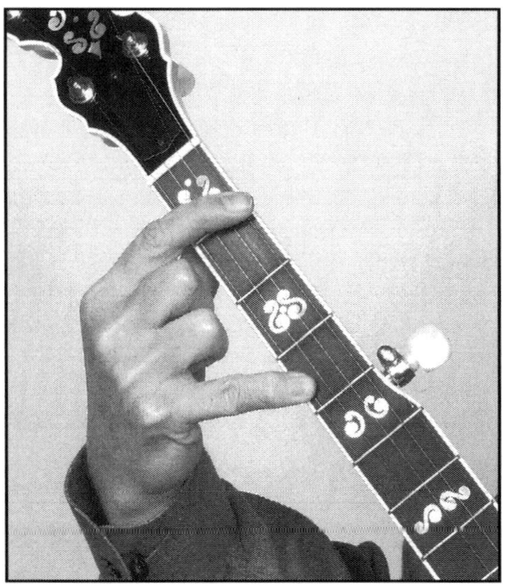

Root - 3rd - 5th - ♭7th
A♭ - C - E♭ - G♭

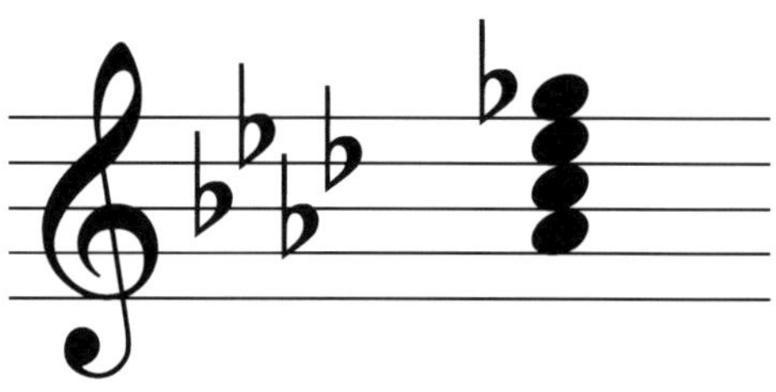

A♭7

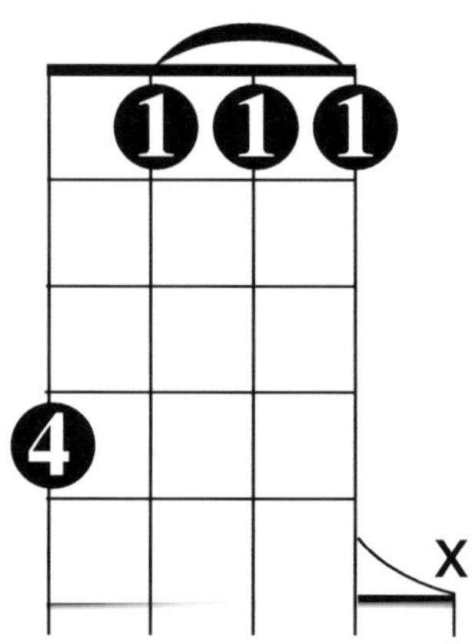

A♭/G♯ Chords

A♭ Diminished

Root - ♭3rd - ♭5th - 𝄫7th
A♭ - C♭ - E𝄫 - G𝄫

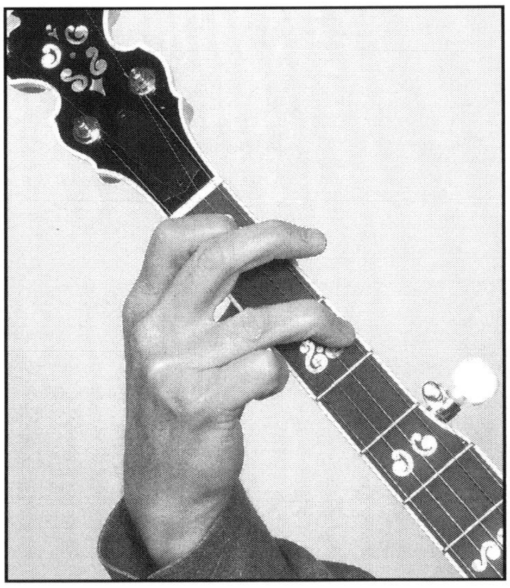

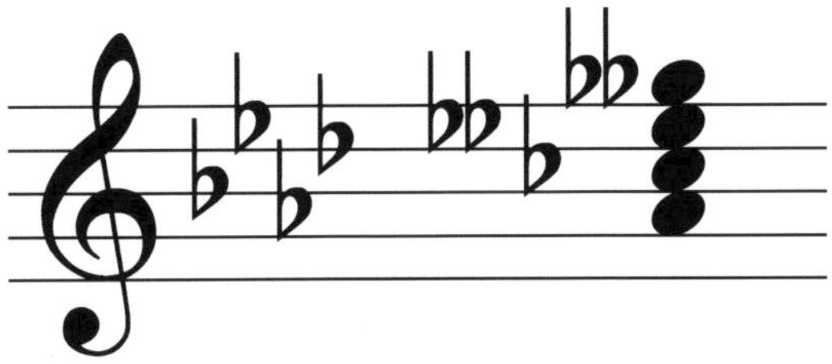

A♭o

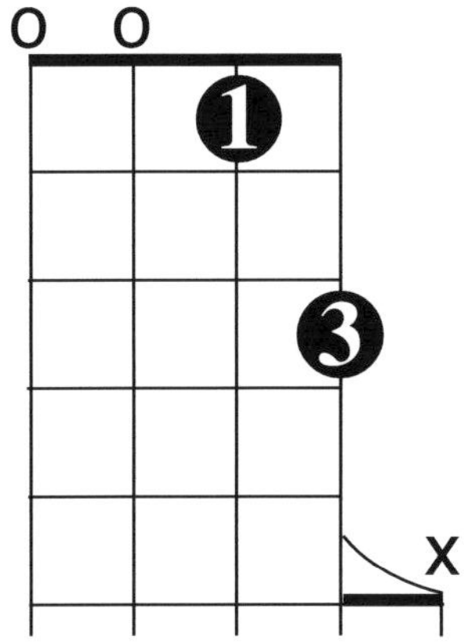

A♭ Augmented

Root - 3rd - ♯5th
A♭ - C - E♮

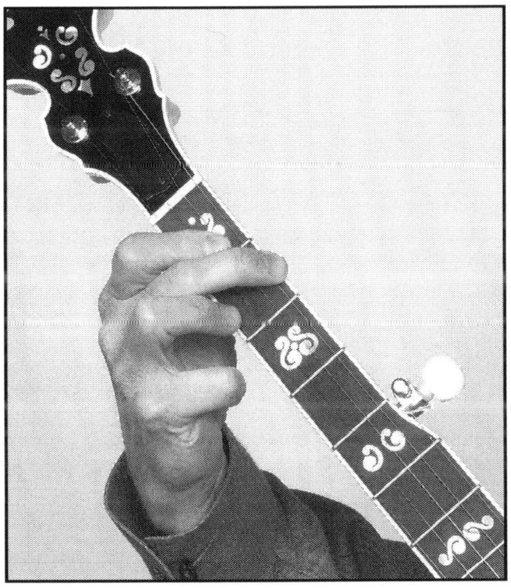

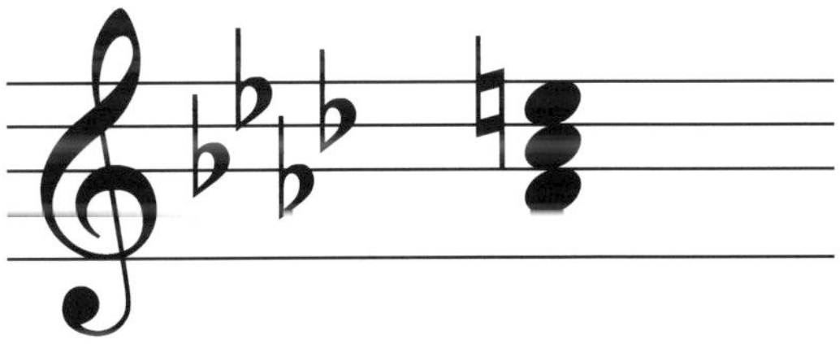

A♭+

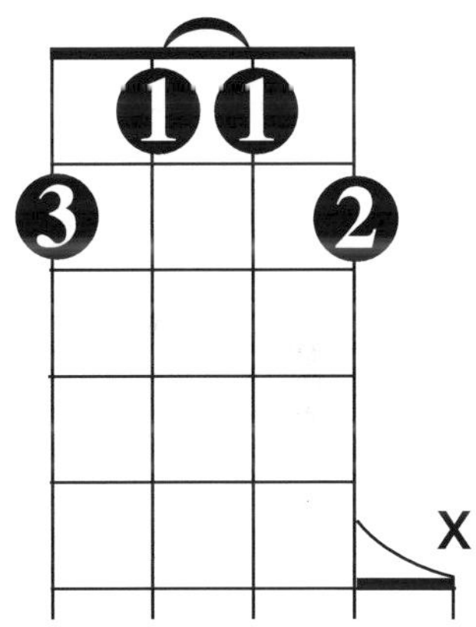

A♭ Sixth

Root - 3rd - 5th - 6th
A♭ - C - E♭ - F

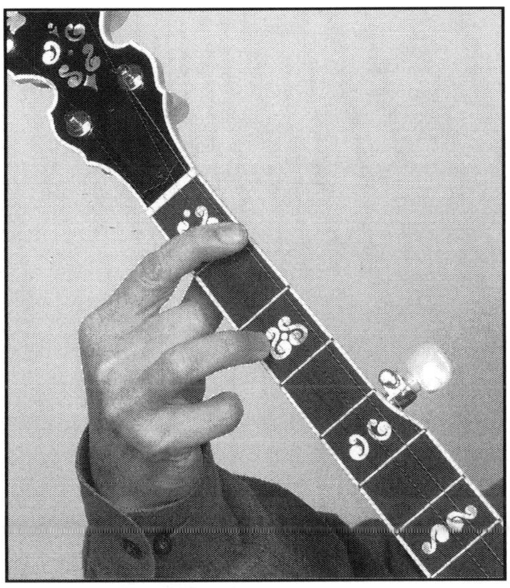

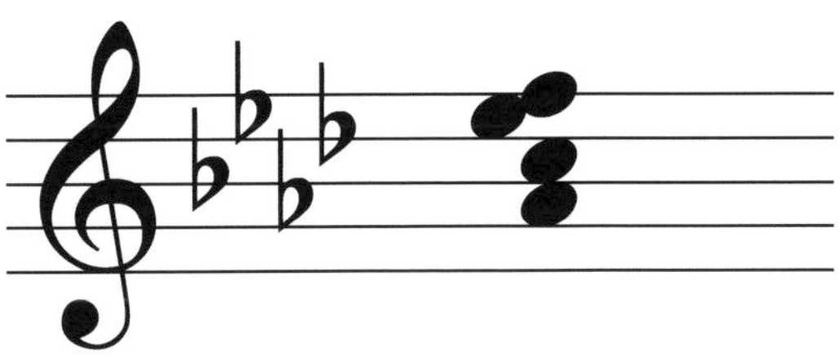

A♭6

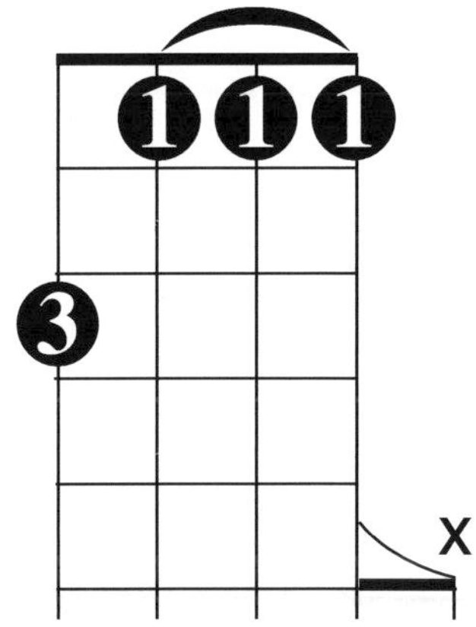

A♭/G♯ Chords

A♭ Minor Sixth

Root - ♭3rd - 5th - 6th
A♭ - C♭ - E♭ - F

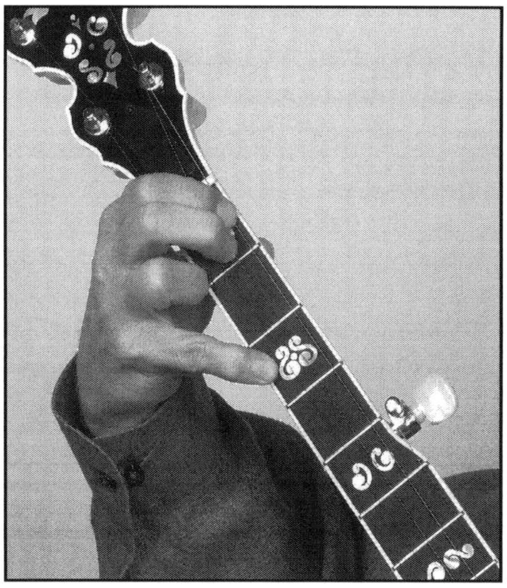

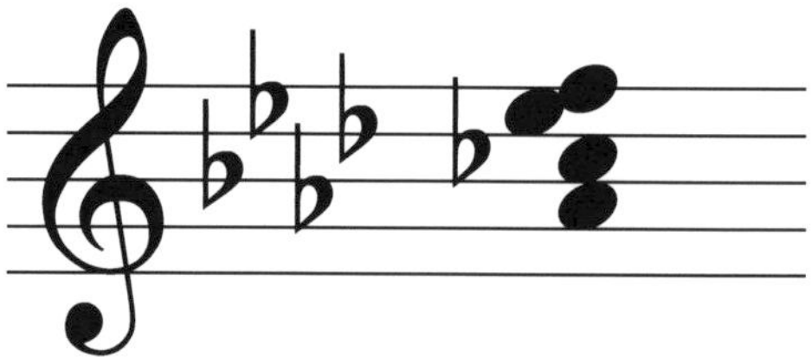

A♭m6

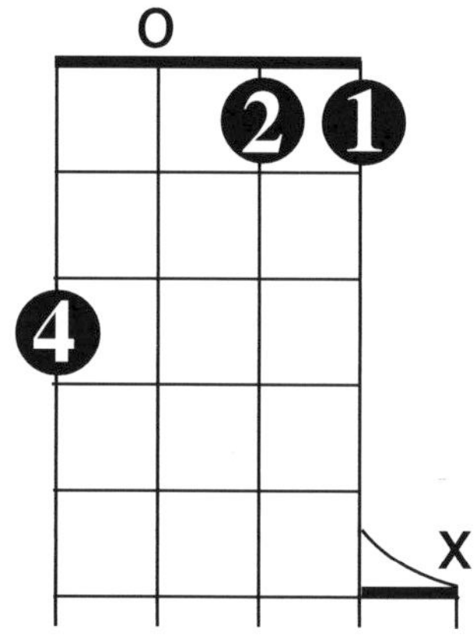

A♭ Seven Flat Five

Root - 3rd - ♭5th - ♭7th
A♭ - C - E♭♭ - G♭

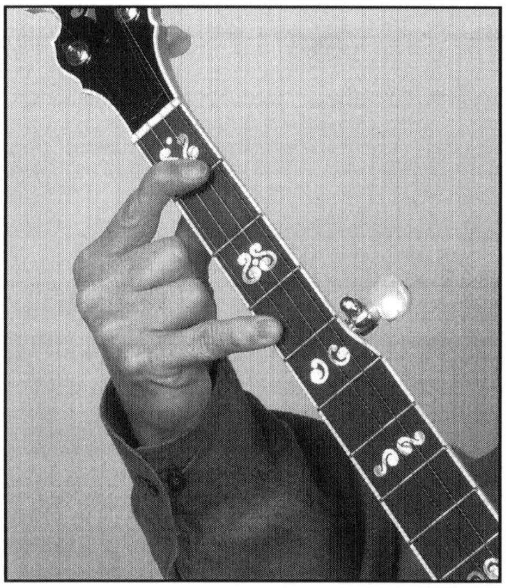

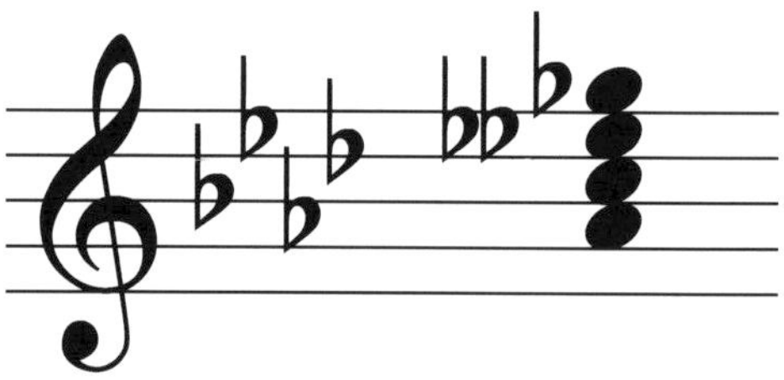

A♭7♭5

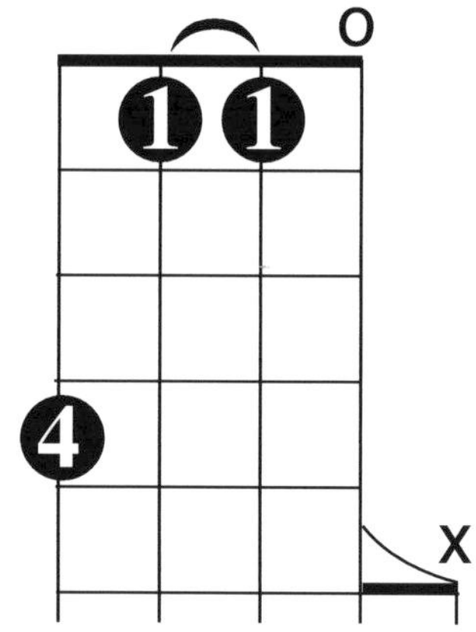

A♭ Major Seventh

Root - 3rd - 5th - 7th
A♭ - C - E♭ - G

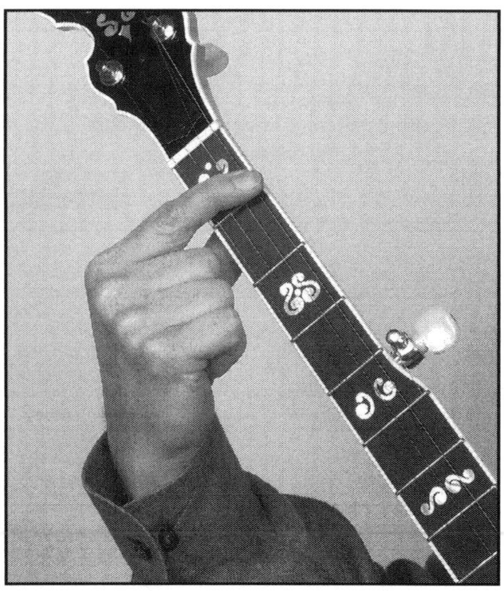

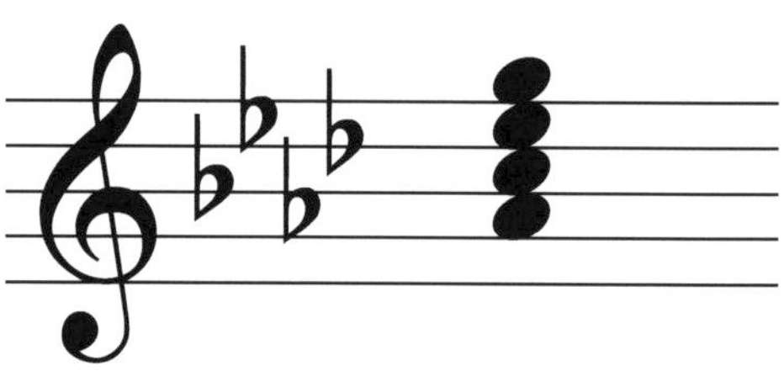

A♭Maj7

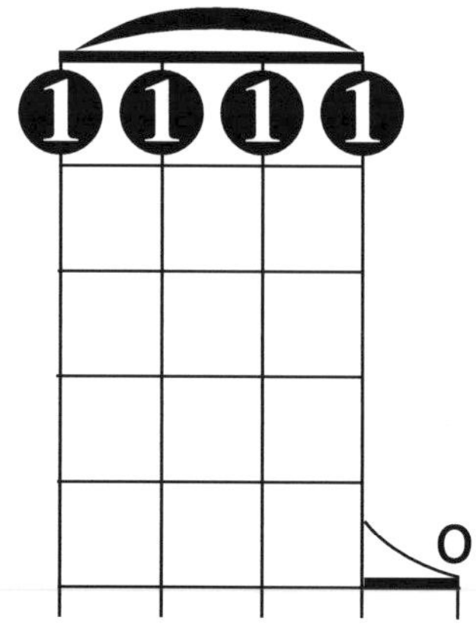

A♭/G♯ Chords

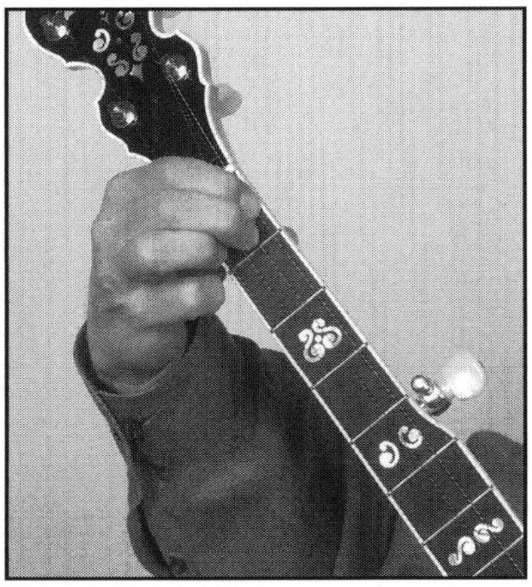

A♭ Major Seventh Flat Third A♭Maj7♭3

Root - ♭3rd - 5th - 7th
A♭ - C♭ - E♭ - G♮

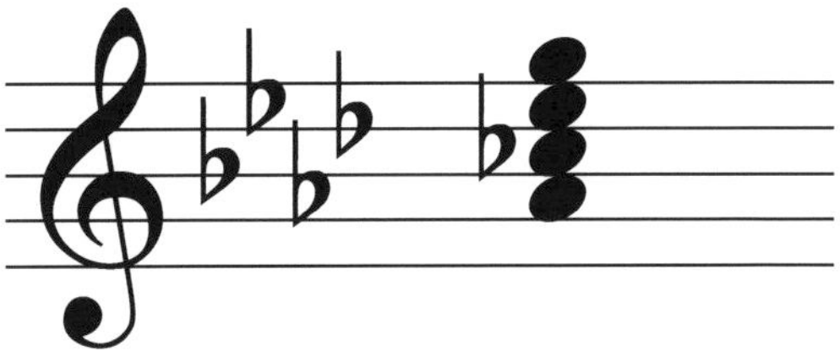

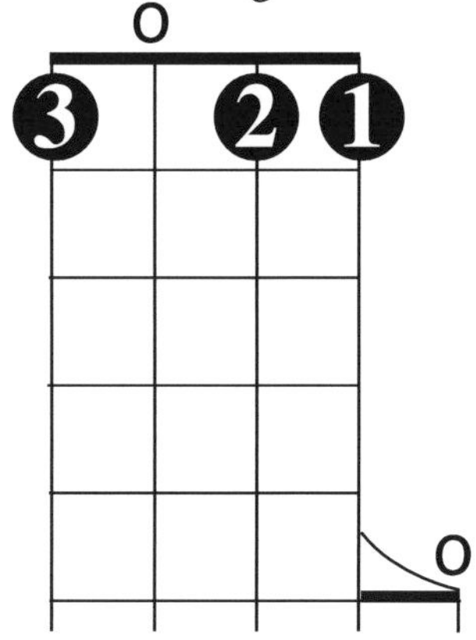

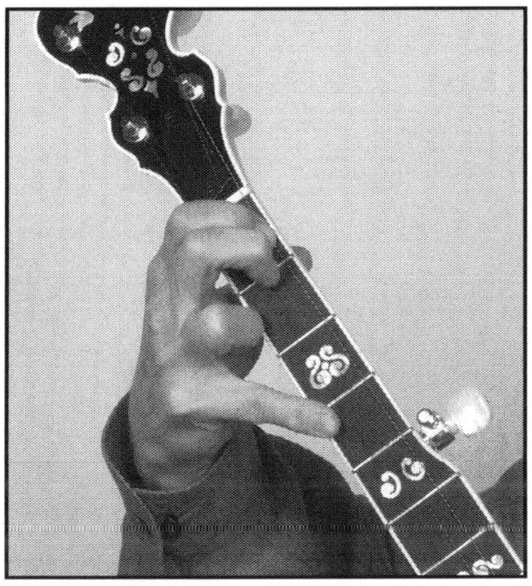

A♭ Minor Seventh

A♭m7

Root - ♭3rd - 5th - ♭7th
A♭ - C♭ - E♭ - G♭

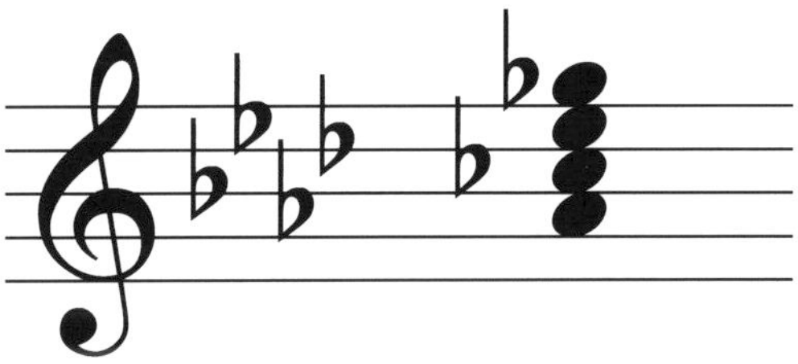

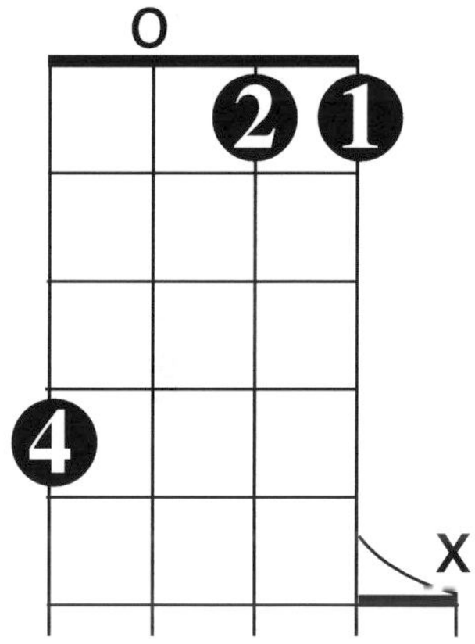

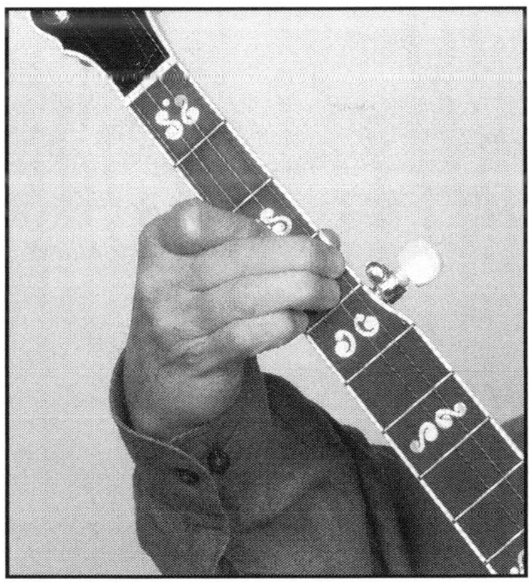

A♭ Minor Seventh Flat Five

A♭m7♭5

Root - ♭3rd - ♭5th - ♭7th
A♭ - C♭ - E♭♭ - G♭

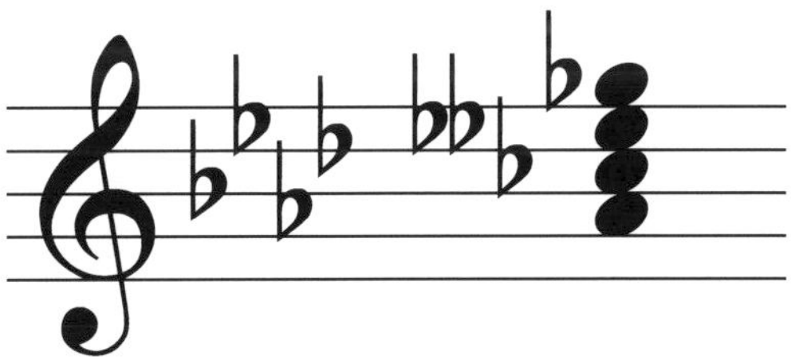

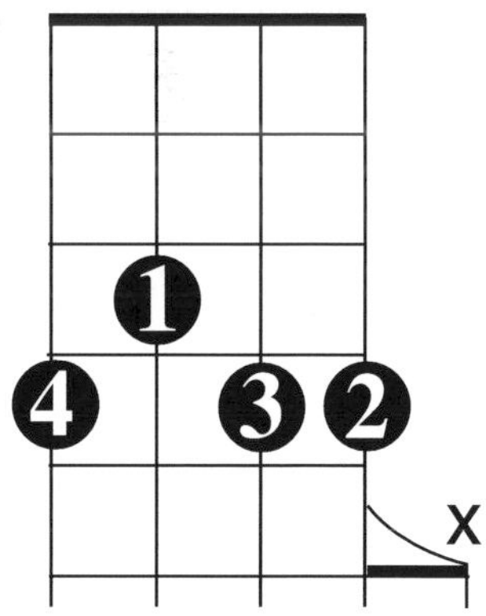

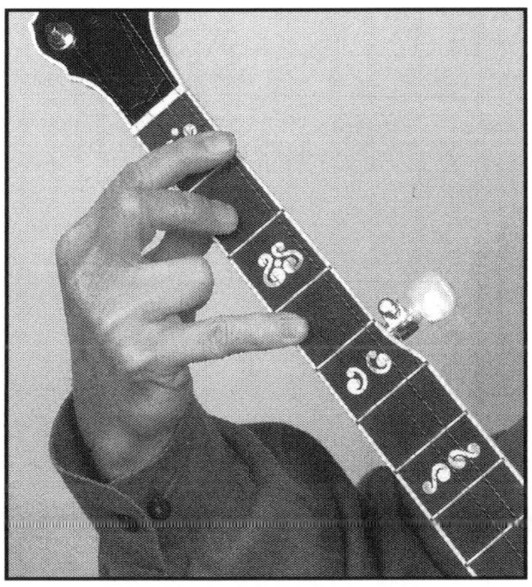

A♭ Seventh Suspended Fourth

A♭7sus4

Root - 4th - 5th - ♭7th
A♭ - D♭ - E♭ - G♭

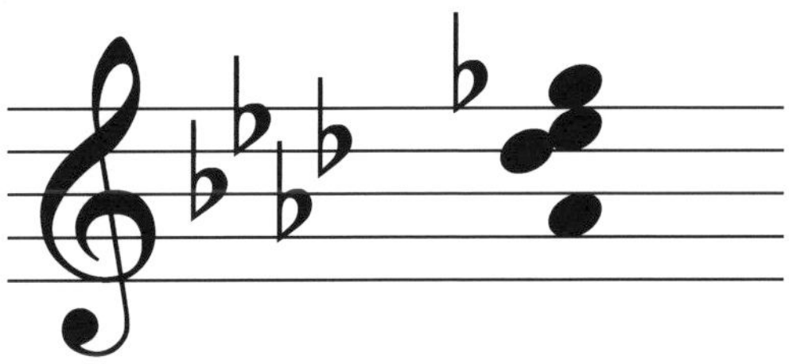

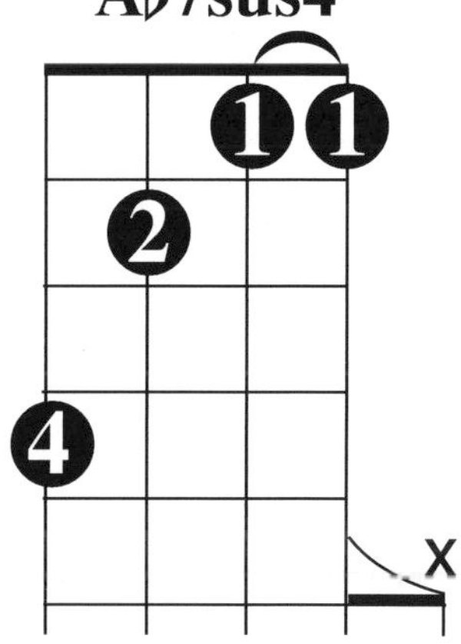

A Chords

A Major

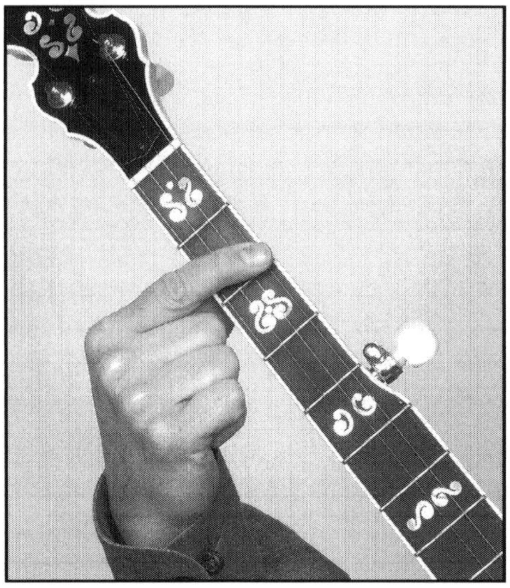

Root - 3rd - 5th
A - C♯ - E

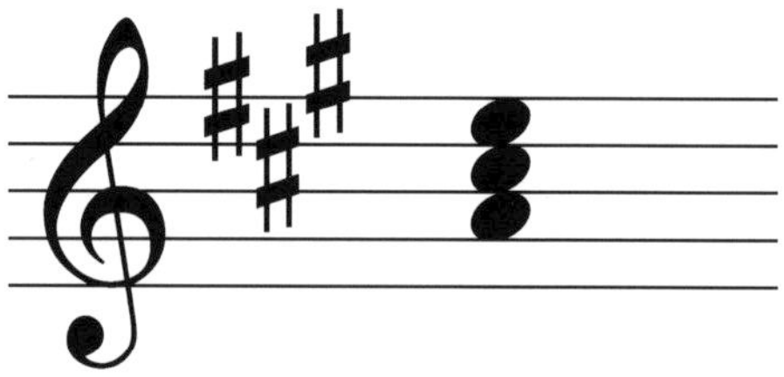

A

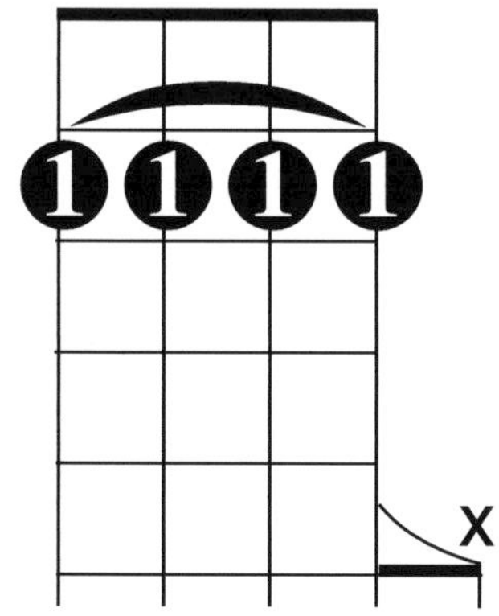

A Minor

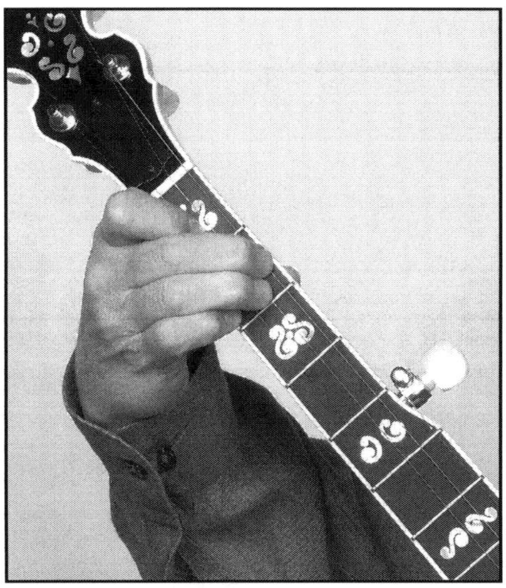

Root - ♭3rd - 5th
A - C♮ - E

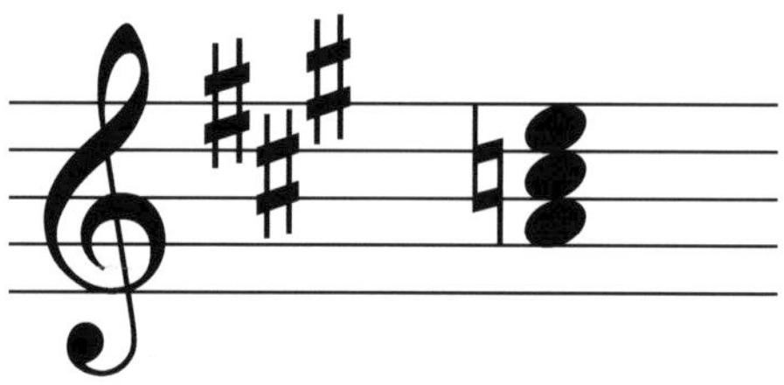

Am

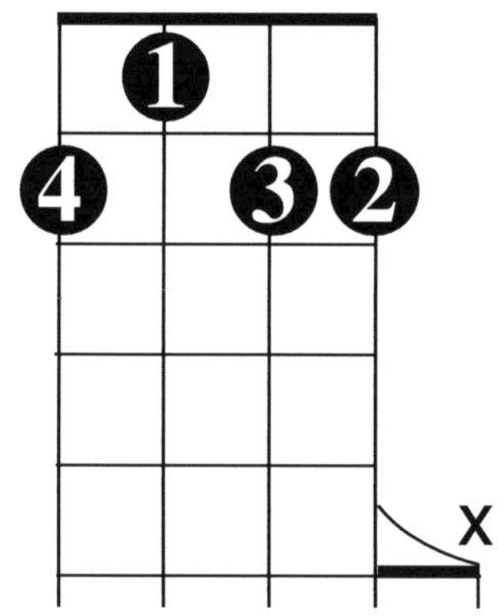

A Seventh

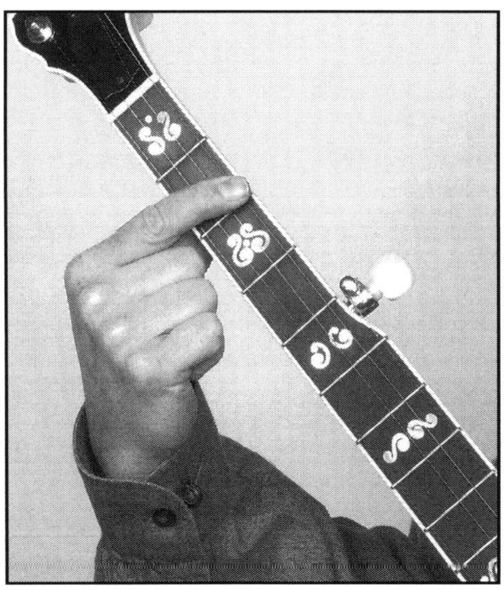

Root - 3rd - 5th - ♭7th
A - C♯ - E - G♮

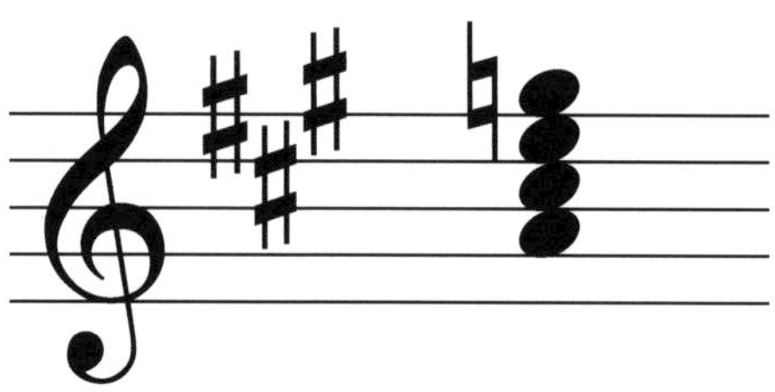

A7

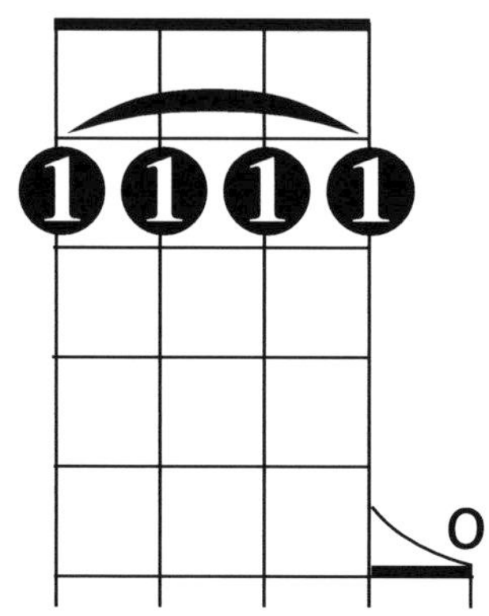

A Chords

A Diminished

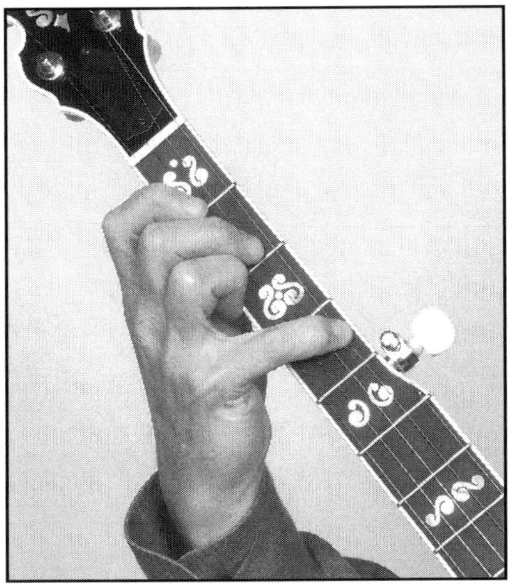

Root - ♭3rd - ♭5th - ♭♭7th
A - C♮ - E♭ - G♭

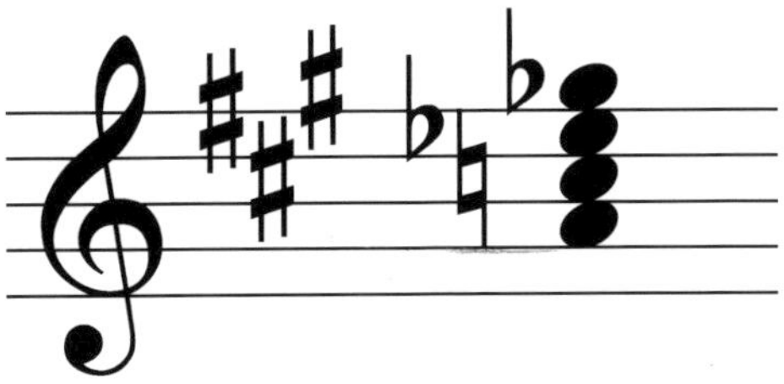

A°

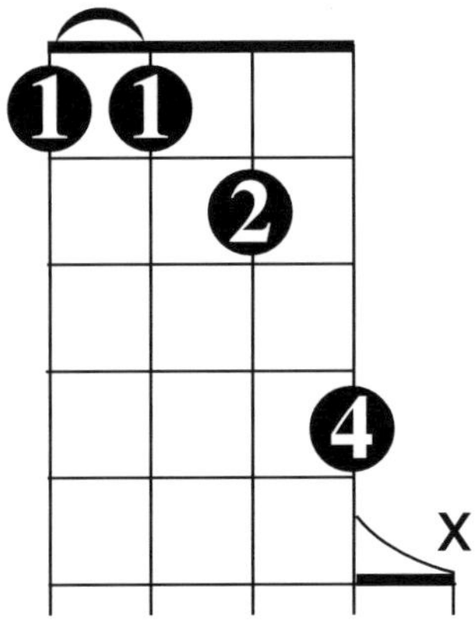

A Augmented

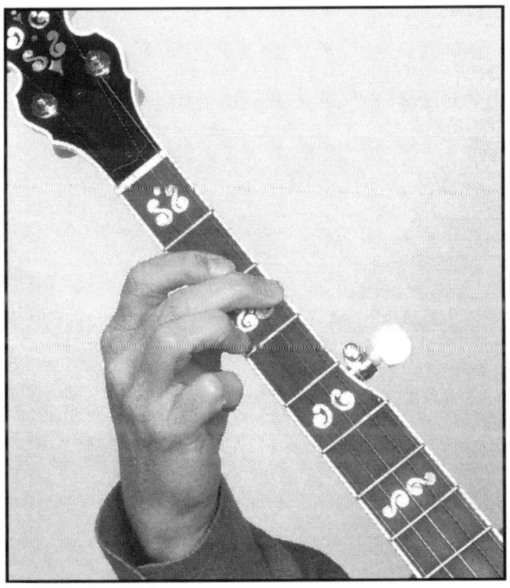

Root - 3rd - ♯5th
A - C♯ - E♯

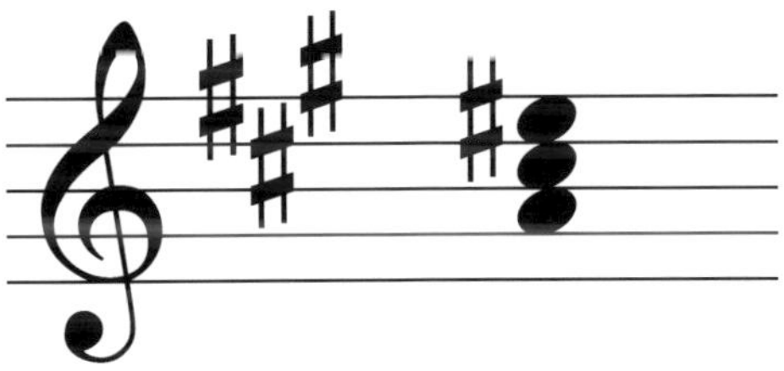

A+

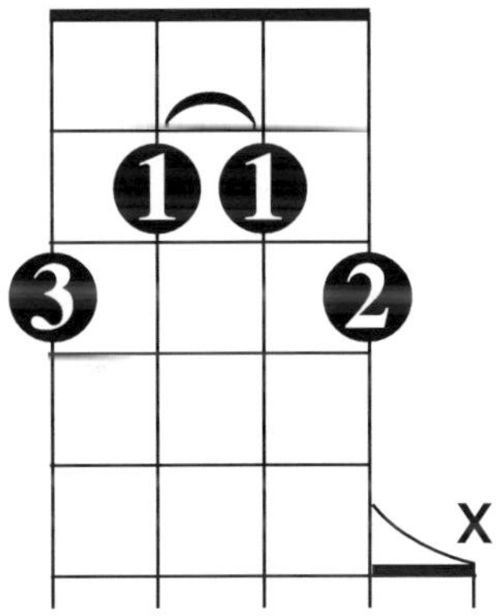

A Sixth

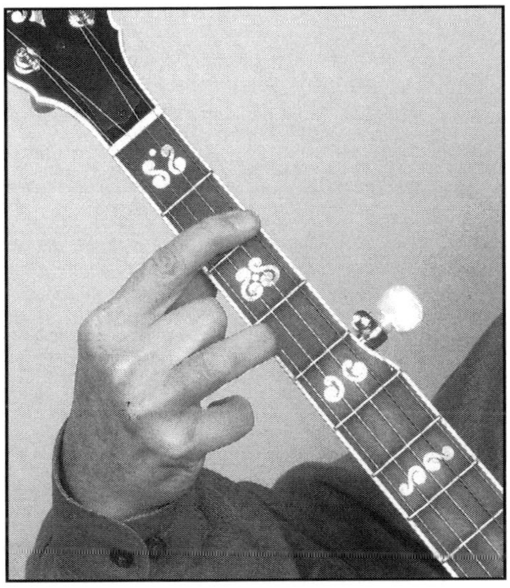

Root - 3rd - 5th - 6th
A - C♯ - E - F♯

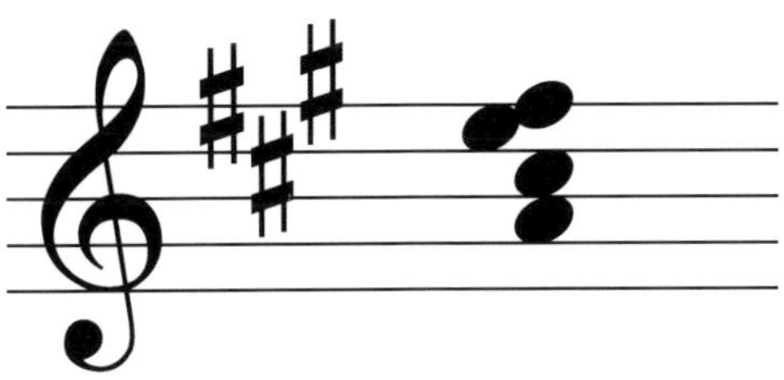

A6

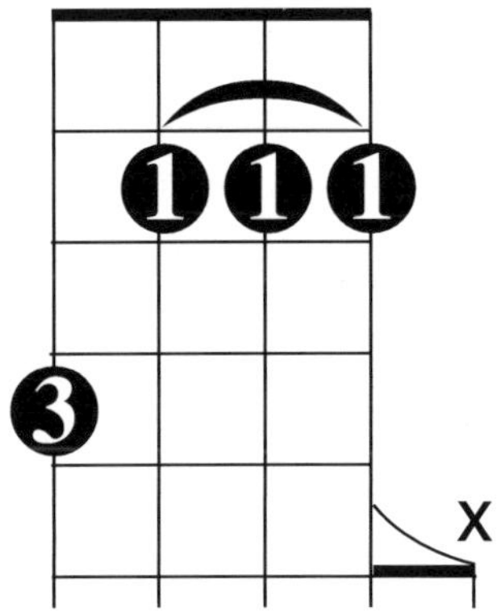

A Chords

A Minor Sixth

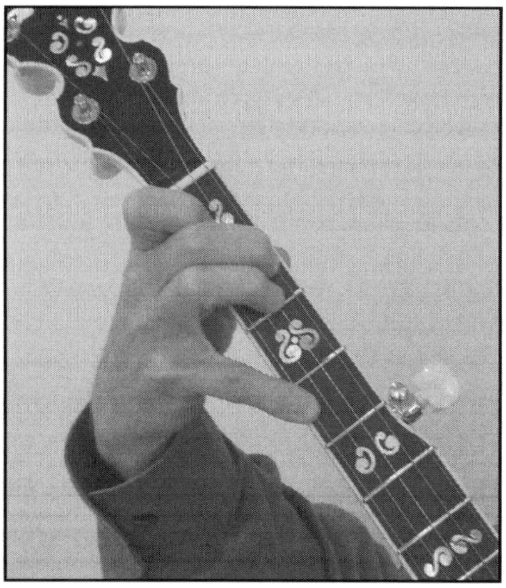

Root - ♭3rd - 5th - 6th
A - C♮ - E - F♯

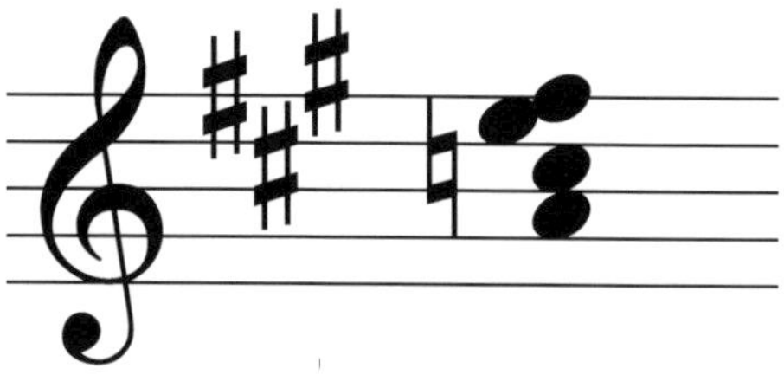

Am6

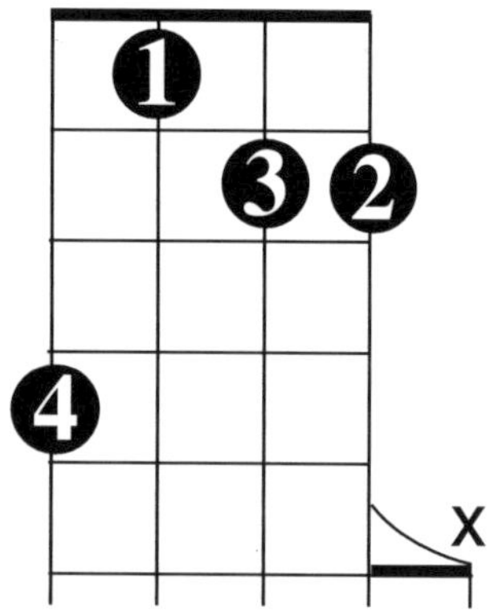

A Seven Flat Five

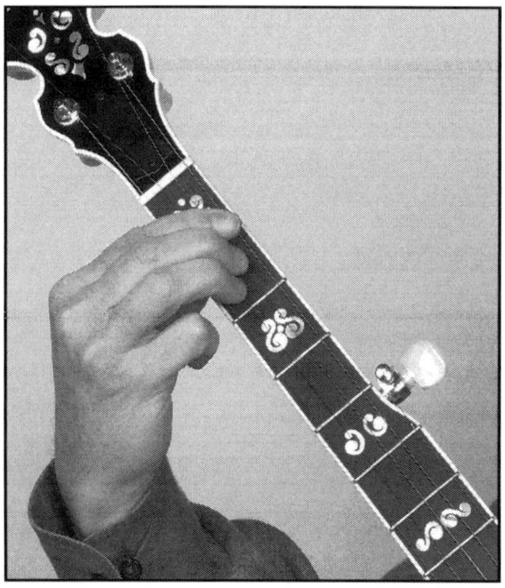

Root - 3rd - ♭5th - ♭7th
A - C♯ - E♭ - G♮

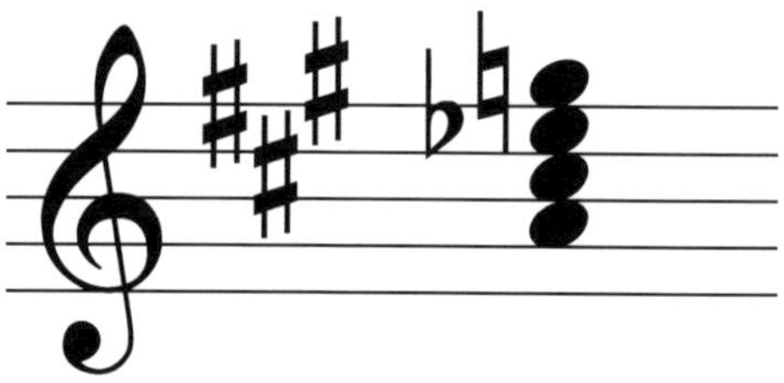

A7♭5

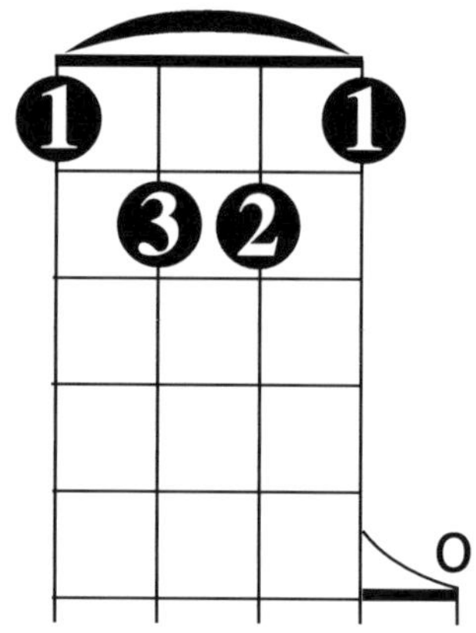

A Major Seventh

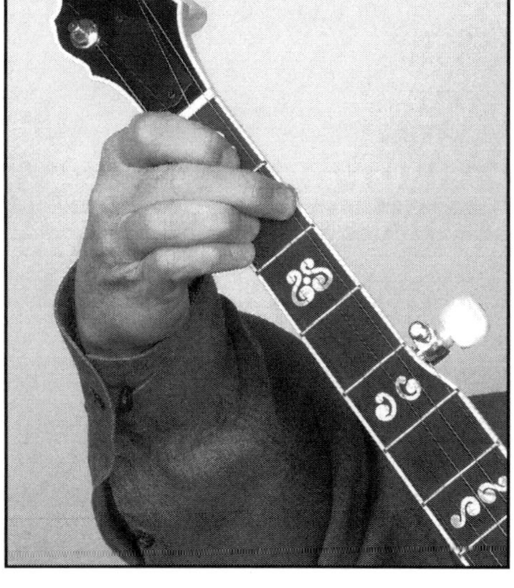

Root - 3rd - 5th - 7th
A - C♯ - E - G♯

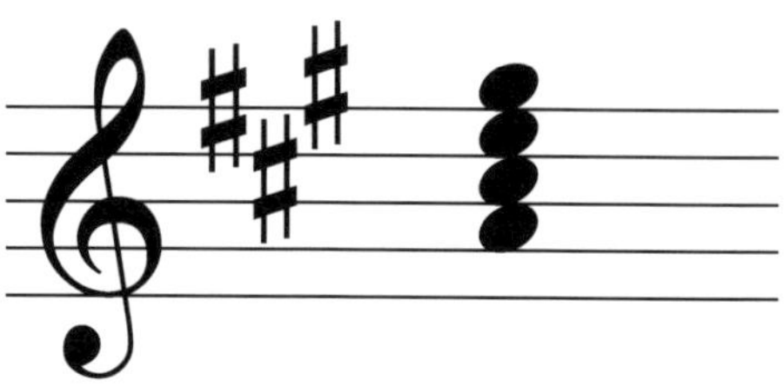

AMaj7

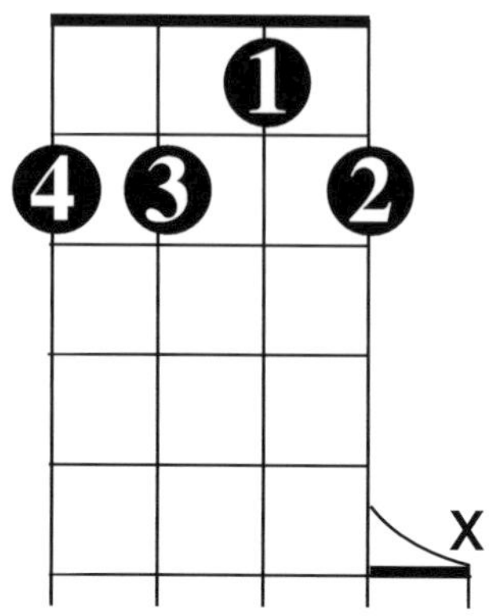

A Chords

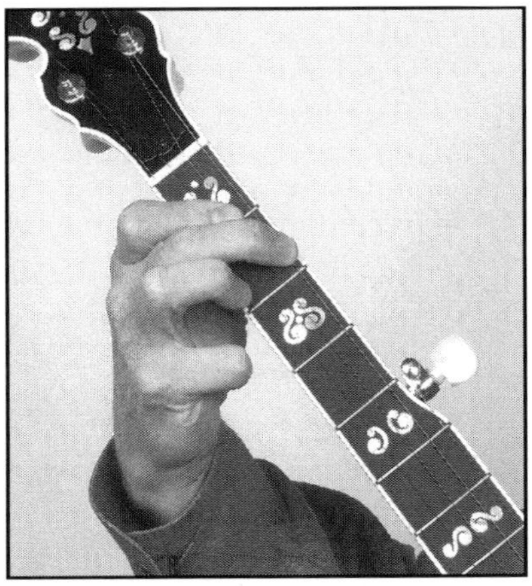

A Major Seventh Flat Third

AMaj7♭3

Root - ♭3rd - 5th - 7th
A - C♮ - E - G♯

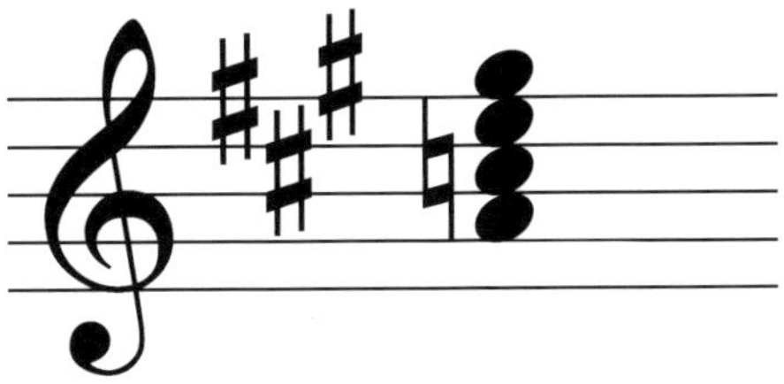

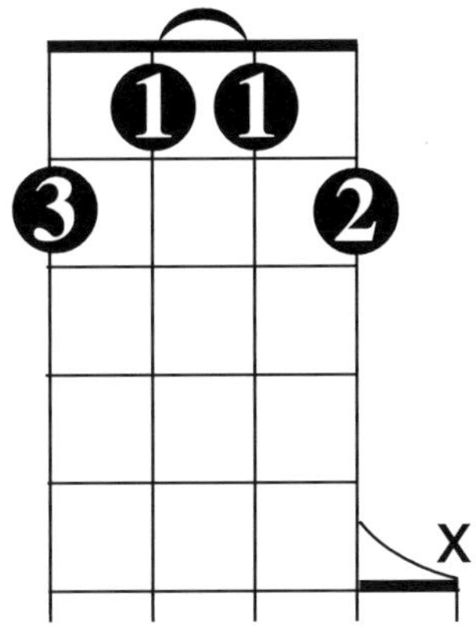

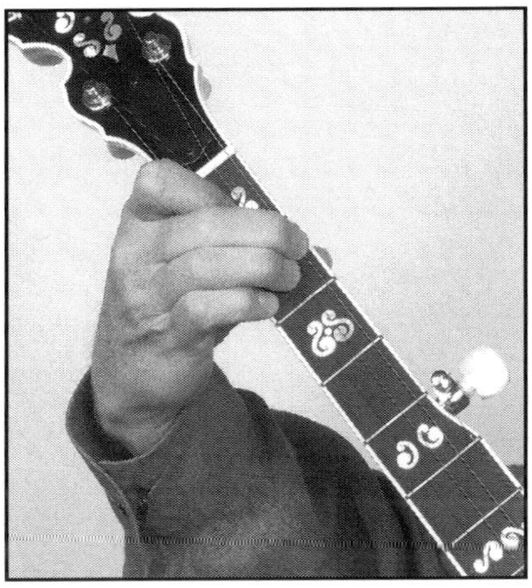

A Minor Seventh

Am7

Root - ♭3rd - 5th - ♭7th
A - C♮ - E - G♮

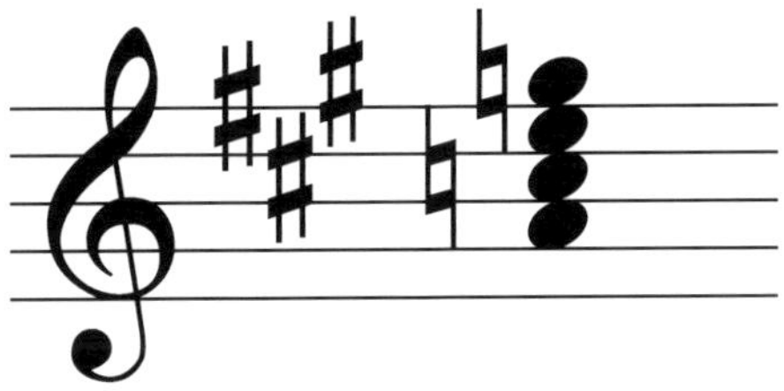

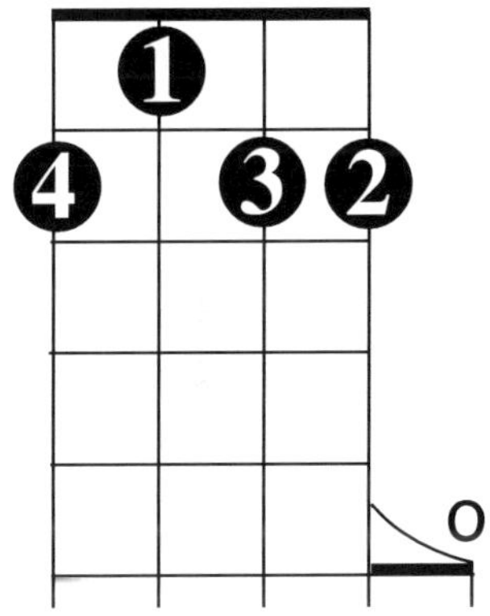

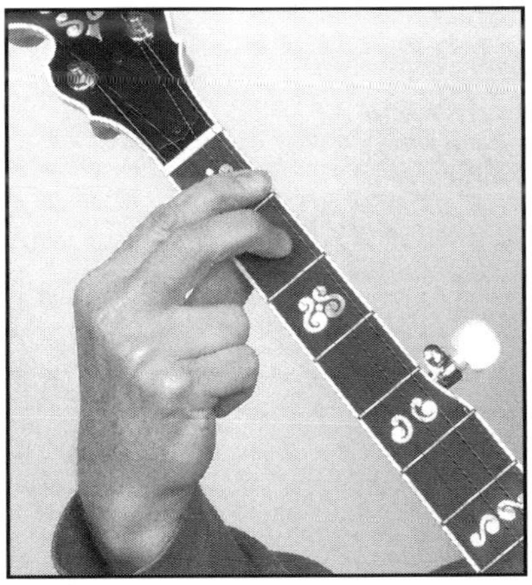

A Minor Seventh Flat Five

Am7♭5

Root - ♭3rd - ♭5th - ♭7th
A - C♮ - E♭ - G♮

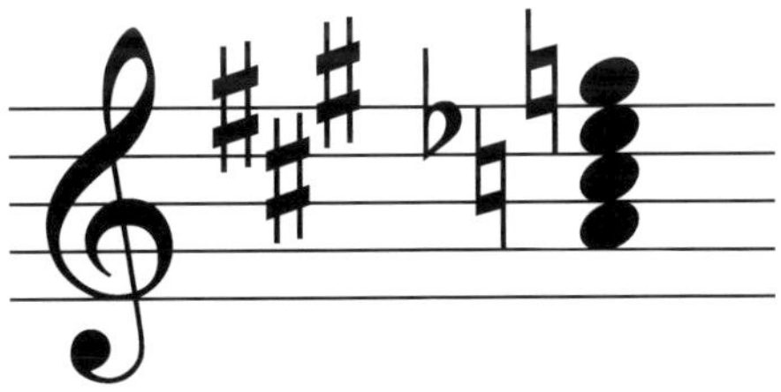

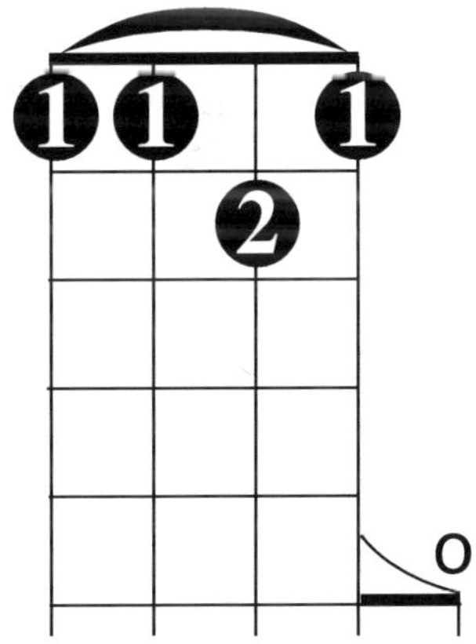

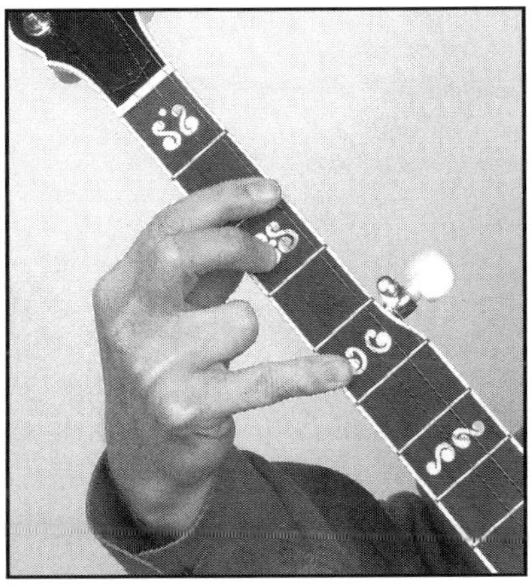

A Seventh Suspended Fourth

A7sus4

Root - 4th - 5th - ♭7th
A - D - E - G♮

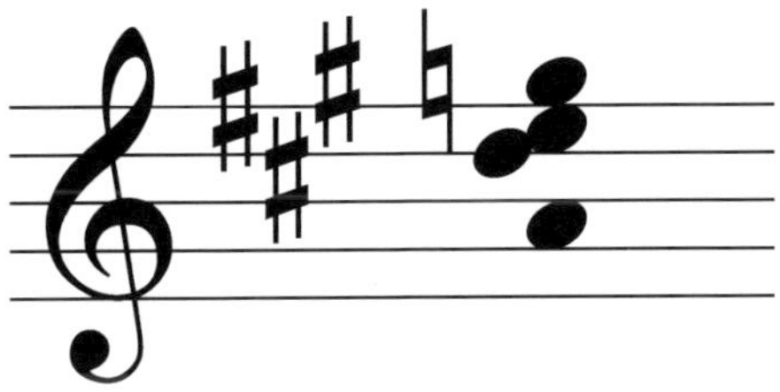

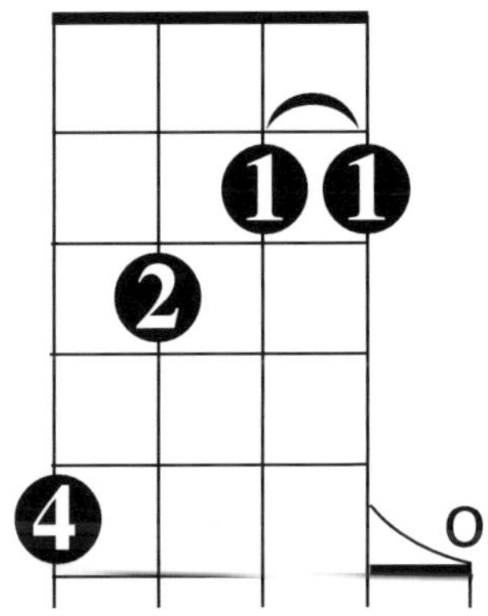

B♭/A♯ Chords

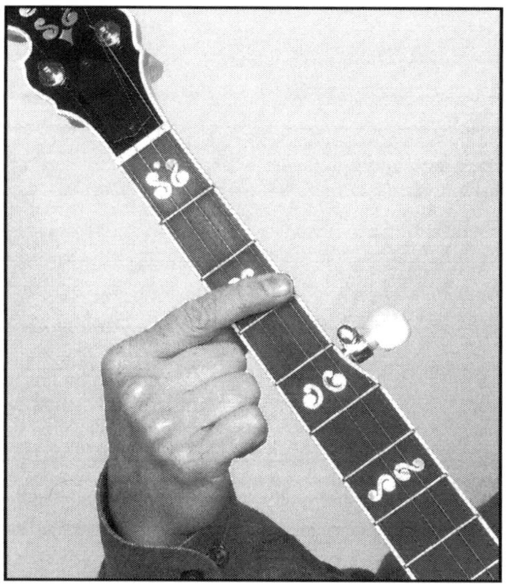

B♭ Major

Root - 3rd - 5th
B♭ - D - F

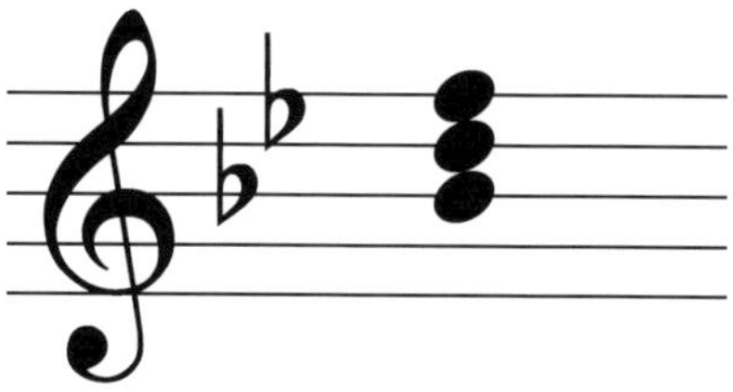

B♭

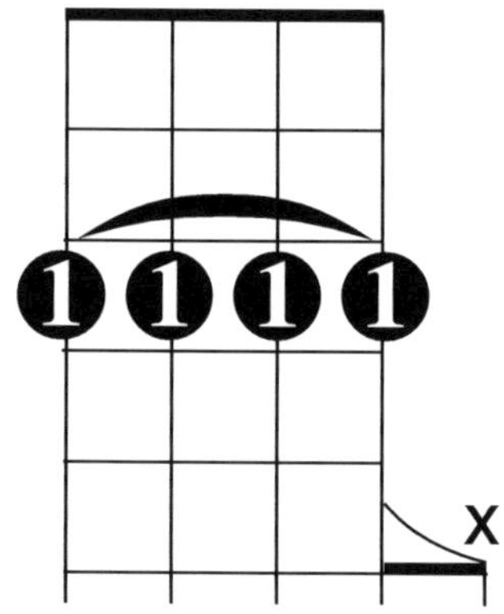

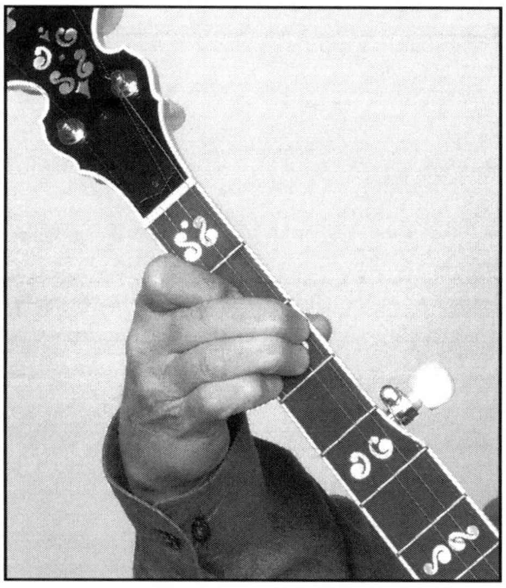

B♭ Minor

Root - ♭3rd - 5th
B♭ - D♭ - F

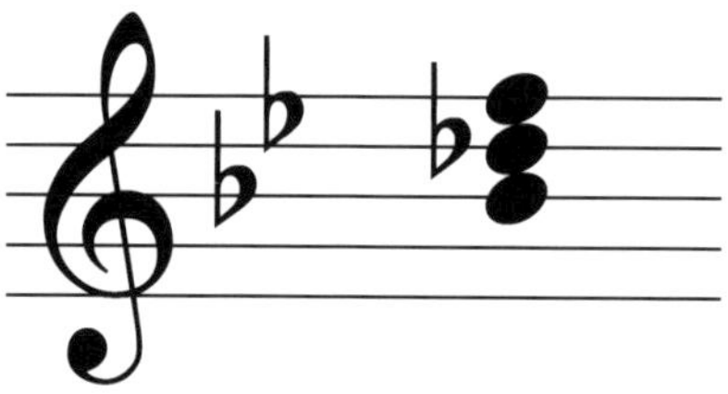

B♭m

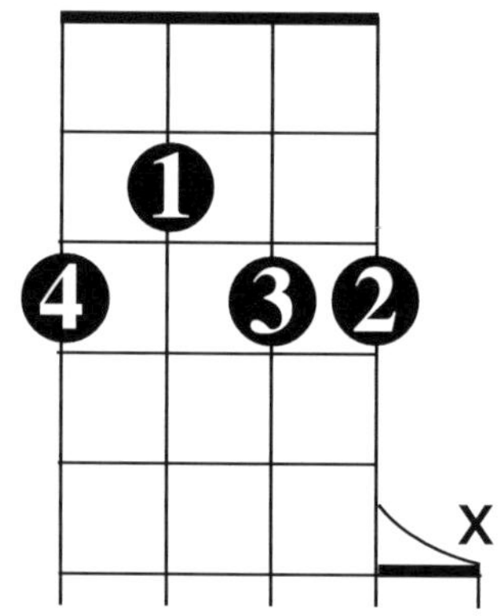

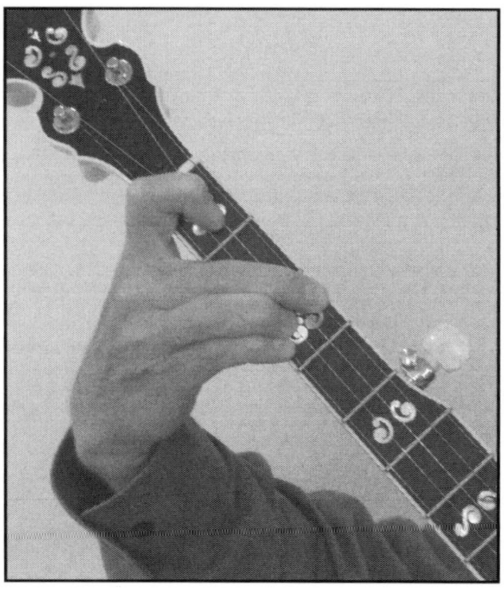

B♭ Seventh

Root - 3rd - 5th - ♭7th
B♭ - D - F - A♭

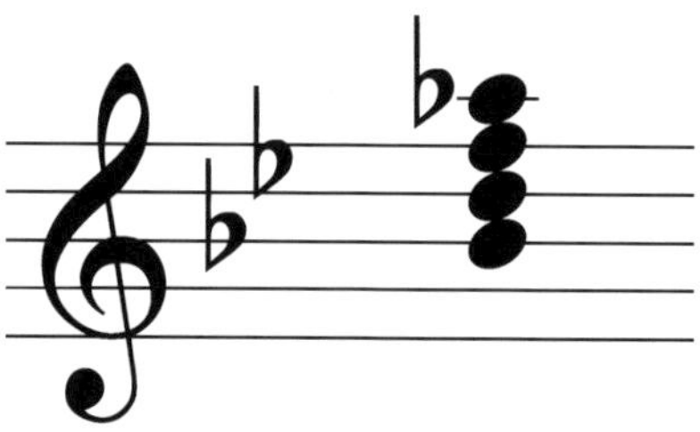

B♭7

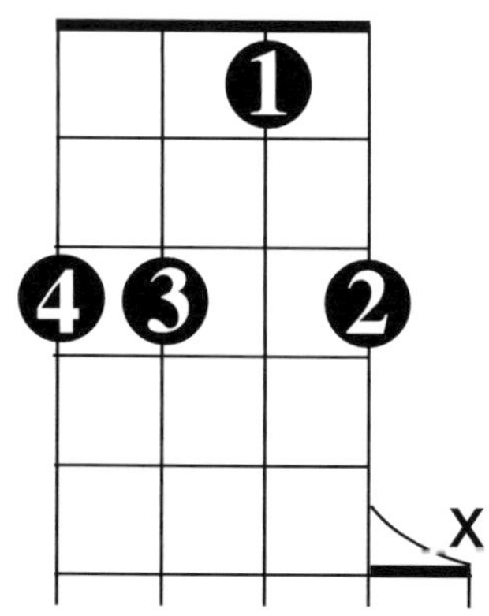

B♭ Diminished

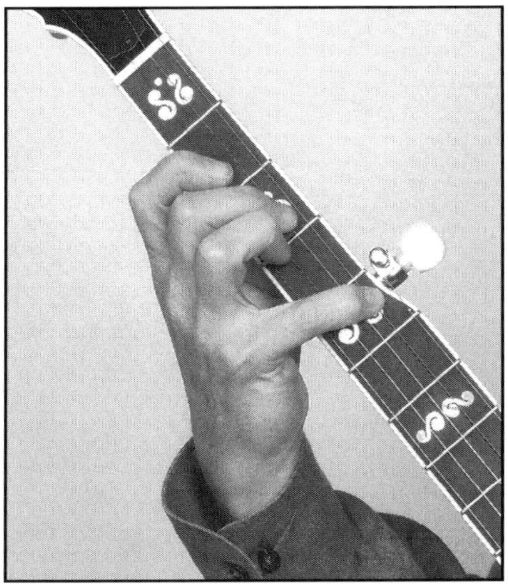

Root - ♭3rd - ♭5th - ♭♭7th
B♭ - D♭ - F♭ - A♭♭

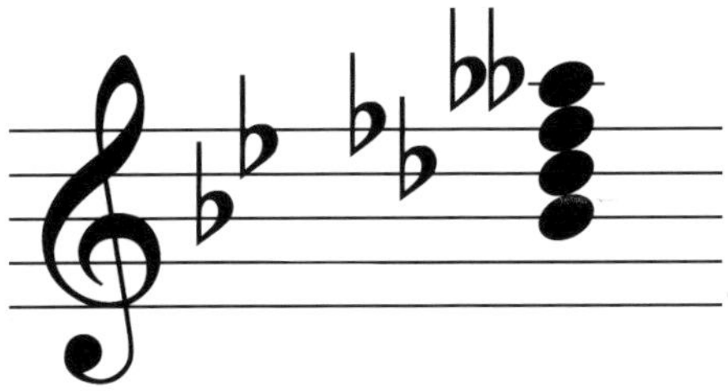

B♭o

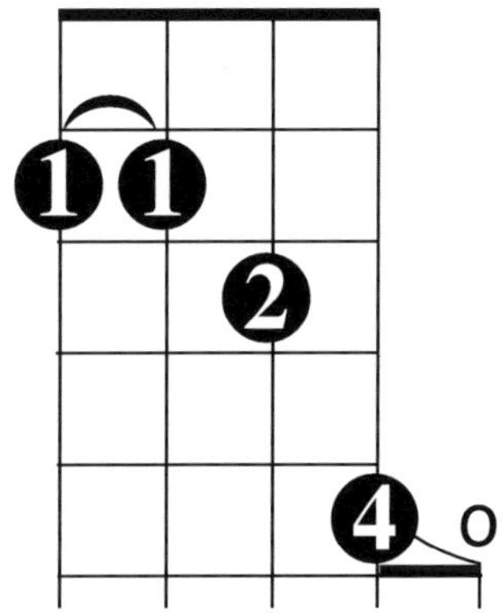

B♭ Augmented

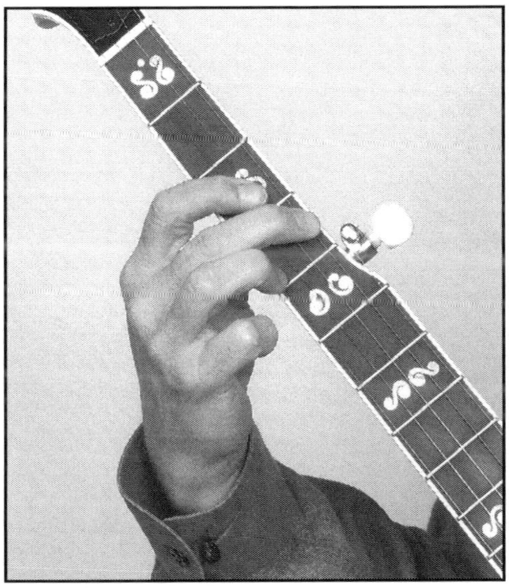

Root - 3rd - ♯5th
B♭ - D - F♯

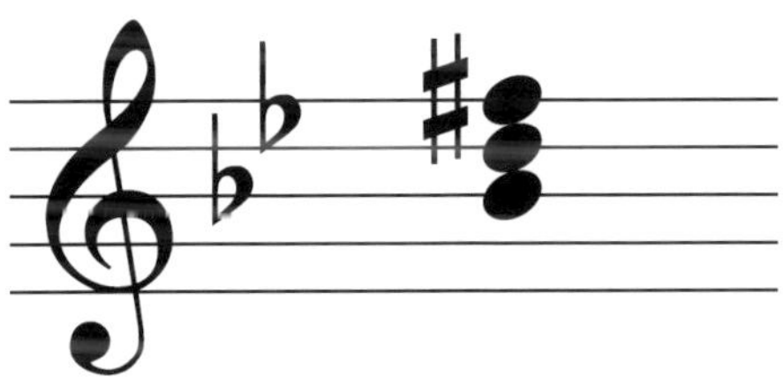

B♭+

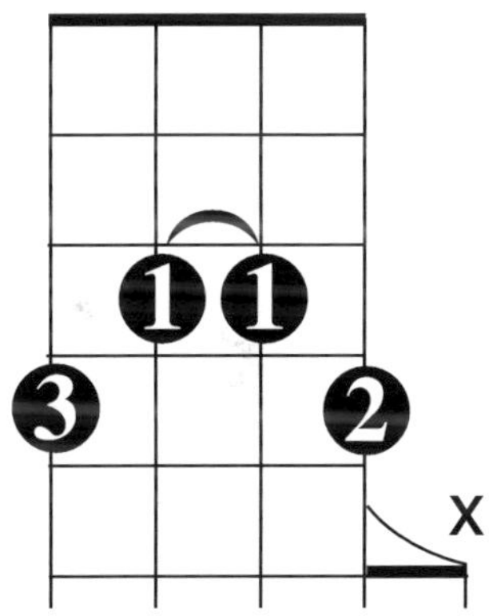

B♭ Sixth

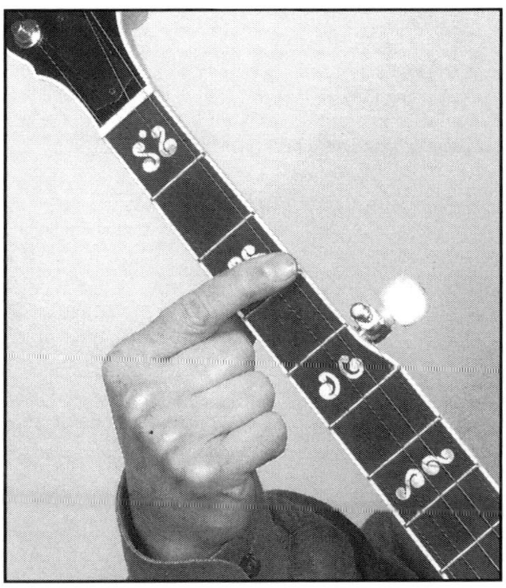

Root - 3rd - 5th - 6th
B♭ - D - F - G

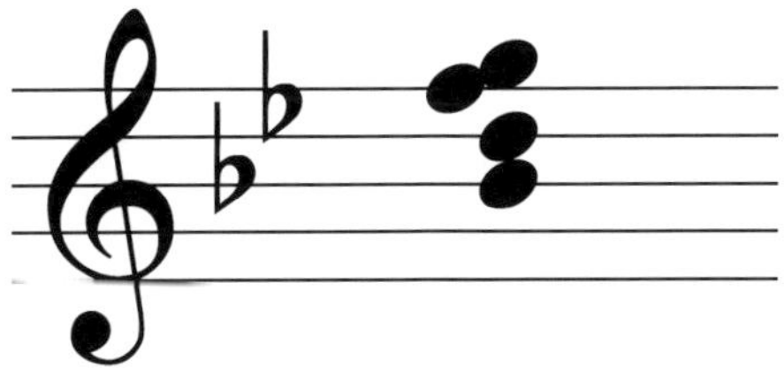

B♭6

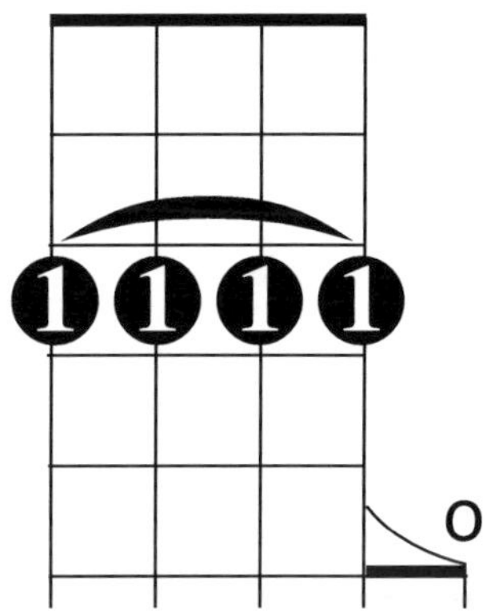

B♭/A♯ Chords

B♭ Minor Sixth

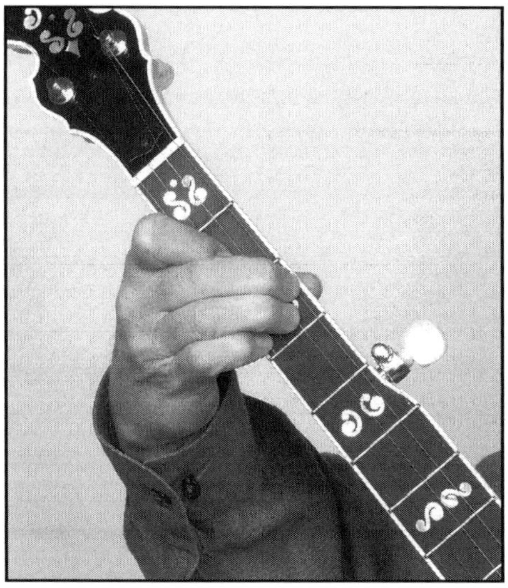

Root - ♭3rd - 5th - 6th
B♭ - D♭ - F - G

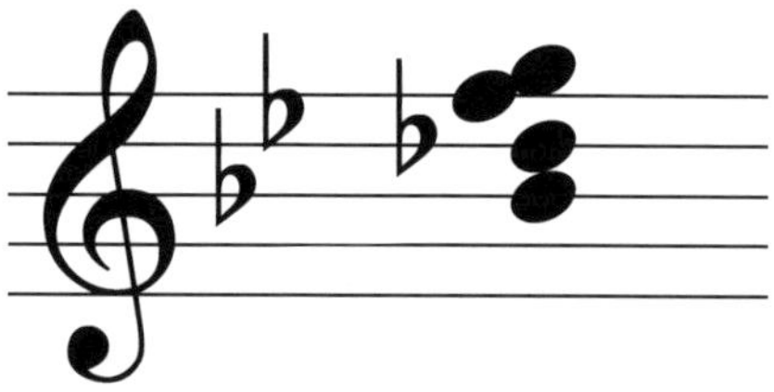

B♭m6

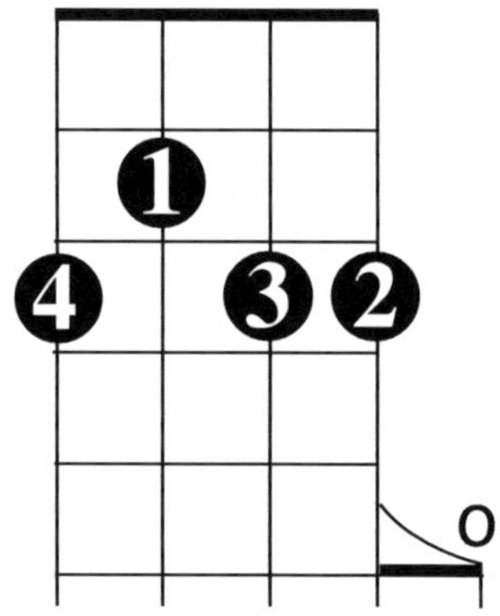

B♭ Seven Flat Five

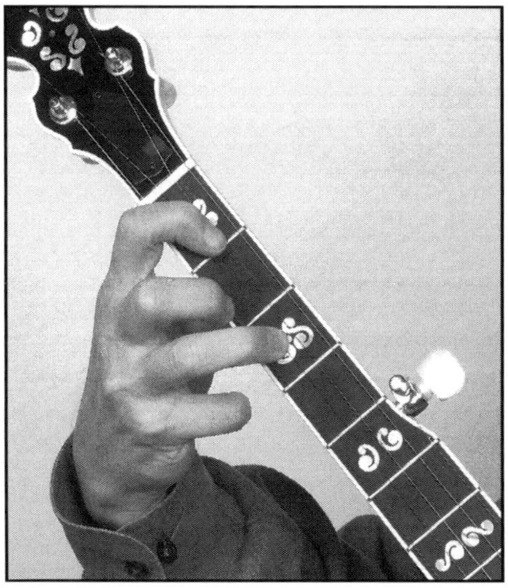

Root - 3rd - ♭5th - ♭7th
B♭ - D - F♭ - A♭

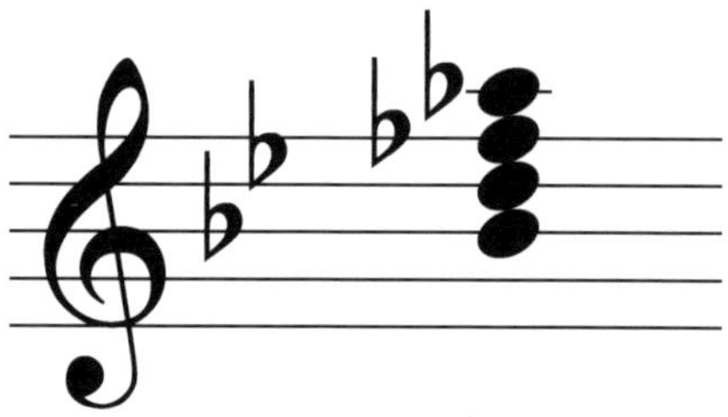

B♭7♭5

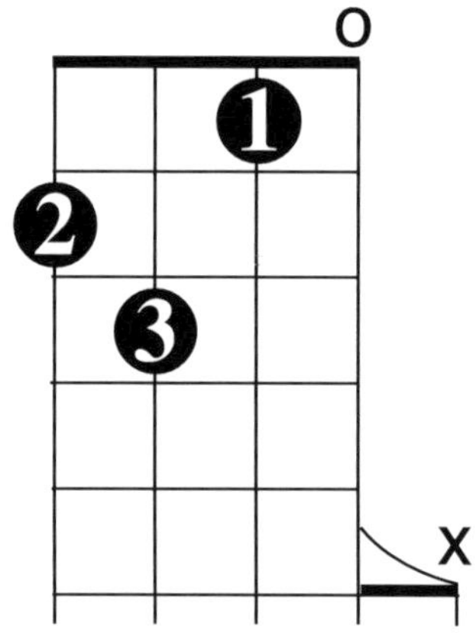

B♭ Major Seventh

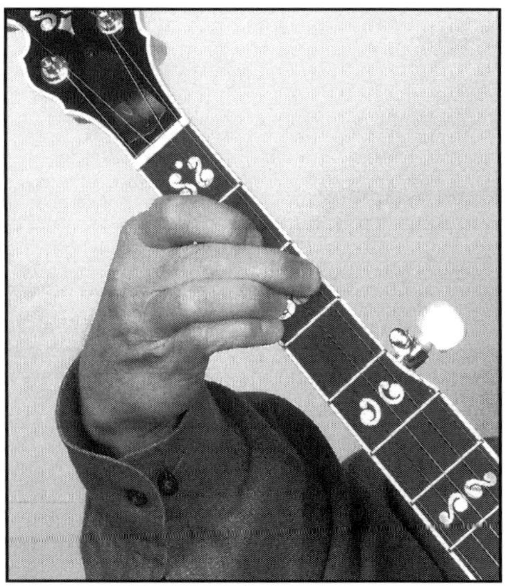

Root - 3rd - 5th - 7th
B♭ - D - F - A

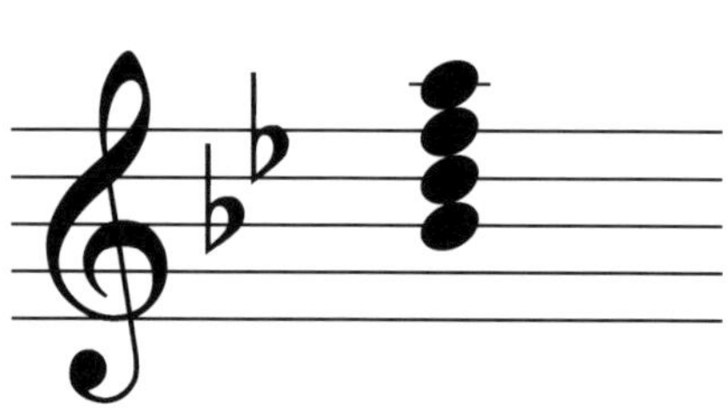

B♭Maj7

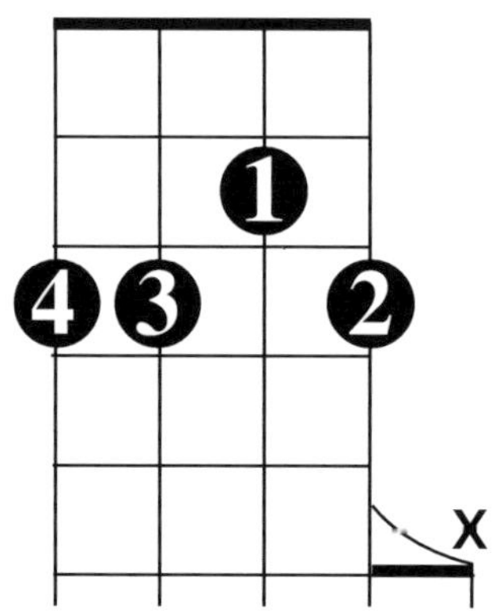

B♭/A♯ Chords

B♭ Major Seventh Flat Third

B♭Maj7♭3

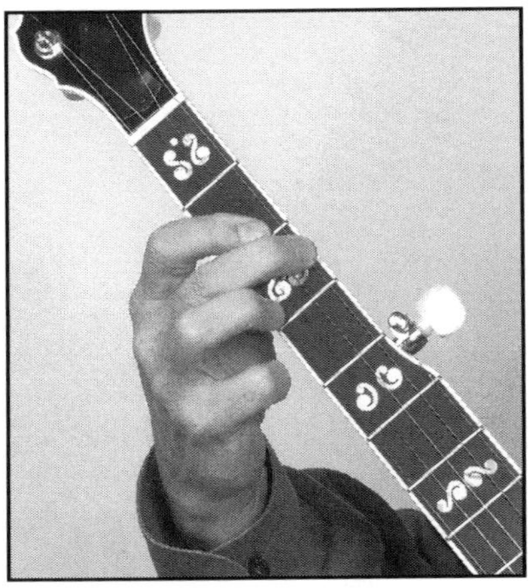

Root - ♭3rd - 5th - 7th
B♭ - D♭ - F - A

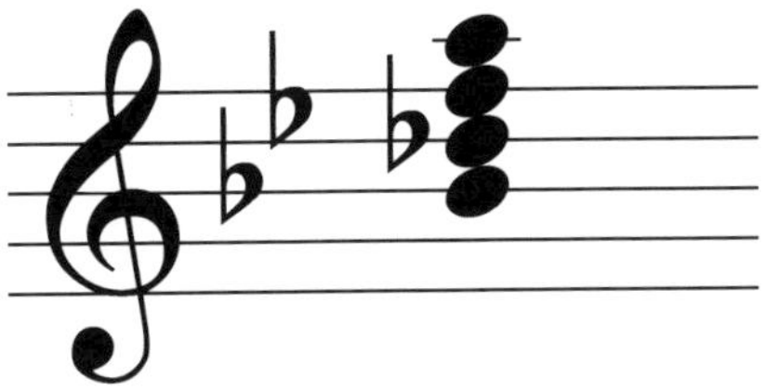

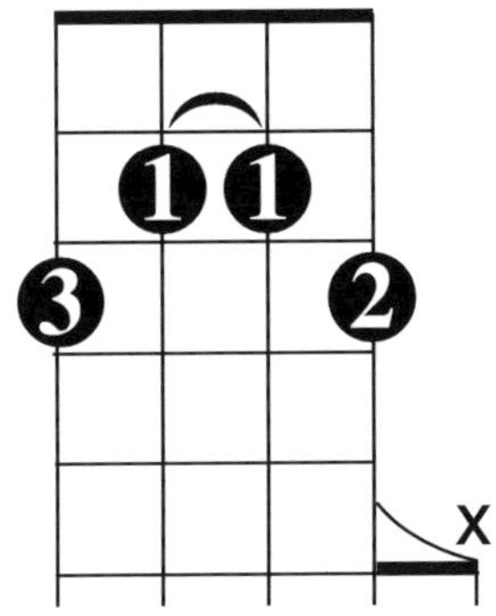

B♭ Minor Seventh

B♭m7

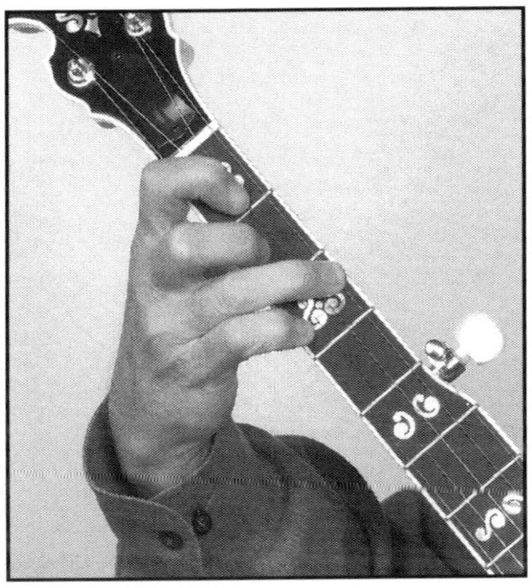

Root - ♭3rd - 5th - ♭7th
B♭ - D♭ - F - A♭

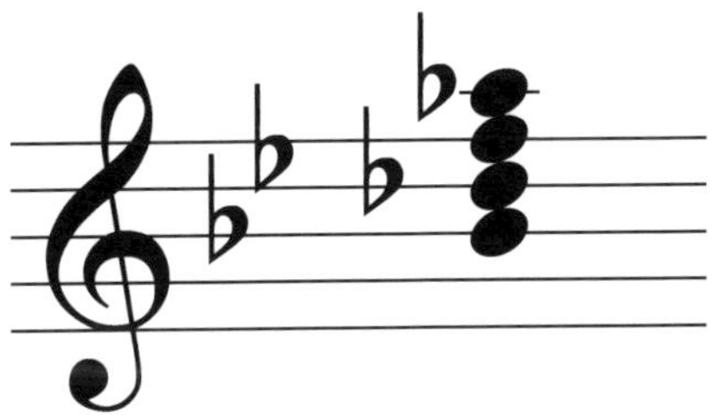

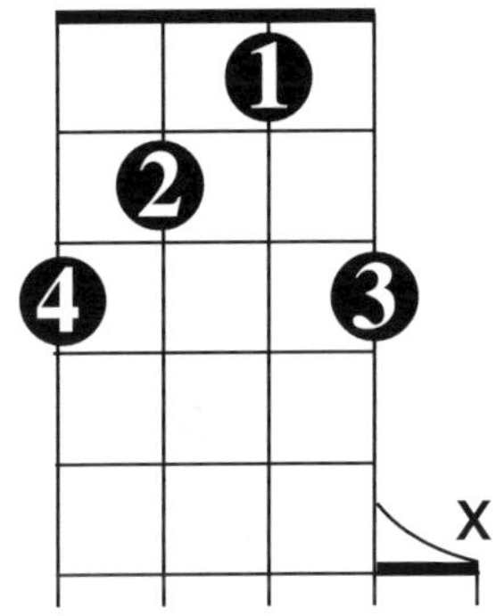

B♭ Minor Seventh Flat Five

B♭m7♭5

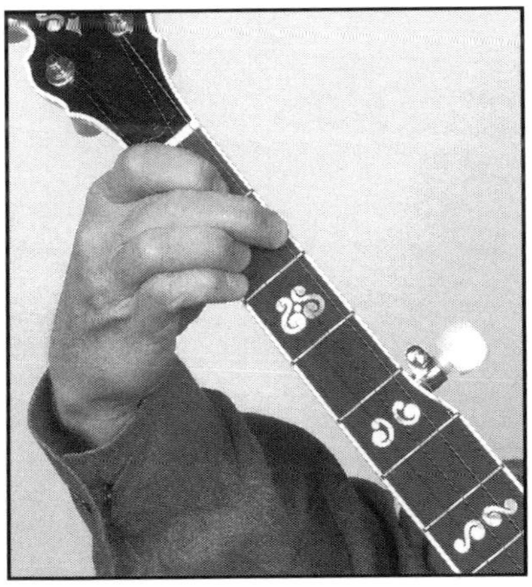

Root - ♭3rd - ♭5th - ♭7th
B♭ - D♭ - F♭ - A♭

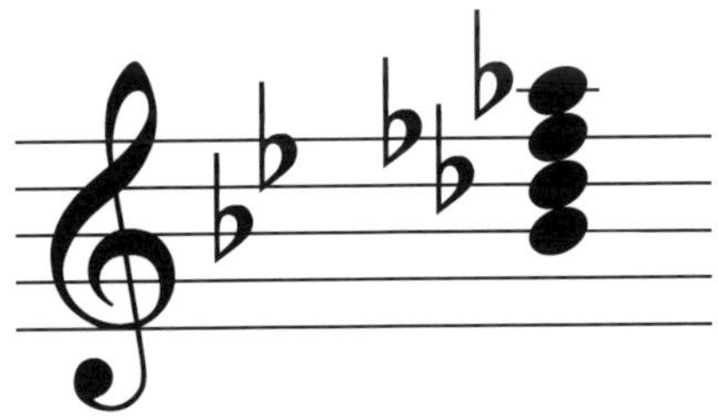

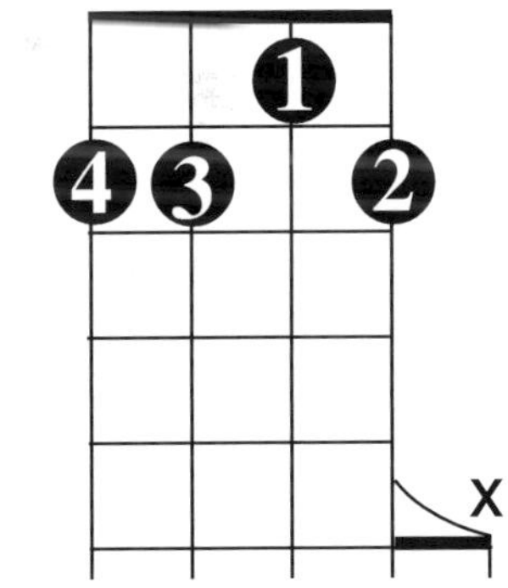

B♭ Seventh Suspended Fourth

B♭7sus4

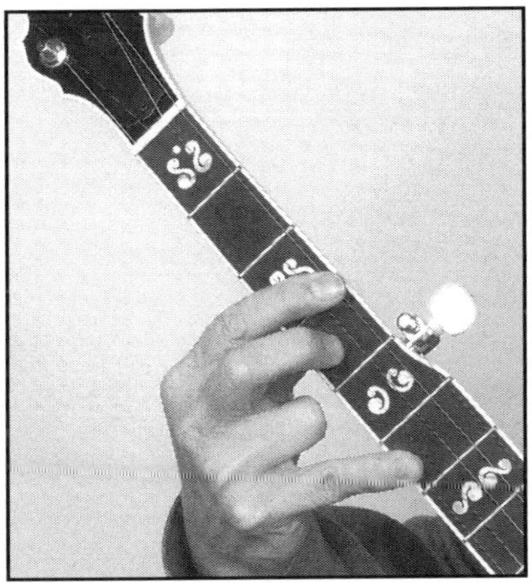

Root - 4th - 5th - ♭7th
B♭ - E♭ - F - A♭

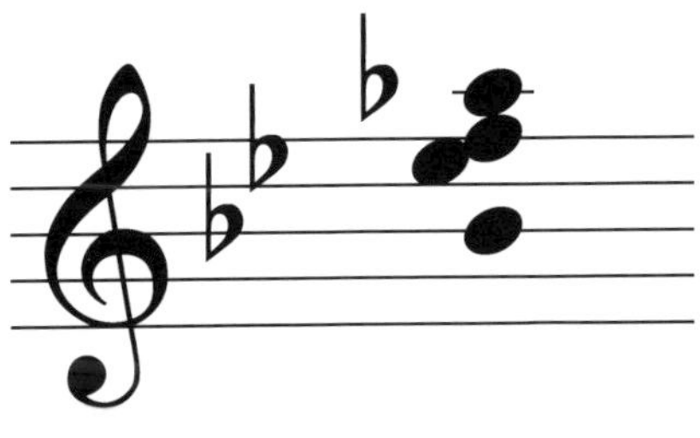

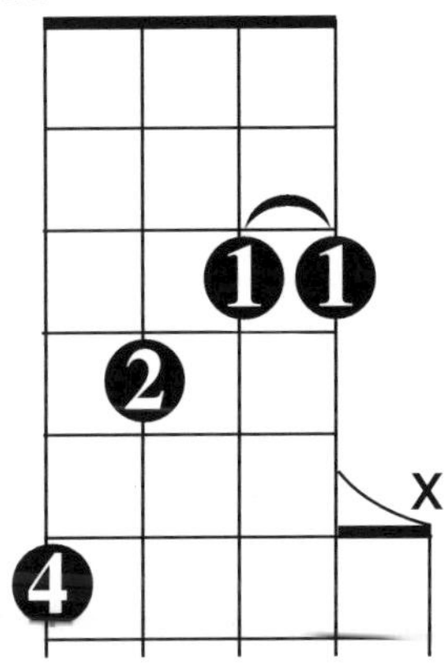

B Chords

B Major

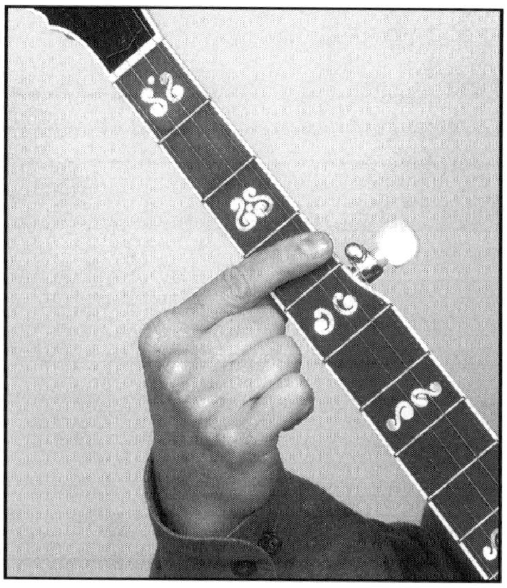

Root - 3rd - 5th
B - D♯ - F♯

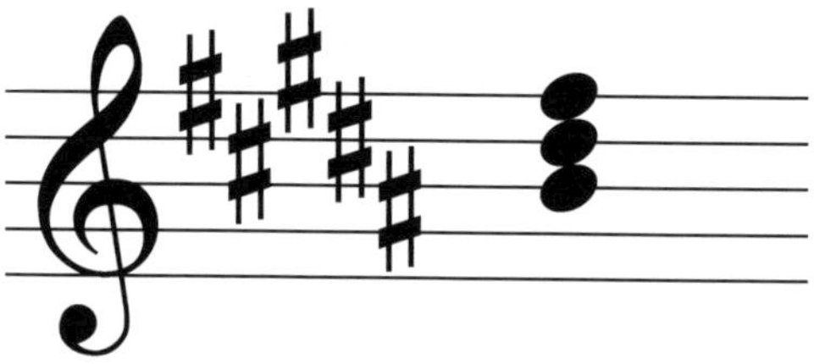

B

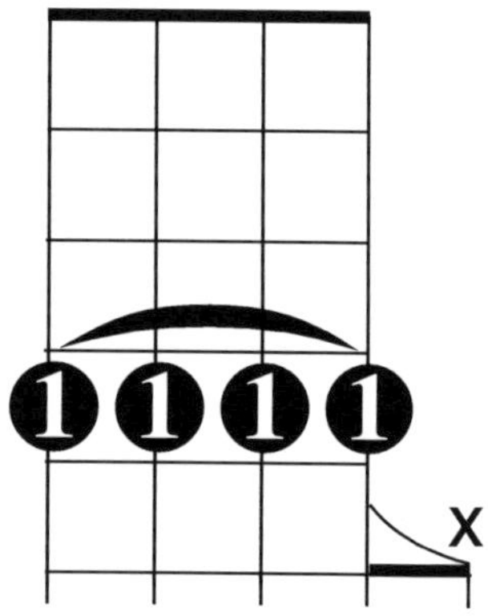

B Minor

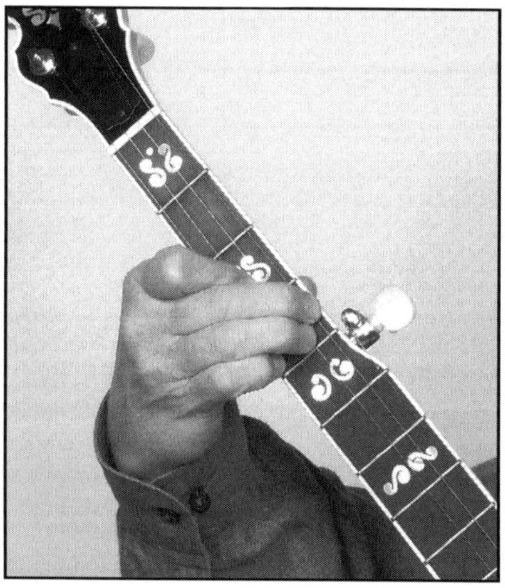

Root - ♭3rd - 5th
B - D♮ - F♯

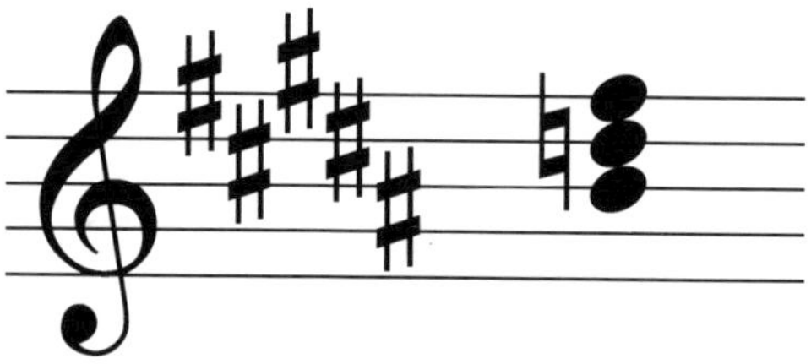

Bm

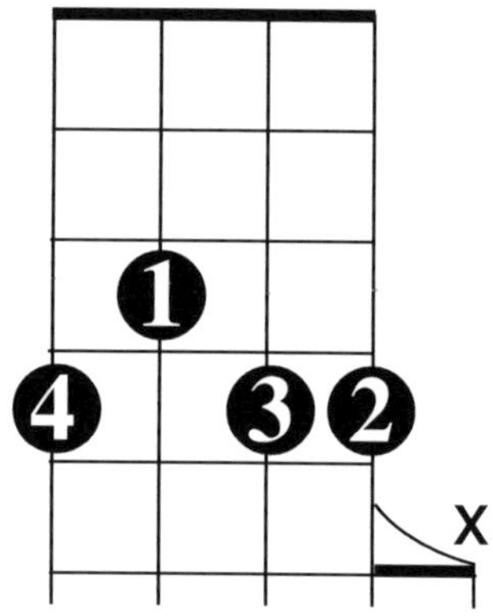

B Seventh

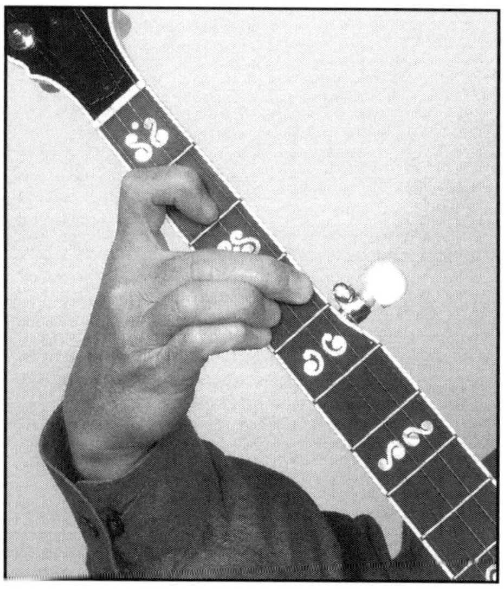

Root - 3rd - 5th - ♭7th
B - D♯ - F♯ - A♮

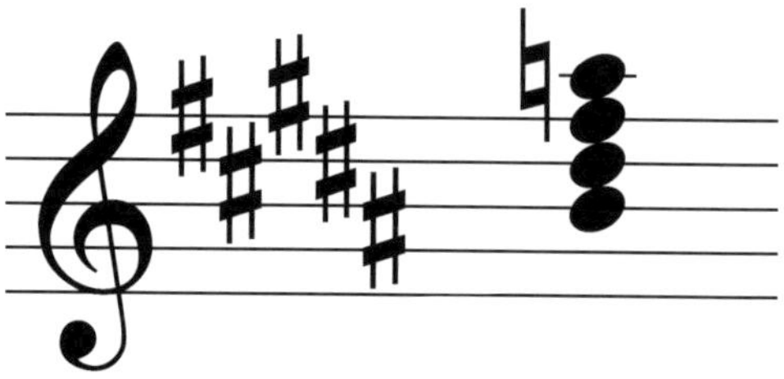

B7

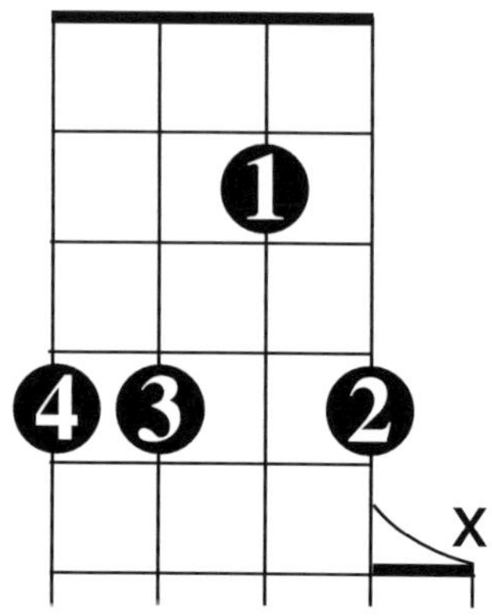

B Chords

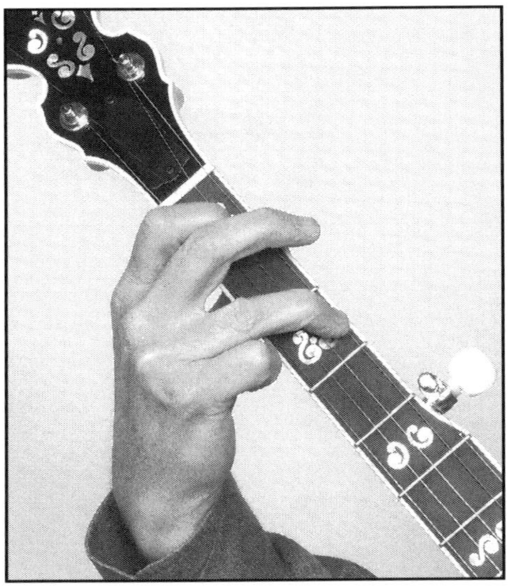

B Diminished

Root - ♭3rd - ♭5th - ♭♭7th
B - D♮ - F♮ - A♭

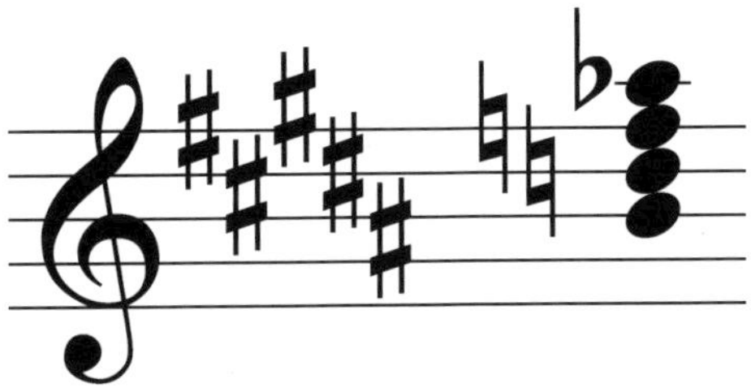

B°

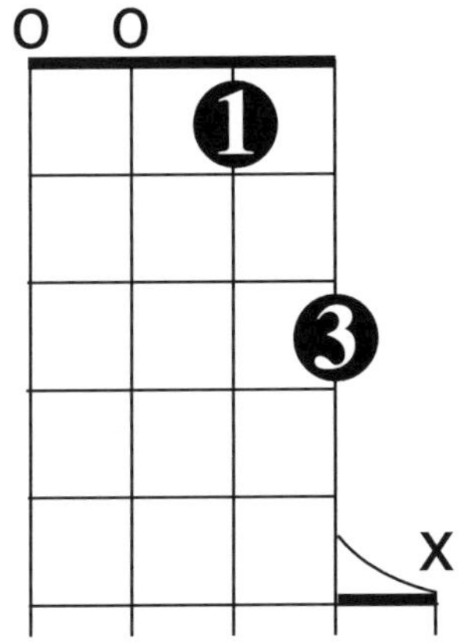

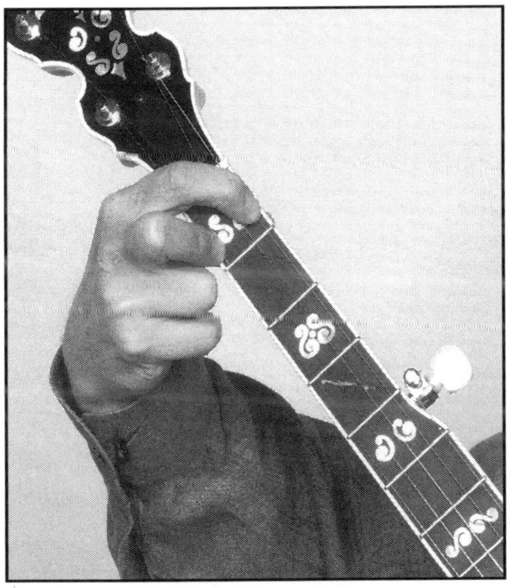

B Augmented

Root - 3rd - ♯5th
B - D♯ - F×

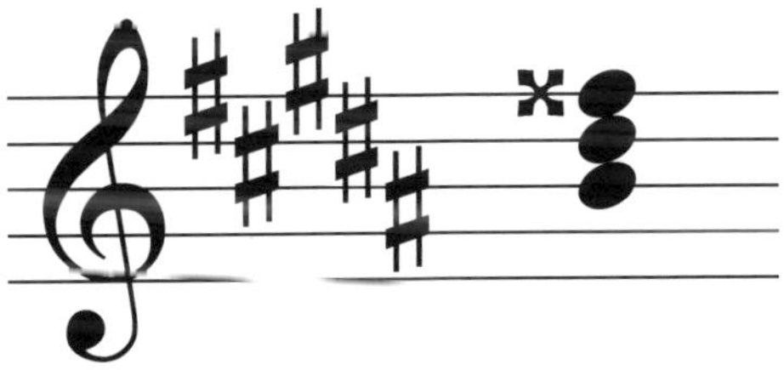

B+

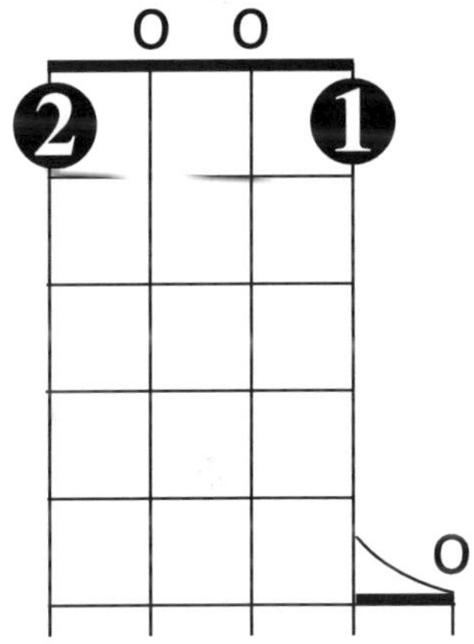

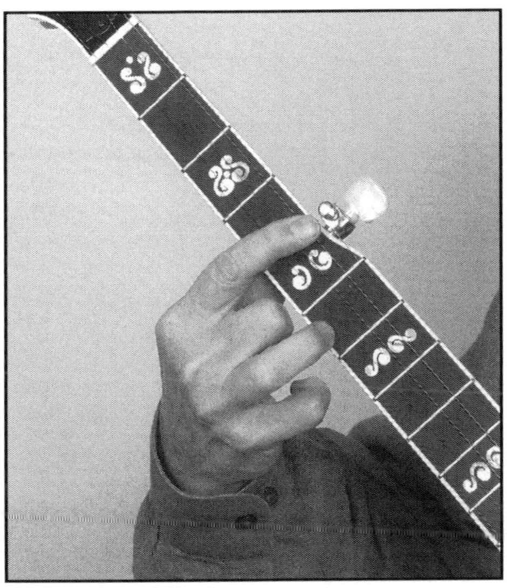

B Sixth

Root - 3rd - 5th - 6th
B - D♯ - F♯ - G♯

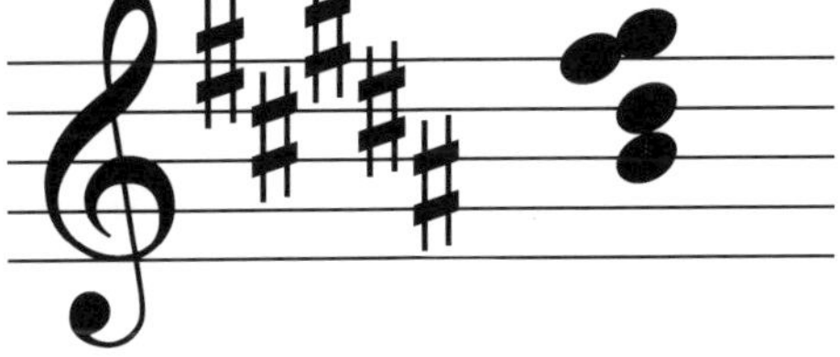

B6

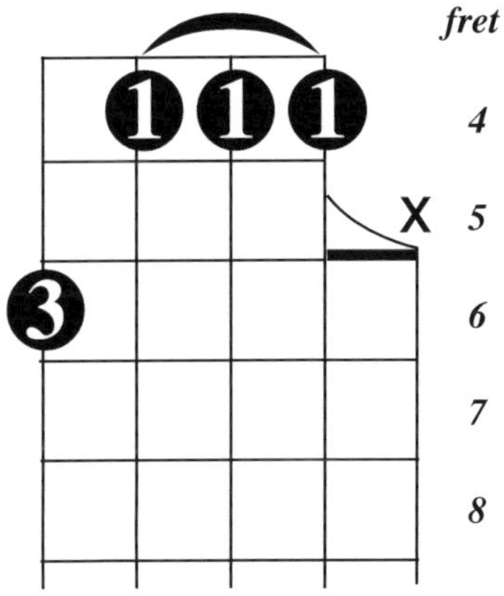

B Chords

B Minor Sixth

Root - ♭3rd - 5th - 6th
B - D♮ - F♯ - G♯

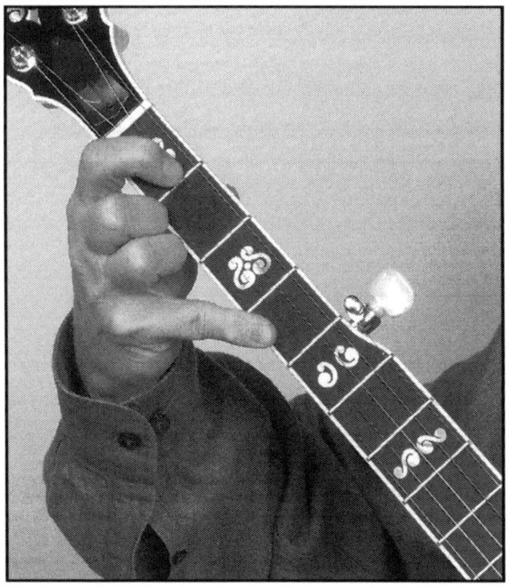

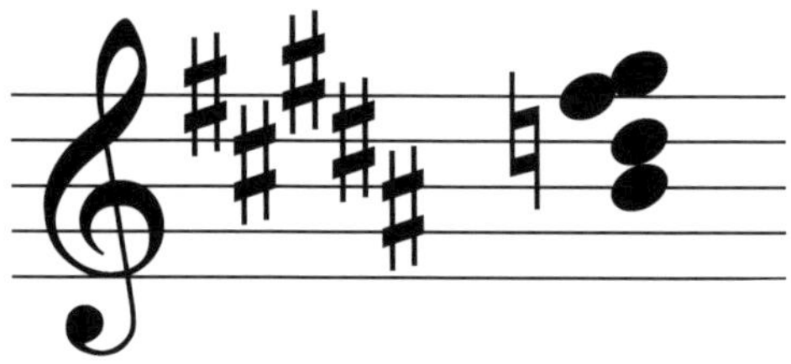

Bm6

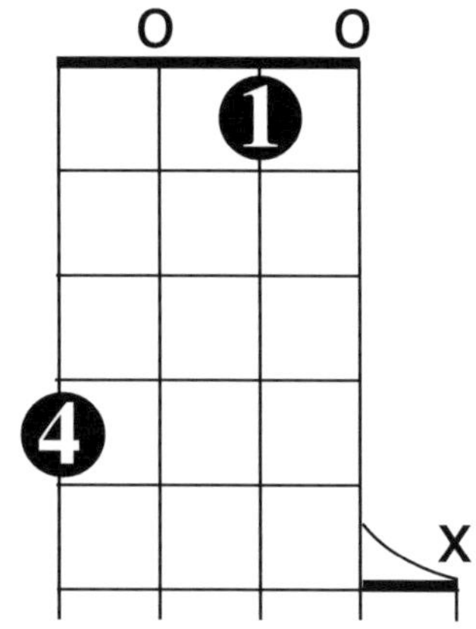

B Seven Flat Five

Root - 3rd - ♭5th - ♭7th
B - D♯ - F♮ - A♮

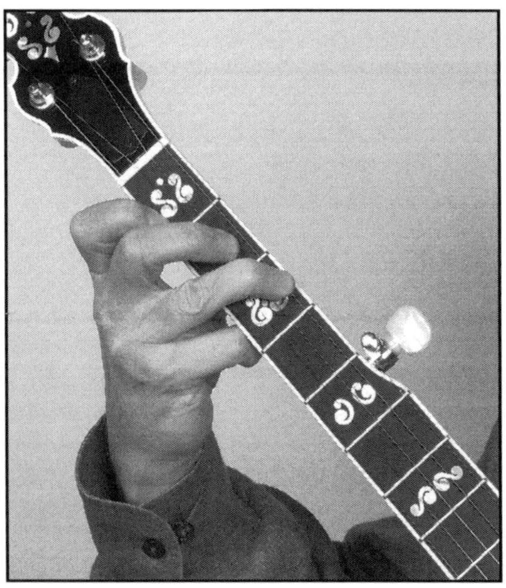

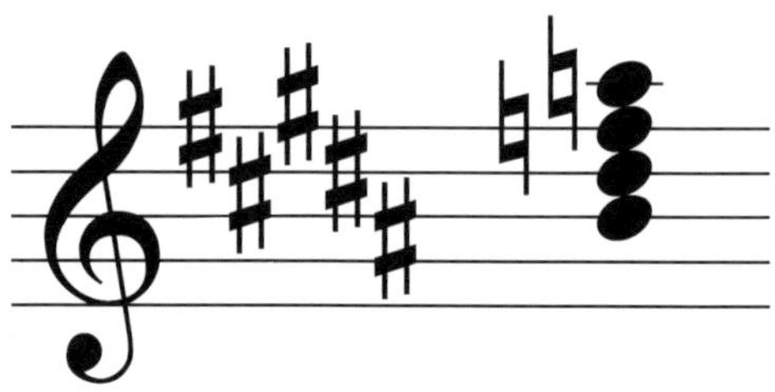

B7♭5

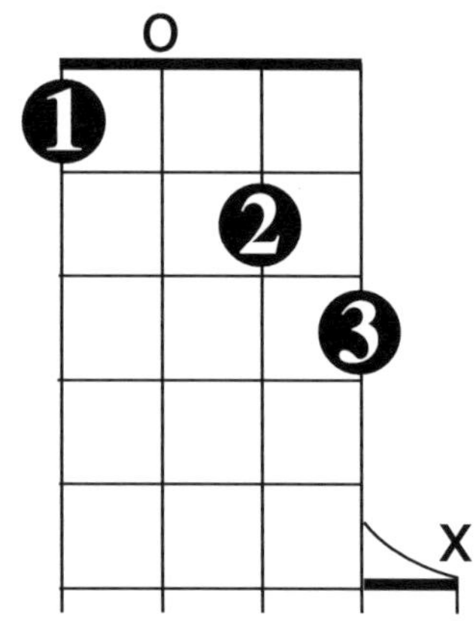

B Major Seventh

Root - 3rd - 5th - 7th
B - D♯ - F♯ - A♯

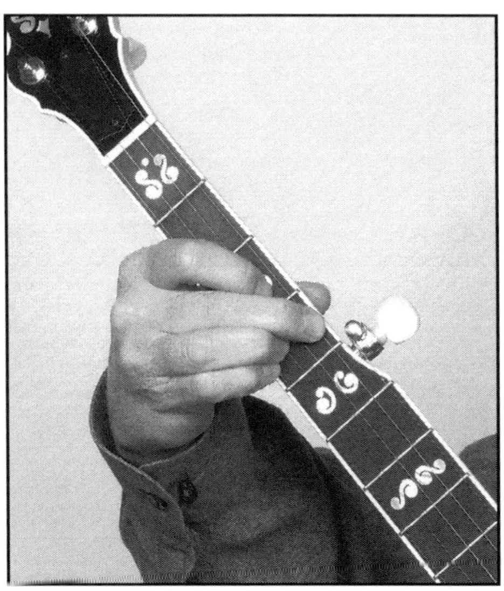

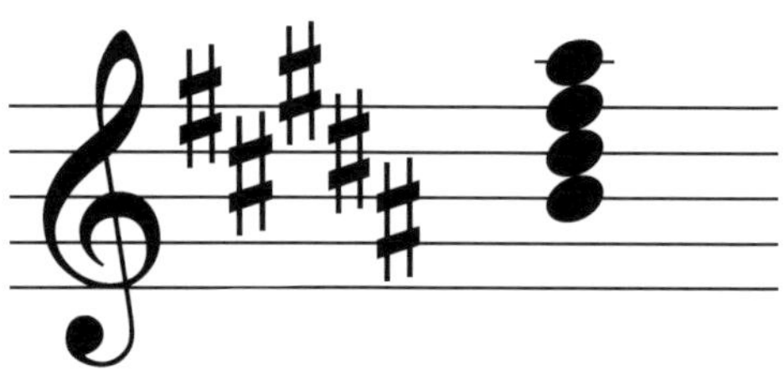

BMaj7

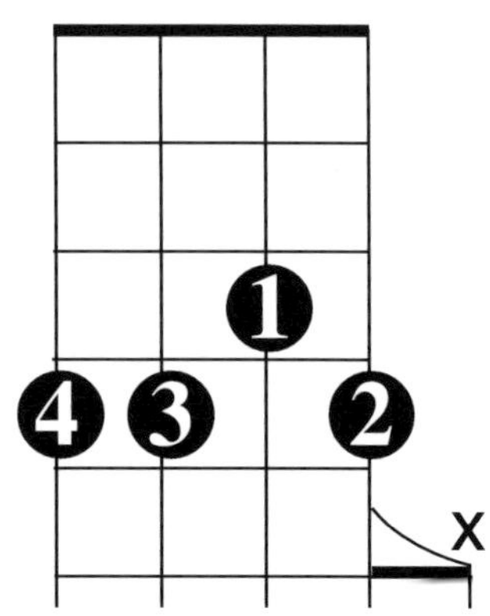

B Chords

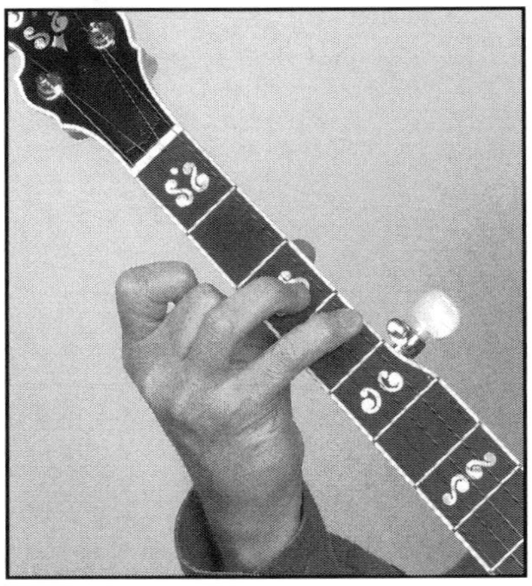

B Major Seventh Flat Third

BMaj7♭3

Root - ♭3rd - 5th - 7th
B - D♮ - F♯ - A♯

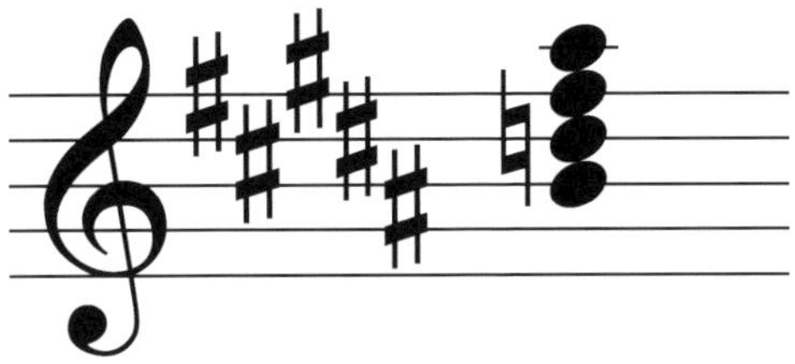

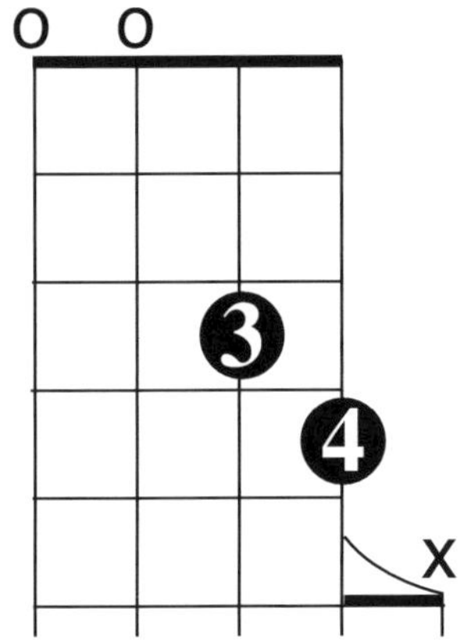

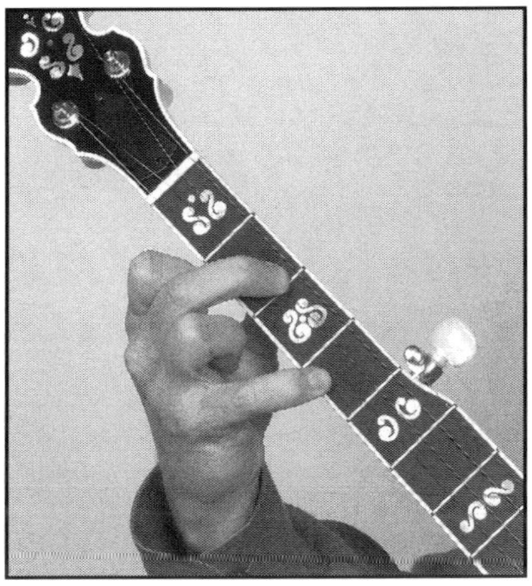

B Minor Seventh

Bm7

Root - ♭3rd - 5th - ♭7th
B - D♮ - F♯ - A♮

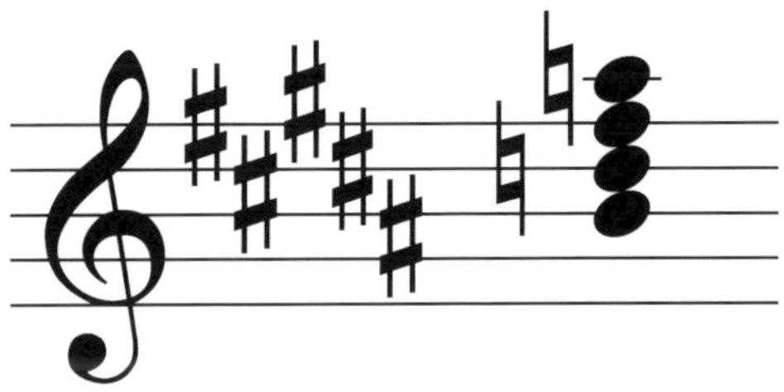

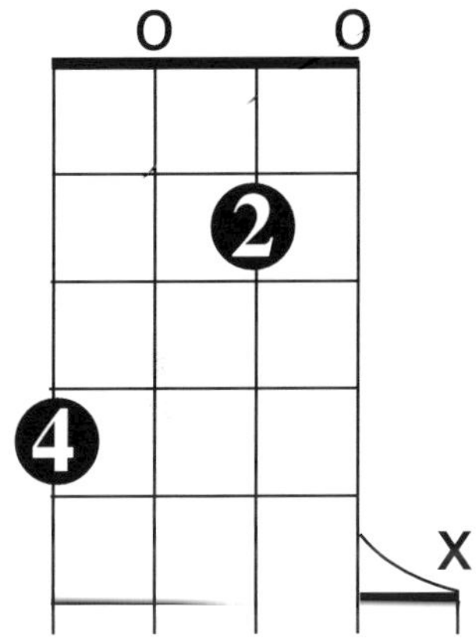

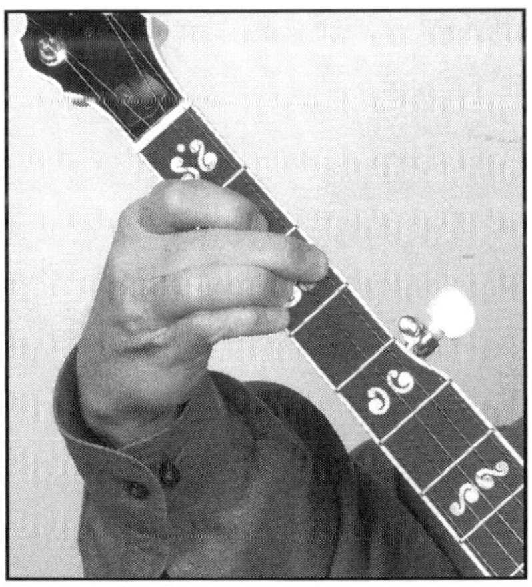

B Minor Seventh Flat Five

Bm7♭5

Root - ♭3rd - ♭5th - ♭7th
B - D♮ - F♮ - A♮

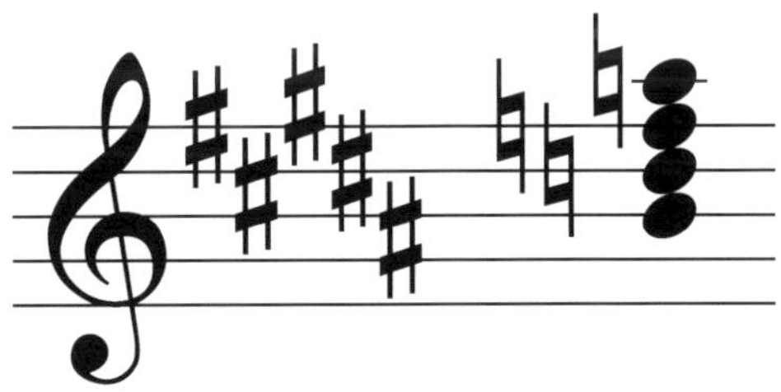

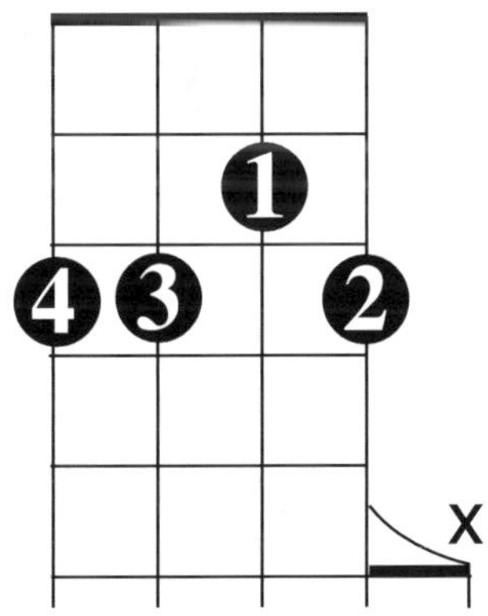

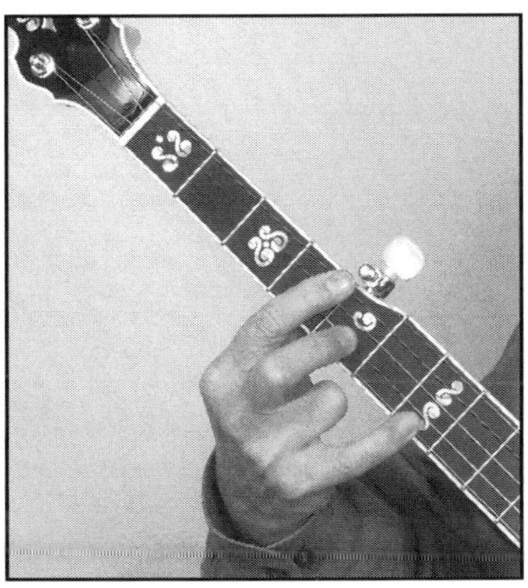

B Seventh Suspended Fourth

B7sus4

Root - 4th - 5th - ♭7th
B - E - F♯ - A♮

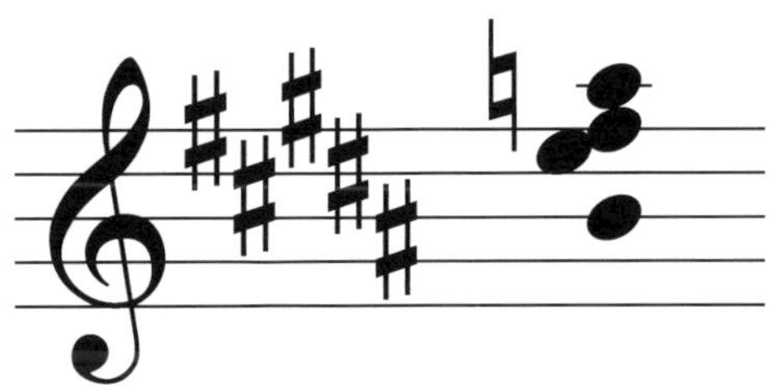

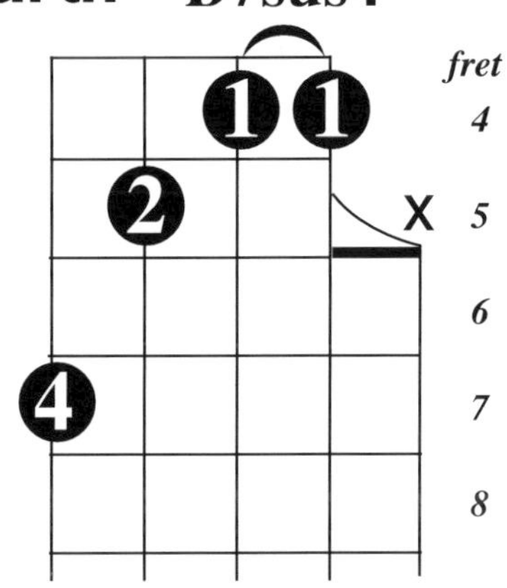

Other Recommended Banjo Books

Easy Banjo Solos (Weissman)

Great Picking Tunes for Banjo (Munde)

My First Banjo Picking Songs (Kaufman)

Banjo Scales in Tab (Davis)

3 Finger Pickin' Banjo Songbook (Bailey)

101 Three-Chord Country & Bluegrass Songs (McCabe)

Bluegrass Standards for Banjo Made Easy (Nickerson)

Gospel Songs for Banjo Made Easy (Nickerson)

Parking Lot Picker's Songbook - Banjo (Bruce and Evans)

Easy Irish and Celtic Melodies for 5-String Banjo (Hanway)

Fiddle Tunes for Banjo Made Easy (Nickerson)

Tony Trischka Master Collection of Fiddle Tunes for Banjo (Trischka)